# LIBERATION IN
# SOUTH AMERICA
## 1806–1827

JAMES PAROISSIEN

# LIBERATION
# IN SOUTH AMERICA
## 1806–1827
### The Career of James Paroissien

BY

R. A. HUMPHREYS

*Professor of Latin American History*
*in the University of London*

UNIVERSITY OF LONDON
THE ATHLONE PRESS
1952

*Published by*
THE ATHLONE PRESS
*at the Senate House, London* W.C.1

*Distributed by Constable & Co. Ltd.*
*12 Orange Street, London* W.C.2

*Printed in Great Britain by*
WESTERN PRINTING SERVICES LTD.
BRISTOL

TO R.H. AND H.M.H.

# PREFACE

In this book I have attempted, not so much to write a biography, as to provide an introduction to the study of one of the great revolutions in modern history. James Paroissien is unknown in England. He is not well-known in South America. But, himself an actor in the drama of South American independence, he was associated with great movements and he was the witness of great events. His career almost exactly spans the years which saw the liberation of South America from European control and the opening of the continent to the trade of the world, and, illustrating these movements, it illustrates also the beginnings of those intimate connexions which were then established between England and South America.

My obligations are many. To Mr. Alfred E. Jones and Mr. W. R. A. Young of the firm of Cunnington Son and Orfeur of Braintree, Essex, I owe a special debt of gratitude, not only for the generosity with which they placed the Paroissien Papers in their possession at my disposal, but also for their continued interest in the progress of my work and for their readiness to help me in every possible way. I am most grateful also to H.E. Sr. Don Manuel Bianchi for his kindness in allowing me to reproduce the portrait of Paroissien which now hangs in the Chilean Embassy in London and which, painted in 1819 by the Peruvian artist, José Gil de Castro, then living in Chile, originally reached England in 1820 as a gift from Paroissien to his sister. Mrs. M. Blanco Fombona de Hood, of the Venezuelan Embassy in London, kindly allowed me to make use of the engraving of Bolívar, in her possession, which Bolívar himself presented to Sir Robert Wilson. The two Brazilian illustrations I owe to the courtesy of Mr. Rex Nan Kivell and Mr. Sidney F. Sabin. I am indebted to Mr. G. Nothman, of the Brazilian Embassy in London, to Mr. Stephen Clissold, of the British Council, and to Dr. Eugenio

Pereira Salas, of the University of Chile, for providing me with photographs; and for permission to reproduce works in their possession I wish to thank Messrs. Frank T. Sabin, the Trustees of the National Maritime Museum, Greenwich, and the Director of the Museo Histórico Nacional, Chile.

Many people have been generous of their time in answering my inquiries and providing me with information. In the Americas I am much indebted to the kindness of Dr. Emilio Ravignani, of the Instituto de Investigaciones Históricas of Montevideo, Dr. Eugenio Pereira Salas, of the University of Chile, Professor James F. King, of the University of California, and Mr. Arthur Richardson, of the British Council. In England it is a pleasure to record, in particular, my obligations to Mr. F. G. Emmison, the Archivist of the County of Essex, who first drew my attention to the existence at Braintree of a collection of papers relating to South America; to Mr. W. G. Fairchild, the Librarian of the Borough of Barking; to the late Sir Henry Hake, of the National Portrait Gallery; to Miss Helen M. Briggs, the Secretary of the Huguenot Society; and to Miss Hilda Clark, the Medical Librarian of the British Council. Mr. G. R. Versey, of the Department of Geography at University College, drew the maps. The index, and much else besides, I owe to my wife.

R. A. H.

# CONTENTS

I  The Invasions of the Río de la Plata, 1806–7    *page* 1

II  Trade and Politics in Brazil, 1807–8    15

III  Montevideo and Buenos Aires, 1808–10    33

IV  Buenos Aires and the Provinces, 1810–16    48

V  The Liberation of Chile, 1817–20    65

VI  The Liberating Expedition to Perú, 1820–1    82

VII  Politics and Diplomacy in South America, 1822    100

VIII  The Mission to England, 1822–3    116

IX  El Dorado, 1824–5    133

X  Catastrophe, 1826–7    145

Appendices
  i Note on the Territorial Organization of the
    Spanish Empire in South America    163

  ii Glossary    164

  iii Note on Sources    165

Index of Authors and Short Titles    167

General Index    169

## MAPS
*at the end*

1  The Spanish and Portuguese Empires in South America in 1808

2  The Invasion of Chile

3  The Invasion of Perú

4  South America in 1826

# ILLUSTRATIONS

James Paroissien                                           Frontispiece
From a painting by José Gil de Castro, 1819. The Chilean
Embassy, London.

1. Rio de Janeiro from the island of Villegagnon       16
From a painting by A. Müller, probably executed in the
eighteen-thirties or eighteen-forties. By permission of Frank
T. Sabin, London.

2. View from the summit of the Corcovado Mountains
near Rio de Janeiro                                    17
From a water colour by Augustus Earie in the collection of
Rex Nan Kivell, Esq. Probably executed in the early eighteen-
twenties.

3. A View of the Town and Harbour of Montevideo, 1807   32
From an aquatint engraved by J. Merigot. National Maritime
Museum, Greenwich.

4. General View of Buenos Aires, from the Plaza de Toros   35
From E. E. Vidal, *Picturesque Illustrations of Buenos Ayres
and Monte Video* (London, 1820).

5. José de San Martín                                     48
From a painting by or after José Gil de Castro, circa 1818–19.
Museo Histórico Nacional, Chile.

6. Travelling Post                                         49
From E. E. Vidal, *Picturesque Illustrations of Buenos Ayres
and Monte Video* (London, 1820).

7. View of the Great Chain of the Andes taken from the
Plain of the Maipú                                    64
From Alexander Caldcleugh, *Travels in South America,
during the years 1819–20–21* (2 vols., London, 1825).

8. The Mint of Santiago 65

From a lithograph by G. Scharf after a drawing by James Paroissien. Peter Schmidtmeyer, *Travels into Chile, over the Andes, in the years 1820 and 1821* (London, 1824).

9. Bernardo O'Higgins 80

From a painting by José Gil de Castro, 1820. Museo Histórico Nacional, Chile.

10. The Cañada, Santiago 81

From a lithograph by G. Scharf after a drawing by James Paroissien. Peter Schmidtmeyer, *Travels into Chile, over the Andes, in the years 1820 and 1821* (London, 1824).

11. Valparaíso Bay 96

From Alexander Caldcleugh, *Travels in South America, during the years 1819–20–21* (2 vols., London, 1825).

12. The Cutting Out of the Spanish Frigate *Esmeralda* from under the Forts of Callao on the night of the 5th November 1821 97

From a water colour by Charles C. Wood. National Maritime Museum, Greenwich.

13. Dom Pedro I of Brazil as he appeared on the day of his coronation 112

From a water colour by Augustus Earle in the collection of Rex Nan Kivell, Esq.

14. Simón Bolívar 113

From an engraving by Charles Turner after a painting by José Gil de Castro. Published in 1827 and inscribed by Bolívar 'Al Señor General Sir Robert Wilson. Retrato mío hecho en Lima con la más grande exactitud y semejanza'. Now in the possession of Mrs. M. Blanco Fombona de Hood.

15. Lima, with the Bridge over the Rimac 128

From Alexander Caldcleugh, *Travels in South America, during the years 1819–20–21* (2 vols., London, 1825).

16. Scene in the Carnival at Potosí 129

From Edmond Temple, *Travels in Various Parts of Peru, including a year's residence in Potosi* (2 vols., London, 1830).

# PRINCIPAL ABBREVIATIONS

Ad.    Admiralty Records, Public Record Office, London
F.O.    Foreign Office Records, Public Record Office, London
P.P.    Paroissien Papers
W.O.    War Office Records, Public Record Office, London

# CHAPTER I

## THE INVASIONS OF THE RÍO DE LA PLATA, 1806–7

'BY an Express which we have just received from Portsmouth, we have to congratulate the Public on one of the most important events of the present war. BUENOS AYRES AT THIS MOMENT FORMS A PART OF THE BRITISH EMPIRE: and when we consider the consequences to which it leads from its situation and commercial capacities, as well as its political influence, we know not how to express ourselves in terms adequate to our ideas of the national advantages which will be derived from this conquest.'

So wrote *The Times* on 13 September 1806, at a moment when Napoleon was overrunning all Europe and Spain was still his ally. Not quite a year earlier, at Trafalgar, the navies of France and Spain had been shattered. Britain was mistress of the seas. But Napoleon was master of the land, and within a month, as Austerlitz had followed Ulm, Jena would follow Austerlitz. The last lingering hopes of a European peace were vanishing. Pitt and Fox, both were gone: Fox died, indeed, on this very day. And 'when Europe crouched to France's yoke, And Austria bent, and Prussia broke', no wonder that the report of the capture of Buenos Aires, the gateway to South America, to the wealth, the trade, the resources, of the Spanish empire in the New World, should excite the most ardent hopes.

For Buenos Aires, a city of between 40,000 and 50,000 people, its domes and towers rising above the muddy waters of the River Plate, was the capital of the far-flung viceroyalty of La Plata. Behind it lay the flat immensity of the pampas, those plains on which the wealth of modern Argentina would be built. On the opposite shores of the Río de la Plata, on its 'Banda Oriental' or eastern bank, but more than one hundred miles away and at the river's mouth, stood the fort and city of

B

Montevideo, once only a garrison town, but now a thriving community of some 10,000 souls. And the viceroyalty itself embraced not only the present territory of Argentina but the modern states of Uruguay, Paraguay and Bolivia as well. It stretched from the Atlantic to the Andes and from Patagonia in the south to the high waters of Lake Titicaca and to the basin of the Amazon in the north; and it was larger than the land mass of India and Burma combined.

Before the viceroyalty had been created, in 1776, the region of the Río de la Plata, rich in land and cattle, but poor in mines, had been among the most neglected parts of Spain's vast territories in America. It was a periphery area, politically unimportant, economically insignificant. But Spain, like Britain, had undertaken in the eighteenth century the task of imperial reorganization, and as administrative institutions were reformed and commercial regulations liberalized, a new day dawned over the waters of the great river. The population of Buenos Aires, its exports, its customs receipts, its shipping, its commerce with the interior provinces and with Spain, all alike rapidly grew. Gold and silver flowed down the mountain-sides of the remote mining region of Upper Perú, the modern Bolivia, to find their outlet at the viceregal port; and Buenos Aires, a small village at the beginning of the eighteenth century, had become, at its end, inferior only, in Spanish South America, to the far-famed capital of the viceroyalty of Perú, to that 'city of the kings', Lima itself.

Out of the blue, on 27 June 1806, it was captured. It fell to an expedition undertaken from the Cape of Good Hope by Commodore Sir Home Riggs Popham and Brigadier-General William Carr Beresford. The responsibility for the attack lay with Popham. An able officer, but suspected by contemporaries of confounding public with personal interests, Popham had convoyed the forces of Major-General Sir David Baird (with Beresford as second-in-command) to the conquest of the Cape in January 1806. It was his persuasive reasoning that had secured the co-operation of Baird for this further expedition. His was the mind that planned it, and he acted entirely without instructions.

Yet as Popham knew, and as he pleaded in extenuation of his proceedings, some such enterprise had long been contemplated by successive cabinets in England. It had been proposed, along with other plans to destroy in America the power of Spain in Europe, during the war

of the American Revolution, when Spain had joined with France to promote the independence of England's colonies. It was thought of again in 1790 when England and Spain were once more on the brink of war. When war was declared, in 1796, an expedition was prepared but its sailing cancelled, and, thereafter, an attack on Buenos Aires, as a move in a wider strategy, was frequently and seriously considered by the British Government. Popham and that exiled Venezuelan adventurer, Francisco de Miranda, who had ceaselessly sought to enlist the aid of England in his schemes to revolutionize South America, had been among its most ardent protagonists.

Yet, however much in principle or policy the idea of an invasion of the Río de la Plata had won official approval, the invasion, when it came, was wholly unauthorized. It surprised the British Government no less than the people of Buenos Aires, and its success was short-lived.[1] As the British approached, the Viceroy of La Plata, the Marqués de Sobremonte, fled. The city, ill-protected, ill-defended, fell almost without resistance, and its treatment was not ungenerous. But once the shock was over, the people quickly rallied. The town was soon alive with conspiracy. Juan Martín de Pueyrredón, a young creole merchant, the son of a French immigrant, but Spanish-American native-born, led a rising in the countryside, and Santiago Liniers, a Frenchman, long an officer in the service of the Spanish Crown, crossed the river to Montevideo to return with an army, partly of regular troops, partly of volunteers, swelling as it marched, to conquer the conquerors. On the 12th August Beresford was forced to capitulate. Twelve hundred of his men, contrary to the terms of surrender, were sent as prisoners to towns in the interior, and, while Popham and his fleet remained in the Río de la Plata to blockade both shores and to await reinforcements, Beresford himself was interned near the capital, at the village of Luján.

It was not for some months, however, that this reverse became known in England, and, meanwhile, the news that Buenos Aires had fallen raised extravagant expectations. The merchants of Britain, impatient of the closed commercial monopoly which Spain had erected but could not

---

[1] The best accounts of the British invasions are to be found in Carlos Roberts, *Las invasiones inglesas del Río de la Plata* (Buenos Aires, 1938), and Juan Beverina, *Las invasiones inglesas al Río de la Plata*, 2 vols. (Buenos Aires, 1939).

enforce in her empire in America, had long hoped for direct access to those fabled markets and rich sources of supply, of gold and silver, drugs and dyewoods, hides and skins, other than by the lucrative but still precarious methods of contraband trade or through the commerce of Lisbon and Cádiz. Now, 'at a moment when', as Canning was to say in December, 'the other markets of the world are attempted to be closed against us',[1] when Napoleon was closing the ports of Europe, and the United States, angered by British molestations of American shipping, threatened to close her own, their anxieties were redoubled and their wishes seemed about to be gratified.

The relief was great and the enthusiasm prodigious. 'Peru and her mines', wrote John Parish Robertson (who was to make, and lose, a fortune in South America), 'were held forth to us as open through this channel: we were told that the tropical regions of Paraguay were approachable by ships; that thousands upon thousands of cattle were grazing in the verdant plains; and that the price of a bullock was four shillings, while that of a horse was half the sum.'[2] The Times foresaw, in South America, 'a never failing market' for British commodities.[3] Popham, in a circular letter, which no naval officer should ever have written, and which he dispatched from Buenos Aires immediately after the city had fallen, addressed the mayors and corporations of the principal manufacturing towns in Britain to much the same effect,[4] and the arrival of more than one million dollars' worth of treasure, captured at Buenos Aires from the Spanish Crown and the Royal Philippine Company, lent verisimilitude to his words. Both he and Beresford were honoured, in absentia, with the freedom of the City of London.

The short-lived Ministry of All-the-Talents, which had succeeded to that of Pitt, was less satisfied. The Prime Minister, Lord Grenville, and his new Foreign Secretary, Charles Grey, were seriously disturbed. To what policy had the country thus been casually committed? What consequences might not flow from it? These doubts, however, were not shared by the Secretary at War, William Windham, whose imagination, indeed, was 'greatly heated' by the prospects of indemnity in the New

---

[1] *Cobbett's Parliamentary Debates* (London, 1804–), viii. 58.
[2] J. P. and W. P. Robertson, *Letters on Paraguay*, 3 vols. (2nd edn., London, 1839), i. 94.
[3] *The Times*, 15 Sept. 1806.     [4] Ibid., 20 Sept. 1806.

World for disappointments in the Old; and the cabinet as a whole, 'anxious to court the commercial interest',[1] bowed, though reluctantly, to the popular fervour. Irresolute and divided, however, it did too little and that little too late. In July, a month after the news of the sailing of Popham's expedition reached England, Popham was recalled, to answer for his conduct by court martial. At the same time reinforcements were promised to Beresford. Yet it was not till October that a small force commanded by Sir Samuel Auchmuty left England for the River Plate. And then, so greatly had Windham's imagination been heated, a further expedition was prepared under Brigadier-General Robert Craufurd, to undertake the conquest of Chile.[2] Meanwhile, in September, by Order in Council, Buenos Aires was declared to form a part of the dominions of His Majesty and to be open to trade. More than a hundred ships were soon engaged in fitting out for the 'New Arcadia',[3] and by the end of the year the value of the goods embarked for Buenos Aires, according to the obsolete valuations of the customs' records, was nearly five times as great as the treasure received from there. It amounted to close on £1,000,000.[4]

Among the merchants, traders and adventurers who now flocked to South America—two thousand were reported to have entered Montevideo when, as events fell out, that city was captured in February 1807,[5] and the Board of Trade was anxiously petitioned for posts in Buenos Aires—there embarked at Gravesend in the *Gallant Schemer* (Captain Reach, master), on 9 November 1806, a young man not yet quite twenty-two years old, by name James Paroissien. Of his early career little is known. He came of a respectable Huguenot family originally settled in Normandy. His great-grandfather, Jesse, had been natural-

---

[1] Henry Richard Lord Holland, *Memoirs of the Whig Party*, 2 vols. (London, 1852–4), ii. 112.

[2] Instructions to Craufurd, 30 Oct. 1806, Public Record Office, War Office Records, 1/161.

[3] Robertson, op. cit., i. 94; J. B. Williams, 'The Establishment of British Commerce with Argentina', *Hispanic American Historical Review*, xv (1935), p. 47.

[4] Public Record Office, Customs, 17/28; R. A. Humphreys, *British Consular Reports on the Trade and Politics of Latin America, 1824–1826* (Camden Third Series, lxiii, Royal Historical Society, London, 1940), p. 349. See also D. B. Goebel, 'British Trade to the Spanish Colonies, 1796–1823', *American Historical Review*, xliii (1938), p. 307.          [5] Robertson, op. cit., i. 102.

ized in 1709.[1] His father, Louis, was for a time a schoolmaster at Barking, Essex. His half-brother, George, had been educated at Cambridge and was, for thirty-six years, a curate at Hackney, and at Hackney the family now lived.[2] James himself, however, was born at Barking on 25 or 28 November 1784.[3] He seems to have had a good general education, with some grounding in chemistry, medicine and surgery in particular. He had read fairly widely. He was interested both in mineralogy and painting, and possessed, indeed, some natural talent as an artist. He had had some slight experience of military life, if only as a member of a volunteer corps at a time when Napoleon threatened to invade England. He had fallen in love. And in company with Dr. Daniel Gardner, who was later to lecture on chemistry in Brazil, he sailed to seek his fame and fortune in the New World as a commission agent, or, indeed, in any other rôle that might prove profitable.

Delayed by false starts and contrary winds, it was not till the 31st December that the *Gallant Schemer* finally left Deal Roads. Paroissien had employed the interval in excursions on shore, in sight-seeing and in sketching, and the rumours, just beginning to circulate, late in December, though unconfirmed, that Buenos Aires had been recaptured, seem not to have reached him. His departure was exciting enough: the *Gallant Schemer* was at once engaged with a French privateer. 'It appears', Paroissien recorded, 'there are in the English Channel an immense number of vessels of this description.'[4] But otherwise, the voyage, enlivened by experiments in the dissection of ducks and sharks and Portuguese men-of-war, was uneventful. Brigadier-General Craufurd's force, which had left England in November, en route for Chile by way of Table Bay, but had long delayed in the Cape Verde Islands, was

---

[1] The Paroissien pedigree is in the Wagner Collection among the records of the French Hospital at Horsham, Sussex.

[2] William Robinson, *The History and Antiquities of the Parish of Hackney*, 2 vols. (London, 1842–3), ii. 180. George was admitted to Pembroke College, Cambridge, as a sizar on 11 June 1784, and his father was then described as a schoolmaster at Barking.

[3] James was in the habit of celebrating his birthday on the 28th November. The register of baptisms of the Parish Church of St. Margaret, Barking, Essex, for 25 December 1784, however, contains the following entry: 'James son of Lewis and Mary Paroissien born 25th November.' Mary was the second of two wives who bore the same Christian name.                      [4] Journal, 1 Jan. 1807.

passed on the 2nd February, and on the 18th the *Medusa* frigate, five days out from Montevideo, brought the news, which 'appeared to con- duce to the frustration of our hopes', that Buenos Aires had been lost six months before, but that Montevideo 'had surrendered to the English after a siege of eighteen days'. Sir Samuel Auchmuty, who had arrived, on the 5th January, at Maldonado, near what is now the pleasant watering place of Punta del Este, had in fact taken the city by storm on the 3rd February. But the assault had been costly and the vanquished, the anxious voyagers were informed, 'seem'd very hostile indeed to the English'.[1]

With this discouraging information it was as a prey to the most gloomy apprehensions that Paroissien himself finally landed at Monte- video on the 28th February, his mind 'too much agitated with the fear of not being able to sell goods' to permit him to observe much. But the harbour, he noted, 'contained about 150 sail, including prizes', the landing place was crowded with people of all kinds, Spaniards, negroes, Englishmen, the latter 'with faces of disappointment', and, as for the inhabitants, they were, he thought fretfully, 'the filthiest devils exist- ing'.[2] Accommodation was scarce; prices were high; and the principal citizens, he was told, had fled. After a wearisome search he took a house, cheaply as it happened, at $10 a month—'some of my friends pay 140—the generality 50'—and opened a shop.[3]

Paroissien's depression was natural enough. The English, soldiers and merchants alike, had expected to be welcomed with open arms. The information which Popham had acquired in London, on his way to, and at the Cape (he was impressed, particularly, by the views of an American sea-captain, Captain Waine, master of the ship *Elizabeth*, who had three times visited Buenos Aires), was that provided Buenos Aires were opened to trade 'all the inhabitants would willingly acquiesce and keep the place for the British nation without troops'.[4] They were, he had written to the War Office, so averse to their existing rulers that they would 'materially assist in the conquest'.[5] Beresford, in July, thought that the sole reason why the *porteños*, as the inhabitants

---

[1] Ibid., 18 Feb. 1807.                                   [2] Ibid., 28 Feb. 1807.
[3] Ibid., 28 Feb., 2, 3 March 1807.
[4] Waine to Popham, 28 March 1806 (Profound Secret), W.O. 1/161.
[5] Popham to Castlereagh, 30 April 1806, W.O. 1/161.

of Buenos Aires were called, did not openly come forward to express
their joy at the change of sovereigns was the fear of again falling under
the dominion of their late masters.[1] The reports which had reached
England from Buenos Aires had indicated that the people were entirely
satisfied.[2] There had been no seizure of private property. Public
officials had been confirmed in their posts, existing institutions maintained, and the port had been opened to trade under moderate duties.
'Such unexampled generosity and moderation', remarked *The Times*,
would 'doubtless make the inhabitants of the Spanish colonies wish to
be connected with Great Britain.'[3] And the Secretary at War, drafting
in October the instructions to Craufurd for the conquest of Chile, com-
placently expected that the contrast which the Spanish Americans had
already experienced between 'the oppressive dominion of Spain and the
benign and protecting Government of His Majesty' should make
Craufurd's task an easy one.[4]

But this was to reckon without the pride and to misinterpret the
wishes of the Spanish Americans. It was Popham's contention, adduced
in partial justification of his conduct, that the conquest of Buenos Aires
would lay 'a successful foundation' for the 'great enterprize' of Francisco de Miranda,[5] who was leading his own abortive expedition to
liberate Venezuela at the very moment when Popham and Beresford
left the Cape. Everyone was aware of Miranda's activities and many
knew that simultaneous expeditions to Venezuela and the Río de la
Plata had in fact been considered. But whatever the understanding
between Popham and Miranda, conquest in South America had never
entered into that arch-plotter's mind. 'I wish', he wrote indignantly in
1807, 'Sir Home Popham . . . had shewn (when he pretended to have
gone to promote and execute the plans that were preconcerted with me,
by Lord Melville, Mr. Pitt and Mr. Addington etc.) that it ever was a
question of entering that country as masters and confiscators but on the
contrary as allies and supporters of their independency for the benefits
of trade and commerce . . . these may have been the plans of Genl.
Beresford and Sir Home Popham, but they certainly never were those

[1] Beresford to Castlereagh, 16 July 1806, W.O. 1/161.
[2] Robertson, op. cit., i. 93.
[3] *The Times*, 15 Sept. 1806.
[4] Instructions to Craufurd, 30 Oct. 1806, W.O. 1/161.
[5] Popham to Castlereagh, 30 April 1806, W.O. 1/161.

of the British Ministers I have just mentioned, nor of mine!'[1] Here, indeed, was the rub. Conquest was not liberation. Castlereagh, Windham's successor at the War Office in 1807, and the true heir of Pitt, early protested against so absurd a policy, and Auchmuty, who found, after the capture of Montevideo, that the people were 'inveterately hostile', that 'a sullen silence pervaded every rank', clearly perceived that while, in Buenos Aires, England might be welcomed as a liberator, as a conqueror she could expect nothing but enmity.[2]

Nevertheless, the merchants who had followed in the wake of the armies found the occupation of Montevideo profitable enough. By May they had received, through their trading, money or goods to the value of more than £1,200,000,[3] and, plainly, since Montevideo was by itself incapable of such a commerce, the city had become the centre of a far-flung contraband trade with Buenos Aires and other parts of the viceroyalty of La Plata. Ship after ship entered its harbour. The *Southern Star*,[4] which made its bow, on the 23rd May, as the first English newspaper to appear in South America and the first of any kind to be printed in Montevideo, abounded in advertisements for Irish linens and English woollens, hardware and glassware, boots and shoes, French brandies, Stockholm pitch and tar, furniture, bottled porter and 'good old rum'. It was not so difficult to sell goods, after all, and, however Paroissien's finances were managed, he was quite able, in June, to subscribe $50, with his friend Dr. Gardner, on behalf of the widows and orphans of the soldiers and sailors who had fallen when the town was taken.[5]

But these golden times were quickly over. On the 10th May Lieutenant-General John Whitelocke, dispatched with a small force from England in March, arrived in Montevideo to take command of operations in the River Plate. He was joined on the 14th June by Brigadier-General Craufurd, now diverted from his expedition to Chile

[1] Miranda to Alex. Cochrane, 4 June 1807, Cochrane Papers, 2320 f. 114, National Library of Scotland.
[2] Auchmuty to Windham, 7 Feb., 6 March 1807, W.O. 1/162.
[3] Auchmuty to Windham (enclosure), 11 May 1806, W.O. 1/162. For the British export figures as given by the Customs see Humphreys, op. cit., p. 349.
[4] There is a facsimile edition published by the Instituto Histórico y Geográfico del Uruguay (Montevideo, 1942).
[5] *The Southern Star*, 27 June 1807.

and in command of a substantial body of troops. The merchants and clerks in Montevideo were banded into a militia, which Paroissien joined as adjutant surgeon with the rank of lieutenant,[1] and while, in 'exhilarated spirits and elated hopes', they were left, with a body of regulars, to defend Montevideo, the second British attack on Buenos Aires was launched.

Whitelocke landed at the hamlet of Enseñada, near where the city of La Plata now stands, on the 28th June. Altogether he had under his command some nine thousand men, quite apart from those he had left at Montevideo. In Buenos Aires, where the indignant citizens, on the news of the fall of Montevideo, had insisted on the deposition of the incompetent Viceroy, and where Santiago Liniers, the hero of the reconquest and thereafter the military commander of the town, had been made acting captain-general of the viceroyalty, Liniers had at his disposal about eight thousand, of whom very few were regular soldiers. He failed, on the 2nd July, to prevent the enemy from crossing the little Riachuelo and was then rebuffed at Miserere (now the Plaza Once on Calle Rivadavia). But Whitelocke, with inexplicable ineptitude, failed to press his advantage, and meanwhile, Martín de Álzaga, a Basque merchant, and the ambitious and energetic first *alcalde*, or magistrate, of the municipality, who had played no small part in the deposition of the Viceroy, organized the defence of the city. The assault began on the 5th July, and then, the streets barricaded, the roof-tops manned, 'every male inhabitant' fighting 'with a resolution and perseverance' which Whitelocke at least did not expect,[2] the invading army met disaster. Whitelocke, it is true, was only half-vanquished. Many of his troops had not yet been employed. He could still have rallied and laid siege to the city. On the 7th, however, he capitulated. Bitterly as he was to be condemned, it was perhaps his wisest action during the whole campaign. Buenos Aires was immediately evacuated, and within a month of leaving Montevideo in anticipated triumph the British army was back, defeated.

But it was not only Buenos Aires that was to be evacuated under the terms of the capitulation. So also, apparently at the insistence of Martín

[1] *The Southern Star*, 13 June 1807.
[2] *The Proceedings of a General Court Martial . . . for the Trial of Lieut. Gen. Whitelocke . . .* 2 vols. (London, 1808), ii. 727.

de Álzaga, was Montevideo. Bewildered and astounded, the British merchants found that they had two months in which to wind up their affairs, and the last issue of the *Southern Star*, on the 11th July, containing little but notices of sales by auction, tells its own tale. Some of the disillusioned adventurers gloomily prepared to return to England. Others turned to fresh woods and pastures new in Brazil. Paroissien himself crossed the river to Buenos Aires and there petitioned Liniers for permission to settle, to open with his friend, Dr. Gardner, a school of chemistry, and to practice as a doctor.[1] That refused, despite the tolerant attitude which Liniers was inclined to adopt towards British merchants and British trade, he returned to Montevideo, and then he, also, determined to mend his fortunes in Brazil.

But the last few weeks in Montevideo were pleasant enough. There were parties. There was riding in the countryside. There were botanizing and mineralogical excursions to nearby *estancias* with Gardner and John Mawe,[2] a mineralogist who had come out to Montevideo in 1805, and had then suffered imprisonment or detention till Auchmuty's capture of the city secured his release. The people were now both courteous and friendly. 'They never alluded to the subject of Whitelocke's defeat,' wrote J. P. Robertson, who was there at the time, 'and when they spoke of our departure, it was ever with an expression of regret that they were about to lose many personal friends.'[3] 'They confessed', another Englishman recorded, 'that they had never before seen such commerce, that they had never enjoyed under their former government such security and happiness, or known such strict impartiality in the administration of justice.'[4] Something may be allowed for the natural courtesy of the Spaniard, *peninsular* and creole alike, and something also for the natural complacency of the British. Not all impressions, John Mawe's in particular, were equally favourable.[5] Nevertheless, when, on the 9th September, warships, merchantmen,

---

[1] Museo Mitre, *Documentos del archivo de Belgrano*, 7 vols. (Buenos Aires, 1913–17), v. 170–1.
[2] *Archivo de Belgrano*, v. 65; Governor and Junta of Montevideo to Strangford, 25 May 1809, enclosure, Public Record Office, Foreign Office Records, 63/70.
[3] Robertson, op. cit., i. 129.
[4] *Notes on the Viceroyalty of La Plata* (London, 1808), pp. 104–5.
[5] John Mawe, *Travels in the Interior of Brazil* (London, 1812), pp. 45–6.

transports, more than two hundred sail in all, left the harbour, it was with mixed feelings that the people of Montevideo watched the departure of the British.

Two days later the news of what had happened reached England, and it came, to the 'commercial interest', like a thunderbolt. The disaster, declared *The Times*, in language which must have been echoed in many a counting-house, was 'perhaps the greatest which has been felt by this country since the commencement of the revolutionary war'. Whitelocke was held up to universal execration as a coward and a traitor. And not only was Whitelocke condemned. So also was Popham. The whole affair, complained *The Times*, forgetful of its earlier raptures, had been, from first to last, 'a dirty sordid enterprise, conceived and executed in a spirit of avarice and plunder, without a parallel, except in the disgraceful expeditions of the Buccaneers', and the chief source of the calamity lay in the unauthorized beginnings of the invasions. 'Commerce, it seems, was the mistress whom we were to gain; and she, contrary to all former usage, was to be ravished, not wooed.' And commerce should occupy her proper place, in the rear of the army and navy, not in directing them.[1]

For Britain, the invasions of the Río de la Plata were little more than an unfortunate episode in the opening of South America to British trade. But they contained a moral, and the moral was drawn. In 1807 and 1808 other invasions were hoped for, and other expeditions were planned, to Buenos Aires and to Mexico; but their aim was emancipation, not subjugation.[2] Never again would Britain entertain the idea of conquest in South America. But neither would she long endure exclusion from South American trade. Her true interests, indeed, and her real desires, were commercial and strategic, not imperial. She looked not to territory but to trade. Her ends now were to prevent Spanish America from falling, as Spain was about to fall, under the dominion of France, to secure in the New World the bullion supplies which she needed to sustain the struggle in Europe, and to obtain, when she could, the opening of the Spanish-American markets. But for

[1] *The Times*, 14, 15 Sept. 1807.

[2] See Charles Vane, Marquess of Londonderry, *Memoirs and Correspondence of Viscount Castlereagh*, 12 vols. (London, 1848–53), vi. 366, vii. 385, 405, 445, viii. 99; Roberts, op. cit., pp. 319–26; W. S. Robertson, *The Life of Miranda*, 2 vols. (Chapel Hill, 1929), ii. 1–21.

the commercial community the winter of 1807 to 1808 was dark indeed and the outlook dim. 'It is to be feared', wrote the author of the *Notes on the Viceroyalty of La Plata*, 'that our prospects in South America are closed. If this be the case, it must be viewed by everyone who has the public welfare at heart, as a national calamity, the greatest that our country has for many years felt.'[1]

But whatever the gloom in England, in Buenos Aires the rejoicing was great; and the experience of the British invasions left, indeed, a permanent impress on the history of the River Plate. In the viceroyalty of La Plata, Spanish America had witnessed the deposition and imprisonment of the legal representative of the king.[2] It had seen a creole militia defeat a European army. It had seen a colonial port crowded with British ships and flooded with British goods. And the 'Americans', the creoles native-born, had tasted power and felt their strength. Their aspirations had been sharpened, their appetites whetted, and though, at Buenos Aires, the British invasions failed to precipitate the overthrow of Spanish colonial rule, they planted the seeds of revolution and they fertilized the soil.

At Montevideo the results were equally profound. Just as, before the viceroyalty of La Plata had been created, in 1776, Buenos Aires had sought to free itself from dependence on distant Lima, the capital of the once great viceroyalty of Perú, so Montevideo had sought to free itself from dependence on Buenos Aires. The city had enjoyed, during the British occupation, a commercial, indeed a political importance, that it could scarcely hope to enjoy again. It had seen the glory of reconquest and defence go to Buenos Aires, and its own part in those heroic days diminished or ignored; and from the moment that the British occupation ended, the political and economic rivalry between the two towns became more acute. At Liniers's orders, moreover, Francisco Javier Elío, a Spanish officer not long arrived in America, now assumed the governorship of Montevideo. This, as it turned out, was the appointment of an enemy, and the hostility between Elío and Liniers, who, as a reward for his services, was officially appointed Viceroy of La Plata *ad interim*, was soon superimposed on the mounting bitterness between

---

[1] op. cit., p. 101.
[2] Bartolomé Mitre, *Historia de Belgrano y de la independencia argentina*, 3 vols. (3rd edn., Buenos Aires, 1876–7), i. 184.

Montevideo and Buenos Aires. The British invasions of the Río de la Plata had done more than foreshadow the independence of Argentina. They foreshadowed also that separation of the eastern from the western bank of the river which was to result at last in the independence of Uruguay.

# CHAPTER II

## TRADE AND POLITICS IN BRAZIL, 1807-8

IN the company of his old friend, Gardner, his new friend, Mawe,[1] and some other of the English merchants Paroissien left Montevideo on the day fixed for the evacuation of the city, the 9th September, in a Portuguese vessel, the *Vencedor*, amidst, wrote Mawe, 'the malignant and hostile taunts of those very men who had of late expressed themselves our friends and well-wishers'.[2] Whatever the regrets of a few or the reservations of many, bonfires and illuminations, a popular patriotism, were the order of the day. The voyagers watched with melancholy the departure of the English fleet, and then, on the 11th, themselves left the Río de la Plata for the island of Santa Catarina.

Here they arrived on the 29th September, greatly impressed by the grandeur of the scenery. The town, Mawe noted, 'consists of several streets, and may contain from five thousand to six thousand inhabitants'. It afforded, he added, 'an agreeable retirement to merchants who have discontinued business, masters of ships who have left off going to sea, and other persons, who, having secured an independence, seek only leisure to enjoy it . . . it is enlivened by the numerous coasting-vessels from Bahia, Pernambuco, and other ports, bound for the Plata, which frequently touch here; and it is amply provided with artisans of all description . . . the ladies are handsome and very lively'.[3] A convenient centre for smuggling, Canning was to have his eye on it as a possible free port for the entry of British goods destined for the Spanish colonies.[4] Its people were friendly and its climate was agreeable, and here, welcomed and well-treated, Paroissien remained for

[1] Paroissien to his father, draft, 4 Sept. 1808, Letter Book, 1808–9. Paroissien Papers, hereinafter cited as P.P.

[2] Mawe, *Travels in the Interior of Brazil*, pp. 45–6.

[3] Ibid., pp. 47–8.

[4] Canning to Strangford, 17 April 1808, F.O. 63/59.

several weeks until, at the end of the year, he made his way to Rio de Janeiro, where he arrived on 15 January 1808.[1]

The move was deliberate and the time opportune. Six weeks earlier, Dom João, the Prince Regent of Portugal, his demented mother, Queen Maria I, his extraordinary wife, Carlota Joaquina, the daughter of Charles IV of Spain, the rest of the royal family, and an immense crowd of courtiers, fleeing the tide of Napoleon's invasion of the Peninsula, had embarked in the Tagus to seek refuge in Brazil. The fleet, convoyed by British warships, and carrying a great quantity of treasure, was dispersed by storms. Some of the vessels made Rio de Janeiro on the very day that Paroissien himself arrived. The Prince Regent, however, first touched Brazilian soil at Bahia on the 21st January, and there, on the 28th, he issued the famous *Carta Régia*, declaring the ports of Brazil open to the trade of all friendly nations. Once more embarking, he reached Rio de Janeiro on the 7th March, to land, amid scenes of great enthusiasm, on the following day.

The effects of this royal hegira, of the arrival of the Court, and of the opening of the ports, were immediate and profound. Rio de Janeiro, which, barely half a century before, had become the capital of Brazil and the residence of the viceroy, now became the capital of Portugal and the seat of the sovereign. Within a few years of the arrival of the Court the sleepy colonial town, in its incomparable setting, with its great aqueduct, its fine convents and its filthy streets, was transformed into what was perhaps the most cosmopolitan of Latin-American cities. Its population—some 50,000 when Paroissien arrived—doubled.[2] A bank was founded, a printing press introduced, a royal library opened, a gazette established. Foreigners were invited to enter the country, industry was encouraged. An impulse of new and vigorous life was transfused throughout the colony. Brazilians, in their own eyes and in those of the world, acquired a new dignity; and while, between native-born Brazilian and Portuguese immigrant, a bitter rivalry soon became evident, a new era in the history of Brazil opened.

So long as the Napoleonic wars continued, and so far as Europe was concerned, it was, of course, only to England that the ports of Brazil

[1] Draft letter by Paroissien, unaddressed, n.d. [1808]. P.P.
[2] J. B. von Spix and C. F. P. von Martius, *Travels in Brazil in the Years 1817–1820*, 2 vols. (London, 1824), i. 143–4.

RIO DE JANEIRO FROM THE ISLAND OF VILLEGAGNON

VIEW FROM THE SUMMIT OF THE CORCOVADO MOUNTAINS
NEAR RIO DE JANEIRO

were now opened.[1] And to the British merchants, plunged in gloom by
the débâcle in the River Plate, excluded from Lisbon and the ports of
Europe, and threatened, by the Non-Importation Act and the American
Embargo, with the loss of their trade with the United States, Brazil was
now the land of hope and promise. By August there were in Rio some
hundred and fifty or two hundred English 'adventurers'.[2] The market
was instantly overstocked. 'So great and so unexpected', wrote Mawe,
'was the influx of English manufactures into Rio de Janeiro, within a
few days after the arrival of the Prince, that the rent of the houses to
put them into became enormously dear. The bay was covered with
ships, and the custom-house soon overflowed with goods: even salt,
casks of ironmongery, and nails, salt-fish, hogsheads of cheese, hats,
together with an immense quantity of crates and hogsheads of earthen
and glass ware, cordage, bottled and barrelled porter, paints, gums,
resin, tar, etc. were exposed, not only to the sun and rain, but to general
depredation.'[3] When John Luccock, a partner in the firm of Luptons of
Leeds, arrived in June (bringing, incidentally, letters for Paroissien),
he found the 'town heaped high with cloth, ironmongery, clothing and
earthenware. The stock of fine cloth was sufficient "for several years".'[4]
Stays and coffins (neither of which happened to be used in Brazil),
saddles, even skates, glutted a market in which they could never be sold
and to which they should never have been sent;[5] and while the prices
of imported goods naturally fell, those of native produce rose. 'Many
goods of British manufacture', wrote Paroissien in April, 'are selling
here at about 50 per cent on the cost prices. How commerce can be supported in this way I am at a loss to determine.'[6] Smuggling, he noted,
was practised 'to a most extraordinary degree—tho much less during
the administration of the last Viceroy than formerly'.[7] And the
jealousy of the Portuguese for the British merchant, which was to grow
stronger as a result of the privileges granted to British subjects under

[1] Cf. Alan K. Manchester, *British Preëminence in Brazil, its Rise and Decline*
(Chapel Hill, 1933), pp. 70–3.
[2] Paroissien to J. Gardner, draft, 23 Aug. 1808, Letter Book, 1808–9. P.P.
[3] Mawe, op. cit., p. 324.
[4] Herbert Heaton, 'A Merchant Adventurer in Brazil, 1808–1818', *Journal
of Economic History*, vi (1946), p. 9.
[5] Mawe, op. cit., pp. 325–6.
[6] Journal, 30 April 1808.  [7] Ibid., 20 May 1808.

C

the Anglo-Portuguese commercial treaty of 1810, was naturally and quickly aroused.[1]

The total turnover of trade was, of course, extensive. Between July and December 1808, the value of British goods arriving at Rio de Janeiro exceeded £788,000, though some £114,000 worth of this merchandise consisted of goods imported in transit for the River Plate,[2] and according to the custom house returns in England, the value of all the goods exported to Brazil as a whole in 1808 amounted to the enormous total of nearly £2,380,000, a figure not exceeded or even equalled till 1818.[3]

But though extensive sales were made, commerce, Paroissien was to find, went on 'very badly',[4] and certainly for a casual trader, unable to stand losses or give long credit, the opportunities turned out to be less favourable than might have been supposed. An attempt to sell goods, other people's goods, in exchange for coffee, at Magé, not far from Rio de Janeiro, by no means improved Paroissien's opinion of Brazilians, who seemed to think, he wrote, that his sole purpose was that 'of taking the people in'.[5] But the practice of medicine, which he had begun on his arrival at the capital, proved even less lucrative, and an essay in the business of auctioneering similarly failed.[6] His friend, Dr. Gardner, left for the west coast of South America and Paroissien himself early toyed with the idea of returning to Santa Catarina and settling there as a merchant. By good fortune, however, a singular opportunity presented itself. The Prince Regent, 'the most humble man I ever conversed with',[7] needed butter. He possessed at Santa Cruz, to the south-west of Rio de Janeiro, a fine estate at which it could be made. Mawe, at the solicitation of João's Foreign Minister, Rodrigo de Souza e Coutinho, soon to be created Conde de Linhares, was persuaded to inspect the property and to establish a dairy. In this task Paroissien, whose 'amiable disposition and scientific pursuits rendered him', wrote

---

[1] Journal, 10 Aug. 1808; Paroissien to Gardner, draft, 15 Aug. 1808, Letter Book, 1808–9. P.P.

[2] Strangford to Canning, 1 March 1809, F.O. 63/68.

[3] Customs, 17/30. For the figures for 1812 to 1830 see Humphreys, *British Consular Reports*, pp. 344–9.

[4] Journal, 10 Aug. 1808.      [5] Ibid., 30 April 1808.

[6] Paroissien to his father, draft, 4 Sept. 1808, Letter Book, 1808–9. P.P.

[7] Journal, 7 July 1808.

Mawe, 'a very useful companion',[1] was perfectly ready to help. A
bargain was struck, and, accompanied by a sergeant and riding the
Prince Regent's horses, the two men left for Santa Cruz late in May.

Here Paroissien remained for a couple of months, making butter,
botanizing, and collecting shells, insects and birds, his life diversified by
excursions to Rio de Janeiro and by visits from the Prince Regent and
his son, the future Dom Pedro I—'a fine promising boy',[2] from members of the Court, and from English naval officers on the Brazil station.
But, whatever the pleasures of country life, Paroissien's heart was
never in Brazil, and his impressions of the people he met, Brazilians
and Portuguese alike, were not the most favourable. They were, he
noted to their credit, 'infinitely more temperate' than the English, and
were shocked at the drunken conduct of the British sailors who rolled
'about the streets like beasts'.[3] But he found them, also, inclined to
jealousy and suspicion of the British. The clergy were 'flagrantly
immoral', and, except for a minority who were freemasons and conspicuous for learning, sunk into 'Gothic barbarism'.[4] The people, particularly the slaves, were lazy and idle. 'There is not a farmer's man',
he noted, 'or even a working mechanic in England who can be half as
idle as a slave', though he noted also that if the 'labouring poor' in
England worked harder, they also lived worse 'than the major part of
the slaves in this country'.[5] On the whole, and despite the acquaintances he made both at Santa Catarina and Rio de Janeiro, Paroissien
much preferred his Spanish friends. The Spaniards, he wrote, 'seem a
kind of common mean between the Portuguese and English':[6] and it
was, indeed, in Buenos Aires, not in Brazil, that he wanted to be, and
to Buenos Aires that he intended to go so soon as he could, 'for several
reasons', as he told his father, 'but principally as I think most money is
to be made there'.[7]

So disposed, he eagerly seized on every rumour that Buenos Aires was
to be again attacked by the British or, at the least, would be opened, by
the colonial authorities there, to British trade. The arrival of Admiral
Sir Sidney Smith, on the 17th May, to take command of the Brazil

---

[1] Mawe, op. cit., p. 106.
[2] Journal, 6 July 1808.
[3] Ibid., 1, 19 May 1808.
[4] Ibid., 28 July, 8 May 1808.
[5] Ibid., 22 July 1808.
[6] Ibid., 3 May 1808.
[7] Paroissien to his father, draft, 4 Sept. 1808, Letter Book, 1808–9. P.P.

naval station, was one cheering event. It portended, he hoped, a further expedition against the city.[1] As for trade, everyone knew that under the tolerant eye of Santiago Liniers, the new Viceroy at Buenos Aires, the Spanish navigation laws might easily be evaded. Commerce between Rio de Janeiro and Buenos Aires was actively encouraged and was valued at the figure of £120,000 in the three months between March and June 1808 alone.[2] Nevertheless, for a Briton the risks were considerable. Britain and Spain were still at war. Paroissien's departure would have been precipitate and possibly ill-advised.

In July, however, occurred one of the most dramatic reversals of alliances in modern history. In March 1808 Charles IV of Spain abdicated in favour of his son, Ferdinand the Well-beloved. A few days later a French army entered Madrid. In May both Charles and Ferdinand, lured by Napoleon to Bayonne, renounced their rights, and in June Joseph Bonaparte was proclaimed king of Spain and the Indies. But Napoleon reckoned without the Spanish love of independence. The Spaniards rose, as Spaniards will always rise, against an alien hand. Juntas of resistance were spontaneously formed. In May the Junta of Asturias, and in June the Junta of Seville, declared war on France. Deputies were sent to England. On the 4th July peace between Spain and England was formally proclaimed in London, and on the 12th the expedition which Wellesley was preparing at Cork for the liberation of Spanish America sailed to liberate, not Spanish America from Spain, but Spain from France. As, wrote Castlereagh on the 20th June, 'by the insurrection in the Asturias, some probability of restoring the Spanish monarchy is revived . . . it is wished to suspend any measure tending to divide and therefore to weaken that monarchy'.[3] Henceforth, ideas of liberation, like those of conquest, in South America were officially renounced. Spain, like Portugal, had become the ally of England, united in a common cause. In the event of the subjugation of Spain, wrote Castlereagh in August, Britain 'would confine her views to forming such a connexion with the Spanish Dominions in South America as might best be calculated to protect their independence and

[1] Journal, 19 May 1808.
[2] Hill to Canning, 2 June 1808, F.O. 63/63; Manchester, op. cit., p. 116; Ricardo Levene, *Ensayo histórico sobre la revolución de mayo y Mariano Moreno*, 3 vols. (2nd edn., Buenos Aires, 1925), i. 180–91.
[3] Castlereagh, *Memoirs and Correspondence*, vi. 375.

resources against the designs of the common enemy',[1] and Canning, at the Foreign Office, laid it down in September that Britain could countenance no designs hostile to the Spanish colonies.[2]

True enough, the reversal of alliances led to no change in Spanish commercial regulations, no breach of the old monopolistic system. The ports of the Indies still remained closed to British commerce except in so far as local regulations might tolerate such trade or local officials connive at it. But the news of the rising in Spain and the break with France, which reached Rio de Janeiro late in August, lifted the British merchants' hopes and lifted Paroissien's. 'The general opinion is', he wrote to his future brother-in-law, Stephen Beuzeville, a silk manufacturer and general merchant of London, 'we shall have B.A. open to our trade which will be a glorious event, perhaps good for you particularly . . .'[3]; and to John Gardner, a relative of his friend, Dr. Daniel Gardner, also a London merchant, he declared: 'In the event of any English getting to Buenos Ayres I know if supported as you can support me I shall stand as good a chance as anyone.'[4] His hopes, in September, were still high. 'If the ports of South America are opened to a free trade with England', he wrote to his sister, 'I shall certainly return to Buenos Ayres',[5] and, by November, he could wait no longer. He entered into an agreement with Ralph Dodsworth Middleton, supercargo of the ship *Mary*, of London, arranged, in return for the sum of £300, to accompany Middleton on a voyage to the River Plate and, if necessary, to the Cape of Good Hope, to help him dispose of his goods, and, on the 5th November, set sail from Rio de Janeiro.[6]

But Paroissien sailed not merely as Middleton's dependant. He sailed as a secret political agent. In these crucial days, when the fate of Spain, and, with it, of Spanish America, hung in the balance, when Napoleon's agents were already arriving in the New World, and when in Brazil itself there was not only a European monarch, but, in the person of his

---

[1] Castlereagh to Sir Sidney Smith, 4 Aug. 1808, F.O. 72/91.

[2] Canning to Strangford, 2 Sept. 1808, F.O. 63/59.

[3] Paroissien to S.B., draft [c. 23 Aug. 1808], Letter Book, 1808–9. P.P. Stephen Beuzeville married Anna Maria Paroissien on 24 Sept. 1808.

[4] Paroissien to J. Gardner, draft, 23 Aug. 1808, Letter Book, 1808–9. P.P.

[5] Paroissien to Anna Maria Paroissien, draft, 30 Sept. 1808. Ibid.

[6] *Archivo de Belgrano*, v. 67–71; Undated, incomplete paper by Paroissien, c. 1809, and Questionnaire, B⁵ Ay⁵, 25 Oct. 1809. P.P.

wife, a representative of the Spanish royal house, Rio de Janeiro was a city of conspiracy. And Paroissien, young, impressionable, slightly gullible, was now to be involved in high politics and in the plots and designs of three very dissimilar but remarkable personages, the Princess of Brazil, Carlota Joaquina, Admiral Sir Sidney Smith, and a middle-aged political exile from Buenos Aires, one Saturnino Rodríguez Peña.

Dr. Saturnino Rodríguez Peña (for he was a doctor of theology), like so many of those ardent spirits who would soon lead Buenos Aires, and South America, on the road to independence, had been educated at the famous Academy of Monserrat in the University of Córdoba (where the future dictator of Paraguay, José Gaspar Rodríguez de Francia, was among his companions) and at the still more famous University of Chuquisaca in the mountain fastnesses of Upper Perú, which was, after the University of San Marcos at Lima, the most celebrated seat of learning in South America. Back in Buenos Aires, where he opened a school, he was one of a small group of like-minded friends who had already begun to dream, even before the British invasions of the Río de la Plata, of the independence of their native land. Buenos Aires invaded, the British defeated, and General Beresford forced to surrender, Rodríguez Peña helped the unfortunate general to escape from the captivity in which he had been improperly placed, in the sincere belief that by so doing he might serve the best interests of his country; and the fact that he then received an allowance from General Whitelocke and a pension from the British Government is no reflection on his patriotism.[1] He fled with Beresford to Montevideo, where Paroissien first met him. On the evacuation of Montevideo he sought refuge in Rio de Janeiro, and here he and Paroissien formed a close friendship. It was in Paroissien's company that Rodríguez Peña, on 19 May 1808, first met Admiral Sir Sidney Smith, who received him, wrote Paroissien, 'as one brother would receive another'.[2] Thereafter the two men met frequently, and Paroissien, as a third party at some of these meetings, found the Admiral 'a most pleasant man'.[3]

---

[1] Beresford to Castlereagh, 12, 28 May 1807, W.O. 1/162; Enrique Ruiz-Guiñazú, *Lord Strangford y la revolución de mayo* (Buenos Aires, 1937), pp. 68–9.

[2] Journal, 19 May 1808.          [3] Ibid., 14 June 1808.

Pleasant or not (and Paroissien later revised his opinion), Admiral Sir Sidney Smith, who had arrived at Rio de Janeiro, as the British commander-in-chief on the Brazil naval station, two months before the British ambassador, Lord Strangford, and who had to be recalled almost a year later on account of his extraordinary indiscretions and his perpetual interference with Strangford's policy, was a brave and energetic officer but an eccentric, vain and theatrical person, captivated, as Strangford justly complained, by romance and singularity;[1] and it is indeed difficult to comprehend the mentality of a man who could discover in the ambitious Carlota Joaquina a 'great perspicuity of genius and liberality of sentiment'.[2] But the strange fact remains that for this mendacious, malignant and despotic woman, now living in a state of scarcely veiled hostility to her husband, the Prince Regent, and prematurely old at the age of thirty-three, Sir Sidney Smith had conceived a romantic devotion. The liking was returned. The two warmly supported each other's plans; and, had success attended their design to erect in Buenos Aires a South American throne for the Princess of Brazil, Smith was to have been rewarded with the title of Duke of Montevideo.

This, then, was the plot (in which Rodríguez Peña was also implicated) and, fantastic as it at first blush appears, the circumstances were equally extraordinary. From its first arrival in Brazil the Portuguese Court had cast longing eyes upon the northern, or eastern, shores of the Río de la Plata, on that territory now known as the independent state of Uruguay. Here, in days gone by, Spain and Portugal had contended for domination, and here considerations of strategy reinforced the disputed claims of history. Portuguese plans were strengthened, or at least seemed to be strengthened, by the fact that England was still at war with Spain and had herself only recently invaded Buenos Aires; and with these facts in mind the Portuguese Foreign Minister, Souza e Coutinho, first attempted to gain his ends by indirection. That failing, and an offer to take Buenos Aires, in these dangerous times, under Portuguese protection having been declined, more forceful measures

---

[1] Strangford to Canning, 29 Nov. 1808, F.O. 63/61.
[2] Smith to Pole, 26 Sept. 1808, Public Record Office, Admiralty 1/19. The apologist of Carlota is J. M. Rubio, *La infanta Carlota Joaquina y la política de España en América (1808–1812)* (Madrid, 1920).

were prepared. The territory of the viceroyalty of La Plata was to be invaded, the town of Asunción, high up on the Paraguay, was to be attacked, the districts of Corrientes and Misiones were to be occupied, and then, while Admiral Sir Sidney Smith blockaded the Río de la Plata, combined operations would be directed against Montevideo.[1] Smith, who affected to fear a French invasion of the Río de la Plata, was quite ready to subserve these plans.[2] Lord Strangford, when he arrived in July and heard of them, was doubtful. The news of the events in Spain and Europe in the spring and summer of 1808, however, led to their frustration. 'The Portuguese look grim', wrote Paroissien, when that news arrived. 'The troops preparing against Montevideo will of course now receive counter-orders.'[3]

The Prince Regent, it is true, had by no means abandoned his intention of extending his dominions to the Río de la Plata. The plan was dear to his heart. And, indeed, when Spain herself was falling into captivity, what an opportunity might now be presented! It was, however, Carlota Joaquina's rather than her husband's opportunity. Carlota Joaquina's moment had come. She now loudly asserted her claims, as the daughter of Charles IV of Spain, and as the sister of Ferdinand VII, to represent, with the Infante Don Carlos, the Spanish royal house, overthrown by Napoleon. In a document which Smith drew up,[4] she solicited her husband to protect her rights, and, through Smith's good offices, broadcast her pretensions and manifestos throughout South America.

Lord Strangford strongly disapproved of these proceedings, and Paroissien's opinion perhaps reflected a general view. 'Ships have been sent to Buenos Ayres', he wrote to his father on September 4th, 'with offers to the People to establish the Prince of Spain (the next heir of the house of Bourbon) in Spanish America as guardian of the Country in trust for the rightful owners when they shall be liberated from the fangs of Bonaparte. I think this offer (tho' tis said 'twill be backed with a force of 20,000 men) will be rejected by the Spaniards who I am per-

---

[1] Strangford to Canning, 25 July 1808, F.O. 63/59. On Portuguese designs see Manchester, op. cit., pp. 113–18, and D. L. Molinari, *Antecedentes de la revolución de mayo*, 3 vols. (Buenos Aires, 1922–6), i. 5–18, iii. 3–7.
[2] Smith to Pole, 5 Aug. 1808, Admiralty 1/19.
[3] Paroissien to J. Gardner, draft, 23 Aug. 1808, Letter Book, 1808–9. P.P.
[4] Smith to Pole, 24 Aug. 1808, Admiralty 1/19.

suaded are more inclined to adopt a Republican form of government than a Monarchical Tyranny especially at the hands of the Portuguese.'[1] But the Princess and the Admiral pressed on with their plans, and far too fast and independently for the liking of Dom João. Towards the end of September Carlota packed her jewels and announced, much to the anger of her husband, that she would proceed to Buenos Aires herself, either accompanied or preceded by Sir Sidney Smith, and that she would then sign a treaty surrendering the Banda Oriental to Brazil provided that the Amazon were opened to Spanish commerce. She would go, she declared in mid-October, 'even although the batteries of Rio de Janeiro should fire upon her at her departure', and at the same moment Smith announced that in his opinion it was quite essential that she should be established as 'Reine Provisoire' in South America.[2]

It was at this point, while Strangford did his best to thwart Carlota's plans and prepared an energetic remonstrance to Canning against the 'perpetual and unauthorized' interventions of Sir Sidney Smith, and while the Prince Regent, angry with his wife, highly annoyed by Smith's conduct, but uncertain what line to follow, was lost in vacillation, that Rodríguez Peña and Paroissien actively entered the story. In Buenos Aires there was a group of persons, old associates of Saturnino Rodríguez Peña, quite prepared, for reasons of their own, to support Carlota's claims to rule. It included his younger brother, Nicolás. It included Juan José Castelli, Saturnino's friend at the Universities of Córdoba and Chuquisaca, and now an advocate of note. It included Manuel Belgrano, born in Buenos Aires—his father was an Italian—but educated in Spain, who had made a name for himself both as secretary to the *consulado*, the chamber of commerce or merchant guild, and as an economist and writer. And there were others. These men, dreamers of dreams, and the political legatees, as it were, of the 'age of enlightenment'—and revolution—would soon play a prominent part in events at Buenos Aires. They looked to the establishment not, of course, of an absolute monarchy in the Río de la Plata but of a constitutional monarchy. They believed that Spain was lost. They saw in the rule of

---

[1] Paroissien to his father, draft, 4 Sept. 1808, Letter Book, 1808–9. P.P.
[2] Strangford to Canning, 24 Oct. 1808, Nos. 23 and 25, F.O. 63/60; Manchester, op. cit., pp. 122–3.

Carlota the means for the peaceful achievement of independence. And in Rio de Janeiro Saturnino Rodríguez Peña shared their views.[1]

Strangford's account of what happened next was contained in a letter to Canning in July 1809. 'Immediately after the formation of the project entertained by the Princess of Brazil of proceeding in person to the Río de la Plata', wrote Strangford, 'it was determined by Her Royal Highness, in conjunction (as it is said) with Sir Sidney Smith, to send a confidential agent to the Spanish Colonies, for the purpose of preparing the minds of the Inhabitants in Her Royal Highness's favour, and of disposing them to receive her with alacrity and joy.' The person selected for this purpose was Paroissien, 'a native of England and a physician by profession', who was recommended to the Princess and to Smith by Rodríguez Peña. Rodríguez Peña, continued Strangford, who was 'known to be the Confidential Agent of the Republican Party in the Spanish Colonies', had, at that time, been reclaimed from his revolutionary principles, by the persuasion of Sir Sidney Smith, and had been induced to espouse the cause and to enter into all the Plans of the Princess. He engaged (at the instance of Sir Sidney Smith) to furnish Parosin [sic] with letters of introduction to all those persons in the Spanish Settlements who might be most likely to forward the Princess's designs.' These persons were Rodríguez Peña's former associates, 'the Republicans of Monte Video and Buenos Aires; whom he hoped to persuade of the absolute necessity of the measures recommended by Sir Sidney Smith, and which that Officer (according to Peña's statement) engaged to support in the name of the British Government'.[2]

Strangford's information was not entirely correct. It may well be that Rodríguez Peña was won over to the support of Carlota's plans by Smith's persuasions.[3] It is possible also—for he wrote of the Princess in singularly exaggerated terms—that he misinterpreted her character and aims. But if he had been converted to the cause of monarchy, he had certainly not been converted to the cause of absolutism, and Car-

---

[1] See Mitre, *Belgrano*, i. 216, and J. C. Chaves, *Castelli. El adalid de mayo* (Buenos Aires, 1944), p. 95.

[2] Strangford to Canning, 2 July 1809, F.O. 63/70.

[3] Smith to Castlereagh, 30 Oct. 1808, W.O. 1/163; Rodríguez Peña to Francisco de Miranda, 28 Aug. 1809, in Vicente Davila and others, *Archivo del general Miranda*, 24 vols. (Caracas and La Habana, 1929–50), xxiii. 281.

lota was an absolutist. Nor had he abandoned his 'revolutionary principles', in so far, at least, as the ultimate independence of his country was concerned; and though it may not have been at once apparent, either to Carlota or to Rodríguez Peña, there was, from the outset, a hostility of purpose between them. Carlota looked to absolute, Rodríguez Peña to constitutional monarchy, the one to the principle of legitimacy, the other to the summoning of a Cortes and the formation of a constitution.

According to his own account, however, Rodríguez Peña now composed, at Smith's instigation, a circular letter, dated at Rio de Janeiro on the 4th October, which Smith approved 'in all its parts',[1] and this was intended for wide distribution. Its references to Carlota Joaquina as a 'singular woman', ready 'to sacrifice everything' for the happiness of others, one 'whom it is impossible to hear without loving', are, indeed, somewhat reminiscent of Sir Sidney's own epistolary style. It referred to the subjugation of Spain and the dangers to be anticipated in the New World from France. It declared that the hour which would decide the destiny of America was at hand, and it exhorted Americans to invite Carlota to the Río de la Plata so that she might be proclaimed regent, a Cortes summoned and an independent empire established. The patriots, it concluded, could count on the protection and help of England.[2]

Further, Rodríguez Peña wrote personal letters to a number of friends and acquaintances in Buenos Aires, his brother Nicolás, Castelli, Martín de Álzaga (who had played so prominent a part in the reconquest of Buenos Aires from the British), and others; letters of introduction to Sir Sidney Smith (ready for delivery on his appearance in the Plate) and to the ineffable Colonel James Burke, an extraordinary character whom Castlereagh had sent out from London to discover the sentiments of the people in South America and to incite them against France, and whom Smith detained at Rio de Janeiro till 1809;[3] and, finally, a secret letter of instructions to Paroissien, who, Rodríguez Peña declared, was 'perfectly instructed' on all the affairs of the day.

[1] Rodríguez Peña to Miranda, 28 Aug. 1809. Loc. cit.

[2] *Archivo de Belgrano*, v. 44–7.

[3] Castlereagh to Burke, 4 Aug. 1808, F.O. 72/91; Smith to Burke, 23 March 1809, F.O. 72/91. For Burke's strange career see Roberts, *Las invasiones inglesas del Río de la Plata*, particularly pp. 44–8.

In this secret letter, dated the 24th October, Paroissien was advised to make immediate contact with Nicolás Rodríguez Peña in order to devise means to win the support of the Viceroy, Liniers, and of Álzaga; he was to approach the ex-Viceroy, Sobremonte (whom Liniers had replaced); he was to propagate the plan 'with a haughty air' as one which would certainly be adopted; and he was, in particular, to take care to indoctrinate the priests, 'who have an incomparable influence, especially among the lower classes', the army officers and officials.[1]

It was not till some five or six days before Paroissien left Rio de Janeiro that Rodríguez Peña asked him to convey these letters to Buenos Aires, together with some trunks—they contained silk stockings and laces—for Nicolás, and the packet was given to him the evening before his departure. Rodríguez Peña then read to him the circular letter, explained that this and other letters were 'approved of by the Princess herself and the Admiral' and that his and their purpose was to preserve 'the integrity of Spanish America', threatened by the intrigues of France, by declaring Carlota 'Regent of the Americas'.[2]

Embarking on the *Mary* in the early hours of the morning of the 5th November, Paroissien placed these papers in a secret drawer of his portable writing-desk. But when the *Mary* sailed later in the day, he was not the sole bearer of dispatches. There also sailed on the same ship a Spanish merchant of Buenos Aires, one Julián de Miguel, who carried a letter from Carlota herself, dated the 1st November, and addressed to Liniers in person. In this the Princess denounced Paroissien as the bearer of documents 'full of revolutionary principles, subversive of the present monarchical order and tending to the establishment of a fanciful and visionary republic'.[3] This letter was given to Miguel on the night of the 4th, together with instructions to the first official who should board the ship on her arrival at port to keep a careful watch on Paroissien until suitable measures could be taken.[4]

Conduct so extraordinary needs no little explanation. What Paroissien later learnt was that 'a fellow of the name of Presas (who had been lifted from the dust by my friend Peña and then by recommendation of

---

[1] *Archivo de Belgrano*, v. 41–3.
[2] Undated, incomplete paper by Paroissien, c. 1809. P.P.
[3] *Archivo de Belgrano*, v. 227–9.
[4] Ibid., v. 20–1, 63–5, 227–31.

Sir Sidney acted as secretary to the Princess of Brazil) informed his Royal Mistress that I was charged with papers relative to the *Independence* of Spanish America'—information, wrote Paroissien, which she later found to be false.[1] Strangford took a similar view. Presas, he wrote, who had been banished from Buenos Aires, and later from Montevideo, for the crime of forgery, inspired the Princess with the belief that Rodríguez Peña was 'acting a double part' and that Paroissien was in fact charged to promote the views of the 'Republican' party. 'The Princess immediately conceived the idea of turning this supposed circumstance to account, and by denouncing Peña and Parosin [*sic*] to the Spanish Colonial Government, of making a merit of her own zeal for the preservation of the Spanish monarchy; furnishing at the same time a positive proof of the danger to be apprehended from the Republicans, and of the urgent necessity that her Royal Highness should proceed forthwith to exercise the functions of Regent in South America.' When Paroissien was interrogated, however, nothing was discovered that could convict Rodríguez Peña and Paroissien of any other designs than those which the Princess herself had confided to them. On the contrary, it appeared that Rodríguez Peña had acted in good faith. Nevertheless, concluded Strangford, the fixed determination of the Princess to subvert the colonial government, and the hopes of English assistance which Sir Sidney Smith held forth, were so manifestly proved that a process for high treason was immediately begun against Paroissien.[2]

This interpretation is supported by the secret memoirs of that born and shifty intriguer, Dr. José Presas himself. A Catalan who had in 1808 removed from the Río de la Plata to Rio de Janeiro and had entered into the service of Sir Sidney Smith and then of Carlota, Presas was, in 1812, given a certificate by the Princess extolling his merits on account, among other things, of his discovery of the seditious designs of the 'traitor Peña'.[3] As for Sir Sidney Smith, he also maintained that Paroissien was arrested at the suggestion of the Princess, Her Royal Highness, he informed the Admiralty, having obtained information

[1] Paroissien to George Paroissien, 9 December 1809, draft, Letter Book, 1808–9. P.P.

[2] Strangford to Canning, 2 July 1809, F.O. 63/70.

[3] José Presas, *Memorias secretas de la princesa del Brasil . . .* (Bordeaux, 1830), p. 206.

that Paroissien had taken upon himself to use the Princess's name as well as Smith's own 'as partisans of the independence of the Spanish colonies'.[1]

That Carlóta and Rodríguez Peña had different ends in view is certainly true. Theirs was an alliance for an immediate common purpose and nothing more. Each was a means for the designs of the other. And though, as Strangford pointed out, there was nothing in Rodríguez Peña's letters actually to convict him of bad faith with the Princess, once Carlota's suspicions had been aroused, her action was of a piece with her character. The part played by Sir Sidney Smith is more perplexing. If Rodríguez Peña is to be believed—and the weight of circumstantial evidence is on his side—Smith had approved the famous circular letter 'in all its parts'. On the 30th October—less than a week before Paroissien left Rio de Janeiro—the Admiral described Rodríguez Peña as a 'worthy man' to whom he paid a pension of £300 a year.[2] On the face of things, it is scarcely credible that he did not know of Paroissien's mission. Yet, he could write to Viceroy Liniers in 1809 that Paroissien was a man 'who never having been able to succeed as a physician to the amelioration of his own affairs has taken upon himself to pretend to apply remedies to the ills of the state committed to your care and management'. 'I have nothing whatever to do', he added, 'with this Mr. Parosin [sic] and his speculative proposals, whatever they may be, nor do I know more of him than his being introduced to me by a Spaniard to interpret between us, which, however, was not necessary, and consequently he never was employed by me even so far as that.'[3] And, if Paroissien's information was correct, Smith gave 'positive orders' to his nephew, Lieutenant Charles Smith, who later visited Montevideo, 'not to say a syllable about my person', although, added Paroissien, 'he, Sir Sidney, was partly the cause of my getting into the hobble'.[4]

That the Princess, in her denunciation of Paroissien, acted without consulting Smith, is likely enough, though it is improbable that the Admiral could long have remained in ignorance of her action. It has

[1] Smith to Pole, 24 Feb. 1809, Admiralty 1/19, F.O. 72/91.
[2] Smith to Castlereagh, 30 Oct. 1808, W.O. 1/163.
[3] Smith to Liniers, 18 March 1809, F.O. 72/91.
[4] Paroissien to George Paroissien, 9 December 1809, draft, Letter Book, 1808–9. P.P.

been suggested that in view of instructions which he had lately received from England, informing him of the state of affairs in Spain, Smith thought that he had gone too far in his promise to Rodríguez Peña of English aid, and that, rather than confess his error, he abandoned Paroissien to his fate.[1] But pusillanimity was not among the Admiral's failings, and however strange his conduct, this explanation scarcely accords with the exalted view which he took, at this moment, of his own powers or with the intemperate manner in which he continued, throughout November, to forward Carlota's designs.[2] He remained her advocate and defender throughout the following months. But his opportunities to fish in the troubled waters of the River Plate were soon to be curtailed. His activities were sternly disapproved in England, and in March 1809 he was recalled, to be replaced by Admiral de Courcy. He left Rio de Janeiro in June 1809. It remained for Strangford, in reply to a communication from Governor Elío of Montevideo giving an account of Rodríguez Peña's plans, which were alleged to have the support of England, to attempt to allay the suspicions which Smith's conduct had aroused, to assure the governor that England would never countenance any project injurious to the honour or integrity of the Spanish nation, and to disavow any person who might have been concerned in any plans to effect changes in the Spanish colonies. Nor, said Strangford, would Britain ever consent that any other State should, under any pretext, disturb the tranquillity of an ally.[3]

As for Carlota, she persisted in her efforts to reach the Río de la Plata. But Strangford was now in control at Rio de Janeiro. Her husband peremptorily forbade her departure, and, with the recall of Sir Sidney Smith, her cause was lost. Her character and her ambitions now became more clearly understood. But she remained, in 1809 and 1810, a centre of intrigue and a disturbing element in the politics of the Río de la Plata and certainly did her best to exacerbate the discord which divided Montevideo from Buenos Aires.[4]

To the fate of Paroissien, of course, both Carlota and Sir Sidney

---

[1] Castlereagh to Smith, 4 Aug. 1808, F.O. 72/91. Cf. Carlos A. Pueyrredón, *En tiempos de los virreyes* (Buenos Aires, 1932), pp. 193–4.

[2] Strangford to Canning, 29 Nov. 1808, F.O. 63/61.

[3] Governor and Junta of Montevideo to Strangford, 25 May 1809; Strangford to Elío, 11 Aug. 1809, F.O. 63/70.

[4] Manchester, op. cit., pp. 124–30.

Smith were entirely indifferent. The unfortunate agent, who had left Rio de Janeiro somewhat hurriedly and had made himself acquainted with Rodríguez Peña's instructions while at sea,[1] had arrived at Montevideo in high spirits on 17 November 1808. With his usual eye for commerce he noted that the *Admiral Berkeley* had obtained permission to land her cargo—valued at £40,000[2]—'in consequence of advancing 20,000 dollars to the Government to pay the troops', and that tallow was extremely scarce, large quantities having been bought up on account of the 'British Government, to be sent home'.[3] He noted also that Montevideo was 'much altered for the better, the streets cleaner, the houses all numbered and the people well dressed.'[4] He failed to note the conduct of Julián de Miguel. Miguel obeyed Carlota's orders to the letter. The port officials were warned, Governor Elío was informed, Carlota's letter to Liniers was sent across the river to Buenos Aires, Paroissien's movements were watched; and, at 11 p.m. on the night of the 19th November, he himself, 'tall, fair, with a scar over the left cheek near the temple', as his description ran, was arrested on board the *Mary* and his papers seized.[5] On the 22nd, after an inventory of the papers had been made and the contents of the secret drawer in his writing-desk, which he had at first refused to divulge, revealed,[6] he was interrogated in the presence of Elío himself, and then, on the charge of high treason, committed to prison.

[1] Undated, incomplete paper by Paroissien, c. 1809, P.P.
[2] For the *Admiral Berkeley* see W.P.S. to Castlereagh, enclosure, 20 Jan. 1810, F.O. 72/157.
[3] Paroissien to Moore, draft, c. 18 or 19 Nov. 1808, Letter Book, 1808–9. P.P.
[4] Paroissien to 'dear Jack', c. 18 or 19 Nov. 1808. Ibid.
[5] *Archivo de Belgrano*, v. 13.
[6] Undated, incomplete paper by Paroissien c. 1809. P.P.; *Archivo de Belgrano*, v. 16–17, 72–4.

A VIEW OF THE TOWN AND

HARBOUR OF MONTE VIDEO

So taken from the spot where the Troops under
the Command of Sir Samuel Auchmuty *were encamped previous to the Assault which took
place on the morning of the 3rd of February 1807.*

BUENOS AIRES, FROM THE PLAZA DE TOROS

# CHAPTER III

## MONTEVIDEO AND BUENOS AIRES, 1808–10

WHEN, in November 1808, Paroissien returned to Montevideo, to imprisonment and the shadow of death, the times were stormy in the River Plate. The tension between Montevideo and Buenos Aires, mounting steadily since the days of the British occupation, had now reached its height. Montevideo bitterly resented the commercial and economic control of its affairs which Buenos Aires attempted to exercise. Opinion in both towns, as almost everywhere else in the Spanish colonies, was deeply confused by the news of events in Spain and by the rival claims of competing authorities to inherit the sovereignty of the Castilian Crown. One after another, emissaries arrived from Rio de Janeiro, from France, from Spain. Every ship seemed to bring a new rumour or the threat of a new danger, and Governor Elío, fearful alike of Brazil and France, regarded with equal suspicion the Court at Rio de Janeiro and the Viceroy at Buenos Aires. Governor Elío and Viceroy Liniers were now, indeed, at daggers drawn. Elío was a Spaniard and an ultra-royalist. Liniers, though he had served the Spanish Crown faithfully and well, was a Frenchman. But what a fatality was this! A Frenchman at the head of the vice-royalty of La Plata at a moment when Napoleon was conquering Spain! And Liniers, whatever his services in the days of the re-conquest of Buenos Aires from the British, had shown, in the view of true-blue Spaniards, a strange partiality for foreigners. Useless to pretend, moreover, that in the viceregal city itself there was not evidence of sedition. There, as throughout Spanish America, the gulf between Spanish Americans native-born and Spaniards born in Spain— between the educated creoles on the one hand, lawyers, landowners and merchants, and the Spanish emigrés on the other, holders of offices, representatives of the great import and export houses of Seville

D

and Cádiz, monopolistic traders, arrogant soldiers—was not only wide and deep, but widening and deepening. Strange doctrines were abroad of free trade and creole rights, and Liniers seemed to lean towards the creole party, the source, indeed, of his own authority. Hot-headed, hot-blooded, and in touch with other Spaniards who were Liniers's enemies in Buenos Aires, Elío openly accused the Viceroy of treason and of con-niving at, or at least tolerating, Napoleon's designs. He flouted the viceregal authority. He rebuffed with violence an official whom Liniers sent to replace him, and, with cries of 'Death to Buenos Aires! Long live our Governor!', the citizens of Montevideo embraced his cause. On 21 September 1808, in *cabildo abierto*, or open meeting of the town council, they repudiated, to all intents and purposes, the authority of the Viceroy and established, in the name of Ferdinand VII, a Govern-ing Junta of their own with Elío at its head. Montevideo had tempor-arily withdrawn from the rest of the viceroyalty of La Plata.[1]

Had the times been normal, a prisoner arrested, as Paroissien was arrested, on a capital charge would, in the ordinary course of pro-cedure, immediately have been sent to Buenos Aires for investigation by the Viceroy and the members of the royal *audiencia*, which was at once an administrative tribunal and the supreme court of justice. But, in these peculiar circumstances, Elío thought otherwise. He forwarded to Spain—proof of his lynx-eyed activity—a full account of what had happened. He transmitted all the details—he could hardly do less—to Liniers, and Carlota's letter to the Viceroy, denouncing Paroissien, was at once delivered. But Paroissien himself he held at Montevideo, thus in the view of the authorities at Buenos Aires paralysing investigations at the capital.

There, proceedings against Nicolás Rodríguez Peña and a long series of interrogations of suspected persons were begun. At both towns officialdom was careful to refrain from openly accusing Carlota herself of any participation in the plot and affected to suppose that it had entirely originated with Saturnino Rodríguez Peña. Saturnino, safe in Rio de Janeiro, could not, of course, be touched, though his extradition was sought, in vain. But Paroissien, as his agent, was in grave danger. A political prisoner, accused of complicity in high treason, he was

[1] P. Blanco Acevedo, *El gobierno colonial en el Uruguay y los orígenes de la nacionalidad* (3rd edn., Montevideo, 1944), pp. 222–5.

beyond the reach of British aid, even if British aid might have been forthcoming, and of this there was no question. Admiral Sir Sidney Smith disavowed him.[1] Lord Strangford, to whom Governor Elío sent a long report of the case, would not, even if he could, intervene. Though he believed that the trial of Paroissien would 'probably terminate in sentence of death being passed upon that unfortunate man',[2] he was only too anxious to repudiate any persons who might have been concerned in any plans to effect changes in the Spanish colonies.[3] Closely confined and later put in irons, Paroissien 'expected his fate in silent despair'.

Elío, however, declined to part with his prisoner, and it may well have been to this recalcitrance that Paroissien owed his salvation. In Buenos Aires proceedings to unravel the conspiracy had to be suspended, in April 1809, for want of Paroissien's presence.[4] Nor was it till Liniers had been superseded, in July, by a new Viceroy sent out from Spain, who brought with him instructions to conclude Paroissien's trial and punish the criminal,[5] that Elío obeyed superior orders and at last dispatched his prisoner to the capital. On 7 October 1809, 'the irons', wrote Paroissien, 'which had been so infamously put upon my legs two months before' (possibly as a result of the communication to Elío of these instructions from Spain) were removed.[6] Paroissien was taken under guard to the Mole and there placed on board a launch for Buenos Aires. At Buenos Aires, on the following day, he was confined in the Ranchería, opposite to the old Jesuit College. And here, in 'a miserable pigstye', which he was, however, allowed to have whitewashed,[7] after rather more than ten months' imprisonment at Montevideo, he was to remain imprisoned for eight months more.

The legal proceedings, suspended in Buenos Aires since April, were now renewed and the business of interrogation began all over again. Paroissien, however, though he complained from time to time of his

---

[1] Above, p. 30.
[2] Strangford to Canning, 2 July 1809, F.O. 63/70.
[3] Strangford to Elío, 11 Aug. 1809, F.O. 63/70.
[4] *Archivo de Belgrano*, v. 165–6. Cf. also J. N. Matienzo, ed., *Documentos relativos a los antecedentes de la independencia de la república argentina*, 2 vols. and index (Buenos Aires, 1912–13), i. 71.
[5] Levene, *La revolución de mayo y Mariano Moreno*, i. 320, note 2.
[6] Journal, 7 Oct. 1809.　　　　　　　　　　　　[7] Ibid., 9 Oct. 1809.

accommodation, of insults and of occasional violence from his guards, and, more particularly, of injury to his health, was not particularly ill-treated. Visitors were denied. But he was allowed to receive and to write letters. He began a series of appeals to successive British naval officers in the River Plate,[1] and in December no less a person than Dr. Juan José Castelli undertook his defence,[2] and an abler advocate than this distinguished creole lawyer Paroissien could hardly have hoped to find.

Meanwhile great events had occurred and were impending at Buenos Aires in 1809, at a time when the structure of colonial government was dissolving but the structure of colonial society remained intact. When, in July and August 1808, the news had arrived, first of the abdication of Charles IV and then of the overthrow of the Spanish royal house, Napoleon's pretensions were indignantly repudiated and the authority of Ferdinand was loyally proclaimed. But, as month succeeded month, excitement and apprehension grew. Ferdinand was a captive, and the prospect must be faced that the cause of Spain was, at least temporarily, lost. But who, then, should rule in America, Spaniards or Spanish Americans, *peninsulares* or creoles? Elío, in Montevideo, had given one answer. Belgrano, Saturnino Rodríguez Peña, and his friends had proposed another. True, properly constituted authorities already existed. There was a viceroy, there was a royal *audiencia*, there were the innumerable officials of a great viceroyalty. But who should govern the governors? The world was being born anew. What if the old Spaniards should seek to maintain the reign of privilege? What if the creoles should assume control and sweep all privilege away? The ferment of ideas had been brewing ever since the days of invasion and reconquest, and now, in confusion and uncertainty, men's minds were torn and their hearts divided. Old loyalties conflicted with new aspirations, established political and economic interests with new political and economic hopes.

Paradoxically enough, it was the old Spaniards who first resorted to revolutionary procedure and the creoles who at first upheld existing order. Of the old Spaniards, the leader was that same Martín de Álzaga who had shared with Liniers the glory of the defence of the city against

[1] Drafts, Letter Book, 1808–9. P.P.
[2] Paroissien to J. R. de Basavilbaso, draft, 16 Dec. 1809. Ibid.

the second British invasion in 1807. Álzaga, wealthy, influential and a magistrate, controlled the *cabildo*. He held to the ideas of Elío; he hated and distrusted Liniers, whose office he had hoped to fill; he enjoyed the powerful support of the bishop; and on 1 January 1809, the day on which the *cabildo* for the coming year should be appointed, Álzaga attempted, with the aid of the Spanish soldiery in Buenos Aires, to depose the Viceroy and to form a junta after the manner of Montevideo. But this plan to establish the ascendancy of the old Spaniards was frustrated. At the critical moment there appeared on the scene the commander of the 'Patrician' regiment of creole troops (which Liniers had organized), Cornelio Saavedra, who, though born in the distant mining town of Potosí, had long been resident in Buenos Aires; and the presence of Saavedra's troops turned the day. Liniers retracted the resignation which had been forced upon him, and while he received a popular ovation, Álzaga was arrested. Packed off by sea to Patagonia, he was promptly rescued by Elío from Montevideo.

The alignment of forces, it is true, was not yet clear and definite. Some of the creoles supported Álzaga and the *cabildo*. Many of the Spanish officials upheld the legal authority of the Viceroy. But the victory, nevertheless, was essentially a creole victory, and the self-confidence and prestige of the creole party were correspondingly enhanced. Six months later, however, it was the turn of the Spaniards to triumph. The so-called 'Junta Central' at Seville now governed what was left of free Spain in the name of Ferdinand VII, though its authority was self-assumed and by no means wholly popular. It had fled from Aranjuez to Seville in December 1808 and, its distrust of Liniers aroused by the reports arriving from America, it had decided in January to relieve the Viceroy of his command, though awarding him the title of Conde de Buenos Aires. His successor, a naval officer, Baltasar Hidalgo de Cisneros, who had fought at Trafalgar, landed at Montevideo on the 2nd July, where the Governing Junta promptly recognized his authority and dissolved itself. At Buenos Aires he found, he wrote, 'two formidable parties' (the Spaniards and the creoles), the viceroyalty convulsed, great diversity of opinions on the fate of Spain, 'intimations of independence', and other evils.[1] He was,

[1] See the *informe* of Cisneros of 22 July 1810 in *Memorias de los virreyes del Río de la Plata* (Buenos Aires, 1945), pp. 569–70.

however, received with acclaim by the Spaniards, and without resistance by the creoles (though resistance was certainly thought of), and he acted, initially at least, with conspicuous moderation.

In June, Manuel Belgrano, so pertinacious an advocate of liberal economic doctrines (as well as of an independent monarchy in the Río de la Plata under the Princess Carlota), had urged upon Liniers the necessity of opening the port of Buenos Aires to British commerce, and Liniers had, in fact, been 'both publicly and privately very friendly' to the British merchants.[1] He had been willing to dispense, in so far as he could, 'with the rigorous Spanish colonial laws',[2] and had 'tolerated' the British flag.[3] In the twelve months between November 1808 and November 1809, indeed, at least thirty-one British vessels arrived at Buenos Aires, with goods to the value of more than £1,200,000, all of which were 'landed by contraband';[4] and Paroissien, on his journey from Montevideo to Buenos Aires in October, himself noted seventeen British merchant vessels lying off the shore 'waiting for permission to land their cargoes'.[5]

It was impossible for Cisneros, fresh from Spain, to approve of this illicit commerce. But the Treasury was empty for want of customs' revenue, since trade with Spain was practically suspended, and the political situation was delicate. When, in August, therefore, two British merchants petitioned for leave to dispose of a cargo of goods recently brought from England, he passed their petition to the *cabildo* and *consulado* for study and advice, proposing that an *ad hoc* committee should be appointed to consider the whole question. The *cabildo* grudgingly conceded that foreign, as distinct from imperial trade was, under existing circumstances, 'a necessary and indispensable evil'. The *consulado*, equally reluctantly, concurred. The representative of the *consulado* of Cádiz, however, violently protested. The old Spanish merchants subscribed a loan of a million dollars to induce the Viceroy to maintain the old exclusionist system.[6] And at this point a young creole advocate, Mariano Moreno, presented, on behalf of the agricul-

[1] William Dunn to Alex. Cunningham, 26 July 1809, F.O. 72/90.
[2] Sidney Smith to Pole, 24 Feb. 1809, F.O. 72/91.
[3] Sidney Smith to Pole, 8 April 1809, F.O. 72/90.
[4] W.P.S. to Castlereagh, Buenos Aires, 20 Jan. 1810, enclosure, F.O. 72/157.
[5] Journal, 7 Oct. 1809.
[6] Mackinnon to Canning, 29 Sept. 1809, F.O. 72/90.

turists and landowners of La Plata, his famous memorial, the *Representación, en nombre de los labradores y hacendados de las campañas del Río de la Plata*.

Dr. Mariano Moreno, who thus, for the first time, appeared as a leader of the creole party, was another of those sons of Buenos Aires who had been educated at the University of Chuquisaca. There he had read theology and law. But he had read also Locke and Raynal, Montesquieu and Adam Smith. Back in Buenos Aires he practised at the bar. Fiery and fearless, restless and tireless, he was, in 1809, only thirty-one years old. Hitherto a genuine antipathy to Liniers had restrained Moreno from throwing in his lot with the creole dissidents in Buenos Aires. But now he leapt to fame, and in a trenchant denunciation of the old monopolistic system and a vigorous plea for free trade, Moreno denied that the *consulado* and the *cabildo*, still less the agent of the *consulado* of Cádiz, represented the true interests of the people of La Plata. Should the Government hesitate, he asked, between the welfare of the wretched labourer who produced the fruits of the earth and that of the monopolistic merchant, the blood-sucker of the state? Why was the Treasury empty? Why were the warehouses filled with native products which could not be exported? Why, when trade with Spain herself was cut off, did a contraband, illicit trade flourish? Because, said Moreno, of an outmoded and tyrannical commercial system, because the interests of a few were placed before the good of the many. The monopolists, turned contrabandists, should blush for shame. But the remedy was at hand. The interests of the Treasury were identical with those of the province. All that was necessary was to open the port to trade with England, that 'rich and generous' country whose aid was absolutely indispensable to Spain. 'My imagination is carried away,' he cried, 'intoxicated by the multitude of benefits with which an active commercial system could achieve our happiness . . . our roadsteads will be crowded with shipping . . . by a thousand channels the seeds of population and prosperity will be dispersed.'

Whatever the effects of the *Representación*—and its influence on the course of events in Buenos Aires is a matter of dispute[1]—it remains one of the most notable documents in the history of Argentine political and

[1] See Levene, op. cit., i. 205 ff., and D. L. Molinari, *La representación de los hacendados de Mariano Moreno* . . . (Buenos Aires, 1914).

economic thought. It was a demand for the economic emancipation of
Buenos Aires, for that freedom of trade which Buenos Aires and
Montevideo, in 1806 and 1807, had briefly tasted and could never
forget. In Buenos Aires it circulated in manuscript. It was translated
and published abroad. And on the 6th November, the consultative
committee convoked by the Viceroy agreed that the port should be
opened to foreign trade under specified duties and regulations, which
were promulgated immediately.

The results were instantaneously beneficial, and the Viceroy was
relieved from his financial difficulties. The Spanish monopolists, however, protested to Spain, and Álzaga, who, together with his fellow
conspirators of January, had been pardoned by Cisneros and restored to
favour, led the opposition. 'To the old Spanish merchants', wrote a
British trader, 'hitherto very profitably employed in a monopoly un-
controlled and unrivalled, our flags of every description and our faces
are very unpleasant',[1] and when, in December, the uneasy Viceroy
ordered foreigners to be expelled from the city and province, it was to
their influence that the move was attributed. So far as the British
merchants were concerned, the Viceroy, it is true, receded from the
rigour of this order. But that the Junta Central of Spain would wish to
restore the old colonial laws, or that the Spanish merchants in Buenos
Aires, detesting the British and creoles alike, would support it, no
one doubted. The days of the Junta Central, however, were already
numbered, and in Buenos Aires, where Belgrano used his new *Correo
de Comercio* to disseminate liberal economic and political ideas, no
Dames Partington and their mops could stem the tide of change.
Nothing could now stand between Buenos Aires and free trade. The
economic emancipation of Buenos Aires was determined before its
political emancipation began.

Buenos Aires, however, was not the only seat of colonial discontents,
and while in Buenos Aires Cisneros, caught between the Spaniards and
creoles, pursued a cautious and wavering policy which satisfied neither,
it was not so in another part of the viceroyalty. In that remote and

---

[1] Mackinnon to Canning, 4 Feb. 1810, F.O. 72/107. See also D. B. Goebel,
'British Trade to the Spanish Colonies, 1796–1823', *American Historical
Review*, xliii (1938), pp. 309–12, and Benjamin Keen, *David Curtis de Forest
and the Revolution of Buenos Aires* (New Haven, 1947), pp. 70–5.

distant region then known as Alto Perú and today as Bolivia, the example of disobedience to constituted authority which Elío had set at Montevideo in September 1808, and which Álzaga had tried to imitate at Buenos Aires in January 1809, had not been lost. Upper Perú, or the presidency or *audiencia* of Charcas, which had formerly owed allegiance to the viceroyalty of Perú, had been transferred to the viceroyalty of La Plata in 1776. Here were the celebrated silver-mines of Potosí. Here was the ancient city of La Paz. And here was the University of Chuquisaca itself. The 'town of four names' (for it has been known in turn as Charcas, La Plata, Chuquisaca and Sucre) was the seat not only of the University, founded in 1624, and of the Caroline Academy attached to it, but of a royal *audiencia* and an archbishopric as well. It contained in 1809 perhaps twenty thousand souls, and on the long road from Buenos Aires to Lima no other town could surpass it in dignity and simple charm.

At Chuquisaca there had arrived in November 1808, one, General José Manuel Goyeneche. American by birth, but an officer of Spain, Goyeneche had been sent to Spanish America by the Junta of Seville —the most important of the provincial juntas of Spain—which had, at this time, asserted its own title to rule both Spain and the Indies. Strangely enough, however, he also brought to Chuquisaca letters from the Princess Carlota Joaquina, in which the Princess offered to take Upper Perú under her protection. The president of the *audiencia* and the archbishop received him with deference. Not so the *audiencia* itself and the doctors of the University, who were already at odds with their superiors. The *audiencia* repudiated Carlota and declined to recognize either Goyeneche as the agent of the Junta of Seville, or the Junta as the repository of the authority of Ferdinand VII. The doctors learnedly debated the juridical effects in America of what had happened in Spain—to reach the conclusion that the American provinces must provide for their own government. The city was set by the ears, and, on 25 May 1809, the *audiencia*, while protesting its loyalty to Ferdinand, deposed its president and took the government into its own hands.[1]

To repudiate Carlota was one thing; the deposition of a royal

[1] See Gabriel René-Moreno, *Últimos días coloniales en el Alto-Perú*, 3 parts (Santiago de Chile, 1896–8), pp. 310, 385 note, 440, 445–58.

governor was quite another. But worse was to come. From Chuquisaca
the agitation spread to La Paz, and there, on the 16th July, the local
governor and the local bishop were overthrown. A junta under the
presidency, not of a Spaniard, not of a creole, but of a mestizo soldier,
Pedro Domingo Murillo, was established. A plan of government was
drawn up; reforms were initiated; and the populace was exhorted 'to
raise the standard of liberty' and 'to organize a new system of government in the interests of our fatherland ground down by the bastard
policy of Madrid'.[1]

This was revolution, and it was premature. Cisneros, newly arrived
in Buenos Aires, and his colleague in Lima, the Viceroy of Perú, combined to stifle it. Cisneros appointed a new President of Charcas,
General Vicente Nieto, who had accompanied him from Spain. The
Viceroy of Perú sent an army under Goyeneche to subdue the revolu-
tionaries of La Paz. 'Some very interesting news is expected shortly . . .
from Potosí', wrote Paroissien from his prison in December. 'The last
accounts we had stated that Gen! Goyeneche had entered La Paz sword
in hand, and hung up several of the principal people there . . . the
major part of the insurgents fled . . .'[2] And Goyeneche, devoid of
humanity as of principle, subdued La Paz with blood and terror. Less
brutal, Nieto's actions in Chuquisaca were equally repressive. And the
news of what had happened in Upper Perú filled the creoles in Buenos
Aires, some of whom, like Castelli and Moreno, had spent their youth
in Chuquisaca, with anger and resentment. How different the treatment of creoles and of Spaniards! For the Americans the gallows or
imprisonment or, at the least, the confiscation of their property, for the
Spaniards, for Álzaga and his fellow conspirators of January 1809,
pardon and oblivion. 'The torch that I have lighted', said Murillo with
his dying breath, 'shall never be extinguished', and in Buenos Aires, in
1810, his words were not forgotten.

There, revolutionary sentiment was mounting. The Viceroy, in his
apprehension, had created in the last weeks of the old year a Tribunal
of Vigilance to arrest the progress of conspiracy, but its efforts were
unavailing. Just as the revolution for North American independence, in
the opinion of John Adams, was consummated in the minds and hearts

[1] Alcides Arguedas, *Historia general de Bolivia* (La Paz, 1922), pp. 10–12.
[2] Paroissien to Baden Powell, draft, 8 Dec. 1809. Letter Book, 1808–9. P.P.

of the people before the war of independence began, so, in Buenos Aires, in the early months of 1810, the revolution was already accomplished in the minds and hearts of the creole leaders. The final step could not now be long delayed, and it was in this tense and expectant atmosphere that Castelli, in March 1810, produced his defence of Paroissien.

Fifteen months had passed since Paroissien, as the agent of Saturnino Rodríguez Peña and, as he believed, of the Princess Carlota and of Admiral Sir Sidney Smith, had been thrown into prison. For more than four of these he had languished at Buenos Aires. The plot in which he had been concerned was still political tinder of an explosive kind, and, in the circumstances of the times, Castelli's defence, both of him and of it, takes on an added significance. It was more than a defence of Paroissien or even of Saturnino Rodríguez Peña: it was a defence of the rights of Spanish Americans, and it was the complement, in the field of politics, to the arguments of Belgrano and Moreno in the field of economics.

Castelli addressed himself to four main points: the opinions of Saturnino Rodríguez Peña on the independence of America; his views on the fate of America and the course that America should follow in the event of the subjugation of Spain; the extent to which Paroissien shared these opinions; and the question of their criminality.[1]

He began by affirming that Saturnino Rodríguez Peña's previous political doctrines, his well-known revolutionary opinions, were irrelevant. Nor was Paroissien concerned in them. The letters and papers entrusted to Paroissien advocated no treasonable plans, no criminal design to overthrow the legitimate sovereign, no revolutionary ideas. It was, declared Castelli, the wish of everyone that if Spain should fall, her free dominions should not fall with her.[2] The plan which Rodríguez Peña proposed, therefore, was to preserve in America the Crown of Spain, to establish a regency in the person of a member of the royal house, not to the exclusion of the rights of Ferdinand VII, not in unison with the Crown of Portugal, not in dependence on conquered Spain, but as regent of a free and independent kingdom whose government, constitution and laws should be regulated by the nation in congress assembled.[3] His crime consisted in proclaiming the inde-

---

[1] The defence is printed in *Archivo de Belgrano*, v. 194–219. There is a copy in the Paroissien Papers. [2] Ibid., p. 205. [3] Ibid., pp. 201, 204–6.

pendence of America under the government of the royal house and opposing 'all adhesion to the fortunes of conquered Spain'.[1]

As for Paroissien, his conduct, asserted Castelli, had been frank and open. He had admitted that he had agreed to promote Rodríguez Peña's proposals. But he had done so in the belief that he thereby 'assisted the cause of Spain, forwarded the views of Great Britain and placed more effective barriers against the intrigues of France'.[2] He had been persuaded of the support of Carlota and of Admiral Sir Sidney Smith. Indeed, the evidence that Sir Sidney Smith approved the proposals had been overwhelming, and that the Princess had entertained such designs was equally true. It could only be supposed that Carlota had been deceived as to Rodríguez Peña's and Paroissien's purposes.[3]

But were these purposes treasonable? The answer led Castelli to the most interesting part of his argument. Not only, he declared, had Rodríguez Peña proposed nothing which was contrary to the rights of the legitimate sovereign, but also he had done nothing which had not been done in Spain itself. There the nation had risen in revolt against the usurpation of the throne. It had ignored the regency which Ferdinand VII had left behind at Madrid. Provincial juntas, and finally a Central Junta, had been formed. These juntas possessed no authority from the Crown; they were unknown to the law and the constitution. But no one presumed to indict the Spanish nation because of their establishment, or the individuals who had, in the most proper manner, advocated the erection of a government thus representative of the Crown. On what grounds, then, could Rodríguez Peña and Paroissien be condemned? When their plans were laid the existence of the Junta Central of Spain was yet unknown, and in any event it was formed without the concurrence of Americans. As for the sovereign pretensions of the Junta of Seville, could it seriously be argued that the peoples of America had not exactly as much right and reason to assume the representation of the sovereignty of the Crown as the Junta of Seville? Nor, moreover, could the constituted authorities already existing in America claim to represent the sovereign will, for their powers were merely delegated powers.[4] And, finally, in so far as

---

[1] *Archivo de Belgrano*, v. 197, 201. The draft in the Paroissien Papers supplies the missing words in the *Archivo de Belgrano*.
[2] Ibid., p. 209.      [3] Ibid., pp. 210–11.      [4] Ibid., pp. 207–9.

the reformation of the constitution was concerned, the juntas in Spain had not ceased to speak of 'cortes and constitution, reforms in the government, barriers to despotism, abolition of tyrannical laws, the regeneration of the state'.[1] Rodríguez Peña had done no more.

Here, within the decorous forms of a legal brief, were the true accents of revolutionary doctrine. Castelli argued, in effect, that since the Crown had fallen into captivity, since the legal government had ceased to exist, power reverted to the people. America was *de facto* independent. Her peoples owed no allegiance to the juntas in Spain. Their destinies were in their own hands. They possessed equal rights with the people of Spain to form their governments and laws. It was the same argument that had recently been heard in Chuquisaca. And it was soon to be vindicated in the events of 22 to 25 May 1810 at Buenos Aires itself.

It is improbable that Castelli's brief greatly impressed the viceregal authorities at Buenos Aires, and certainly the prosecutor of the Crown was quite unmoved. As a result of Paroissien's complaint that the conditions of his imprisonment were affecting his health, orders were given that, if the state of his prison was as he represented it to be, he should be lodged elsewhere. But he was to remain closely guarded and kept *incomunicado*,[2] and, on the 7th May, Cisneros ordered that his case should be remitted for decision to Spain—a procedure which did indeed argue a degree of hesitation, whether from political or legal motives, on the Viceroy's part.[3]

But the day of Paroissien's release was now approaching as events in Buenos Aires moved towards their climax. In January 1810, a French army had occupied Andalucía and Seville. The Central Junta fled from Seville to Cádiz. There it dissolved, arranging for a regency of five to be established in its place. The news reached Montevideo on May 13th though it was not till the 18th that Cisneros published it officially at Buenos Aires. It had, however, been anticipated. A secret society, of which Belgrano, Castelli, and Nicolás Rodríguez Peña were all prominent members, had prepared against this day. Now it acted. Belgrano and Cornelio Saavedra, the creole commander who, more than a year earlier, had prevented the overthrow of Liniers, interviewed the first

[1] Ibid., p. 215.
[2] Ibid., p. 222.　　　　[3] Ibid., p. 260; Levene, op. cit., i. 320, note.

*alcalde* of the municipality, while Castelli interviewed its attorney, to demand that an open meeting of the town council, a *cabildo abierto*, attended by the principal citizens, should be held to discuss this grave event. Late on the evening of the 20th Castelli, now accompanied by Martín Rodríguez, like Saavedra a creole commander, presented this demand in forthright terms to the Viceroy himself. The Viceroy, who had already discovered that, in the event of refusal, he could scarcely count on the loyalty of the troops, reluctantly, and with every premonition of impending evil, granted what he dared not refuse. On the 21st a general congress, as it was called, was summoned, and on the 22nd it met.

It was not a democratic assembly. It represented, for the most part, the classes of 'distinction and name', and even among these many of the more conservative figures were in fact excluded by 'the partiality of the soldiers' stationed at the entrance to the plaza.[1] Nor was it unanimous in opinion. There was a strong body of loyal supporters of the Viceroy, representing, in the main, the old official classes, and reinforced by the bishop. And the patriots themselves were not all of one mind. The critical speech was Castelli's. And it is notable that Castelli returned to the doctrines he had already laid down in his defence of Paroissien. The argument was identical. The sovereign power in Spain, said Castelli, had ceased to exist. The juntas which had been there established were themselves illegitimate. The Central Junta at Seville, in which the Americans were unrepresented, had no power to establish a regency, and now it had fallen. In America, as in Spain, sovereignty had reverted to the people, and it was for the people of Buenos Aires to control their own destinies and to establish their own government.[2]

A 'master of that species of eloquence which captivates the multitude',[3] Castelli fired the enthusiasm of the patriots. But the debate was prolonged, and it was midnight before the assembly broke up, resolving that the Viceroy (who had been appointed by the Junta at Seville) should relinquish his command and that a temporary authority should reside in the *cabildo* until a governing junta could be formed.

---

[1] Levene, op. cit., ii. 36–7.

[2] Only fragmentary accounts of Castelli's speech survive. For its reconstruction see Levene, op. cit., ii. 39–40, and Chaves, *Castelli*, p. 139.

[3] John Miller, *Memoirs of General Miller*, 2 vols. (London, 1828), i. 67.

The assembly was to meet again the following afternoon. The *cabildo*, however, now acted beyond its mandate. It cancelled, on the following morning, the adjourned meeting of the general assembly and proceeded to scrutinize in detail the votes cast on the 22nd May. It then resolved that the Viceroy should not be entirely deprived of his authority, but, on the contrary, should act as president of the proposed junta. On the 24th, it appointed a junta of four, with Cisneros as president and, as a sop to Cerberus, Castelli and Saavedra among its members.

This arrangement, in the words of an English merchant at Buenos Aires, 'gave great and general discontent, as the choice had been made by the magistrates, without consulting the general voice of the qualified inhabitants. The ferment amongst the Creole Patricians had risen to such a serious degree during the 23rd May and all that night, that much address was required to keep them from the commission of tragical acts.'[1] The leading creole patriots met together in the house of Nicolás Rodríguez Peña. They insisted that the junta should not be recognized and drew up a list of the persons who should replace it. Castelli, Saavedra and the other members of the junta nominated by the *cabildo* resigned, and on the following morning, 25th May, the *cabildo*, sitting behind closed doors, was besieged by excited crowds. A petition, bearing 409 signatures, was presented demanding the installation of the junta agreed upon by the patriot committee. The *cabildo* hesitated, but yielded, and that same afternoon the patriot junta was installed. Saavedra was its president. Belgrano and Castelli were among its members. Moreno was one of its two secretaries. It swore to govern faithfully and well in the name of the sovereign king, Ferdinand VII, and with its establishment the first act of the drama of Argentine independence, a drama which had begun when Popham and his fleet invaded the Río de la Plata in 1806, was completed.

As for Paroissien, for him the independence of Buenos Aires—and the revolution of 25 May 1810, though it wore 'the mask of Ferdinand', was, in effect, if not in formal fact, a declaration of independence—meant freedom. He was released under an order signed by Moreno on the 11th June,[2] and, almost at once, attached himself to the friend and protector of the days of his imprisonment—Castelli.

[1] Mackinnon to Canning, 1 June 1810, F.O. 72/107.
[2] Levene, op. cit., i. 320.

# CHAPTER IV

## BUENOS AIRES AND THE PROVINCES,
## 1810–16

THE revolution of 25 May 1810, at Buenos Aires, the deposition of the Viceroy, the establishment of a Junta, took place in the name of Ferdinand VII. In his name the new Government acted, and its loyalty to him was constantly proclaimed. But though, to confuse the waverers and attract the timid, the fiction of allegiance to a captive Crown was carefully maintained, the intent of the May revolution was clear and definite. Whatever the language of 'fidelity and vassalage to our unfortunate Ferdinand', a Government set up by revolutionary procedure in the capital assumed all the authority of the Crown itself. It removed Spanish officials. It shipped the Viceroy and the judges of the royal *audiencia* off to the Canary Islands. It dispatched agents abroad. It prepared to make war, and raised an expeditionary force to carry the revolution to the interior provinces and to enforce obedience to its will. It was quick to give assurances of friendship and 'all the privileges of fellow citizens' to foreigners,[1] welcomed foreign trade, lowered the export duties and opened ports; and in the pages of its new *Gaceta de Buenos Aires*, its secretary, Moreno, who published an edition of Rousseau's *Contrat social* (with the chapter on religion omitted), boldly preached the doctrines of the 'general will', the 'sovereignty of the Nation' and the constitutional organization of the 'State'.

These events in Buenos Aires signalized the final transference of power in the viceroyalty of La Plata from a Spanish to a creole minority. They completed also the transition from the closed to the open door, the destruction of the commercial monopoly of Spain. As at Rio de Janeiro in 1808, so at Buenos Aires in 1810, the market was flooded

[1] Mackinnon to Canning, 1 June 1810, F.O. 72/107.

JOSÉ DE SAN MARTÍN

TRAVELLING POST

with British goods. Skates and warming-pans, of all improbable articles, dangled in the shops.[1] The property which British traders had at stake, wrote a merchant in August, was 'seldom less than £750,000' and 'sometimes exceeded a million'.[2] And while a British colony took root and an American consul soon appeared, the foundations were laid of an Anglo-Argentine commercial connexion, open and recognized, which would never again be broken.

But the revolution had been made at Buenos Aires. If it was a creole it was also a *porteño* revolution. And if at Buenos Aires, though the 'old Spaniards' were much mortified at what had happened, the mass of the population was, in general, 'contented',[3] the question remained, could the Junta succeed to the authority of the Viceroy throughout the length and breadth of the viceroyalty of La Plata? Would the interior provinces accept its jurisdiction? And, across the river, would Montevideo?

The viceroyalty of La Plata in 1810, despite its vast extent, contained fewer inhabitants than did contemporary Scotland. Of its peoples, more than a half, predominantly Indian and mestizo, dwelt in the rich mining area of Upper Perú. The fertile land of Paraguay perhaps accounted for some one hundred thousand, and the pastoral plains and rolling hills of the Banda Oriental of Uruguay, with its chief town Montevideo, for forty thousand more.

In the rest of the viceroyalty, where small cities were separated by great distances and empty spaces, there lived fewer than half a million people,[4] apart, that is, from the Indian tribes on its southern frontiers and its inland plains. Buenos Aires was the largest town, a city which was indeed a city of the river and the plain, with small farms on its outskirts and, beyond, stretching southwards and westwards, the great sweep of the pampa, flat, treeless, unenclosed, a frontier area still occasionally exposed, even at no very great distance from the capital, to the sudden incursions of the pampa Indians. With the opening of

[1] W. R. Manning, ed., *Diplomatic Correspondence of the United States concerning the Independence of the Latin-American Nations*, 3 vols. (New York, 1925), i. 454.

[2] Mackinnon to Canning, 12 Aug. 1810, F.O. 72/107.

[3] Mackinnon to Canning, 1 June 1810, F.O. 72/107.

[4] Cf. Miron Burgin, *The Economic Aspects of Argentine Federalism, 1820–1852* (Cambridge, Mass., 1946), p. 115; Ángel Rosenblat, *La población indígena de América desde 1492 hasta la actualidad* (Buenos Aires, 1945), pp. 146–50.

E

Buenos Aires to the trade of the world, its economic future was assured. The limits of effective occupation were already expanding, and the province, like the city, grew and flourished on foreign trade.

Three great trade routes linked the capital to the inland provinces. The first was the route to the north. With post-houses—'mere mud huts, imperfectly thatched, kept very dirty'—marking the way,[1] it led through Santa Fe, a town of one square and eight streets, where the traveller prepared to cross the river Paraná, to Corrientes, the 'city of the seven currents', near the confluence of the Paraná and the Paraguay, and so to Asunción, the old capital of Paraguay, almost one thousand miles away. And though the land it fringed, Entre Ríos—the territory between the two great rivers, the Paraná and the Uruguay—was no longer pampa but undulating and wooded, this too was cattle country, a land of horses and cows, of *estancieros*, and of *gauchos* almost as wild as the cattle whose life they made their own. As for Santa Fe itself, from there the *yerba maté*, the lumber and the tobacco of Paraguay, floating down the river or brought by land, were distributed to other parts of the viceroyalty, and from Santa Fe great trains of mules left in annual journey across the plains on the way to the mountain provinces of Upper Perú.

The second route was the route to the north-west, to Córdoba and Tucumán, to Potosí and Perú. Córdoba, 'perhaps the prettiest city in South America',[2] and farther from Buenos Aires than is Edinburgh from London, was renowned as the summer retreat of the viceroys, but still more for its convents, its cathedral and its university; and the *cordobeses* not only exported wool and hides, they wove coarse textiles as well. Here the route turned north, fringing the charming Sierras de Córdoba, to traverse a flat country and a sandy soil to the ancient but poverty-stricken settlement of Santiago del Estero. Thence it led to Tucumán, where the Andes begin to lord it over the plains, and to Salta. Tucumán, 'surrounded by groves of citron, orange, fig, and pomegranate trees',[3] and set in a fertile plain, where wheat and sugar-cane, fruit and tobacco, grew, and sheep and cattle roamed, was wealthy

[1] Robertson, *Letters on Paraguay*, i. 190.
[2] *Memoirs of General Miller*, ii. 331.
[3] A. Z. Helms, *Travels from Buenos Ayres, by Potosi, to Lima* (London, 1807), p. 15.

and prosperous. But Salta, in its valley bottom, shut in by mountain ranges, was equally important. It was the great halting-place for travellers to and from the north. From Buenos Aires to Córdoba and from Córdoba to Salta the journey could be made by cart or coach, their huge wheels specially adapted to travel over rough roads and on the plains. But at Salta the carriage must be exchanged for saddle-mules or horses; and from Jujuy, a small but ancient town at no great distance to the north, the old and famous route led upwards through magnificent mountain avenues and steep passes to the great altiplano of Upper Perú, twelve to fourteen thousand feet above the level of the sea. Down this trail the merchants of Buenos Aires had once been compelled to obtain their goods from Spain by way of Lima and the isthmus of Panamá. Up it there toiled the long trains of mules from Santa Fe and Tucumán and Salta, and the trade with Upper Perú had long been one of the most flourishing branches of the commerce both of the interior provinces and of Buenos Aires.

The third of the main trade routes from Buenos Aires was the western route, the route to Chile. It led across the pampas—and the traveller might, or might not, go by way of Santa Fe and Córdoba—to the rough hills of San Luis, and then, by a waterless and dusty *travesía*, to Mendoza, at the foot of the great Cordillera of the Andes. With its low, one-storied houses set in rectilinear plan, Mendoza was an oasis in the desert, a garden city, watered by the melting snows of mountain ranges, where vines and fruit trees flourished. Its wines, like those of its northern neighbour, San Juan, were famous. The gateway to Chile by towering mountain passes, it had at one time formed, with San Juan and San Luis, the Chilean province of Cuyo, and as the capital of Cuyo it was soon to be known again.

Though the *gauchos*, the herdsmen and the peasantry of the country-side, 'thinly strewed over the great pastures'[1] and leading an indolent, half-savage, carefree life, formed a high proportion of the scanty population, the cities, in this imperial domain, were the centres of civilization. Linked only by the ox-cart and the mule-train, they were the capitals of regions, each with its distinctive industries—vine-growing in Mendoza, the making of coarse textiles in Córdoba and Corrientes, sugar-manufacturing in Tucumán. They looked to trade not, like

[1] Manning, op. cit., i. 416.

Buenos Aires, with Europe, but with one another and with Chile and Perú, and their economic interests were by no means identical with those of the capital.[1] Nor were the bonds between them strong. While each city was a jealous guardian of local life, the lowland provinces had little in common with the mountain provinces of Upper Perú, and Paraguay was distinct from both. The viceroyalty of La Plata, held together within the framework of colonial rule, had only a tenuous unity, and, with the revolution at Buenos Aires, its disintegration began.

The process was rapid. Two days after its installation, the Junta at Buenos Aires, already preparing to carry the revolution to the interior provinces by force of arms, invited the other cities of the viceroyalty to send deputies to the capital. In what are today the provinces of Argentina, the invitation was accepted and the Junta's authority admitted. Only at Córdoba, where Santiago Liniers now lived, was resistance contemplated, and there the governor, the bishop, and Liniers himself, to the last loyal to Spain, planned counter-measures. In Upper Perú, however, the colonial officials acted promptly. Upper Perú was reattached to the neighbouring viceroyalty of Perú, to which it had once belonged. And, significantly enough, neither Montevideo, in the Banda Oriental, nor Asunción, in Paraguay, were numbered among the cities which declared their adhesion to the Junta.

In Montevideo, it is true, opinion wavered. The first impulse was to recognize the new government at the capital. But when, on the 2nd June, the news arrived that a regency had been established in Spain, Montevideo, always hostile to Buenos Aires, threw in its lot with the mother country. Six months later, the former governor of the city, Francisco Javier Elío, who had left for Spain before the May revolution began, returned to Montevideo invested with the title of Viceroy of La Plata. This was indeed the enemy at the gates, and henceforth the two cities, whose strife had already begun, were constantly at war. But in the end, neither won the victory, and for Montevideo the fates were harsh. The surrounding population in the Banda Oriental rose under the leadership of an ex-soldier and *estanciero*, skilled in *gaucho* arts and *gaucho* ways, José Gervasio Artigas, who fought first against the royalists in Montevideo and then against the creoles in Buenos Aires.

[1] Burgin, op. cit., pp. 15–16, 119–20.

Montevideo, twice besieged by *porteño* troops, was occupied in turn by the royalists, the *porteños* and the *orientales,* only to fall at last, like the Banda itself, under the dominion of yet a further party. For the strife in the Río de la Plata was the opportunity of the Portuguese, and when, in August 1816, rather more than six years after the May revolution at Buenos Aires, a Portuguese army entered the Banda, at long last the hopes and ambitions of the Court at Rio de Janeiro were to be temporarily fulfilled. A new province was added to the empire of Portugal, and the flag which waved over the Amazon waved also over the waters of the River Plate.

As Montevideo, in 1810, repudiated the authority of the Junta, so also did Paraguay. The creoles of Asunción, like the creoles and Spaniards of Montevideo, had no wish to exchange the dominion of Spain for that of Buenos Aires. They, too, entertained towards the *porteños* an instinctive aversion, born of isolation, of old traditions, and of the exactions which Buenos Aires imposed on Paraguayan trade; and when, in July 1810, a general assembly, convoked by the governor, resolved to recognize the regency in Spain, it was moved less by loyalty to Spain than by dislike of Buenos Aires. With more haste than wisdom, the Junta dispatched a small expedition to Asunción under the command of Manuel Belgrano. But Belgrano, given an impossible task, and himself a novice in the art of war, was, in 1811, twice defeated. In the same year the Spanish Governor of Paraguay was deposed by the creoles of Asunción themselves, and from that moment Paraguay, soon to fall under the dictatorship of the redoubtable Dr. José Gaspar Rodríguez de Francia, the absolute ruler of a subject people, remained independent in fact if not in name. Paraguay, like Montevideo, was for ever lost to the old viceroyalty of La Plata.

But important as it seemed, in 1810, to compel Montevideo and even Paraguay to recognize the authority of the new Junta at Buenos Aires, to carry the revolution to the interior provinces was still more vital; and, early in July, only a few weeks after the revolution had occurred, the liberating—or subjugating—expedition which the Junta had prepared, numbering some one thousand men, began its march. At Córdoba, as the army approached, all resistance vanished. The governor, Liniers, and their fellow conspirators fled. All, however, were captured, and, on the 26th August, both Liniers and the governor were shot. For this act

of terrorism the Junta as a whole was responsible, and Castelli himself proceeded to Córdoba to see the execution carried out. If, as tradition records,[1] Castelli's eyes were bathed in tears when Liniers fell, he might well weep, and the impetuous, generous, unfortunate Liniers, the hero of the reconquest and the loyal servant both of Buenos Aires and Spain, ill deserved the bitter words with which Moreno, in the *Gaceta de Buenos Aires*, attempted to justify his death.

Meanwhile, the liberating expedition pursued its way to Upper Perú. It was under the command of a *porteño* soldier, Antonio González Balcarce. But to strengthen its hand and advance its cause the Junta, in September, delegated Castelli as its political representative, or high commissioner, to accompany and direct the army. Castelli appointed Nicolás Rodríguez Peña (in whose house so much of the May revolution had been plotted) as his secretary, and he took with him, in the capacity of physician, Paroissien, now three months out of prison, doubtless almost penniless, ready for any adventure, and attached by ties of gratitude as well as interest to the advocate who had been so suddenly elevated to responsibility and power. Together, on 22 September 1810, the three men left the capital on the long north-west road to Upper Perú.

The travellers moved fast. Córdoba was reached in six days, Salta and Jujuy by the end of October. Here they came up with the rearguard of the liberating army, and on the 7th November its vanguard, scaling the formidable passes which led to the great table-land above, defeated on the field of Suipacha a royalist detachment sent to contain it. Suipacha was the first victory won by an Argentine army. It opened the doors of Upper Perú, and on the 25th November, two months after leaving Buenos Aires, the Junta's high commissioner, endowed with almost absolute powers, entered Potosí in triumph.

In the imperial city of Potosí, two and a half miles above the level of the sea, dominated by its famous silver mountain, and the seat of an equally famous royal mint, Castelli was received with enthusiasm. The events of 1809 at Chuquisaca and La Paz, those fatal movements so hopefully begun, so tragically repressed, the ruthless tyranny of Goyeneche, the severity of General Nieto, now President of Charcas, were fresh in mind, and despite the vigilance of the colonial authorities,

[1] Chaves, *Castelli*, p. 170.

the towns of Upper Perú had not waited for Castelli and the liberating army before they began to assert their independence. To the east, the populous city of Cochabamba, in its fertile agricultural valley, had revolted in September. To the west, the mining centre of Oruro, on its bleak plateau, also rose. Chuquisaca in the south and La Paz in the north each declared their support of the Junta, and Castelli, three days after his arrival in Potosí, was able to affirm that all the provinces of Upper Perú, to the very limits of the viceroyalty of Perú itself, sustained and recognized the revolution at Buenos Aires.[1]

In the great square of Potosí, on 15th December, the governor of the city, the President of Charcas, and the commander of the royalist troops suffered the fate of Liniers and the Governor of Córdoba, and for this second act of terrorism once again the Junta at Buenos Aires was directly responsible. But this time Castelli shed no tears, and, during the six months which he spent in visiting and reorganizing the cities of Upper Perú, neither his own political fanaticism, nor the conduct of the *porteño* troops, nor his impious entry into La Paz on Ash Wednesday (for so the *paceños* regarded it), endeared the liberators to the liberated; and meanwhile, on the other side of the Desaguadero River, flowing from the inland sea of Lake Titicaca, no great distance away, the royalist forces under Goyeneche were preparing for attack. Castelli, dreaming now of carrying the revolution to Perú itself, crossed the high flat plain towards the river, and there, on the 20th June, at Huaquí, Goyeneche surprised and defeated him.

Huaquí was Castelli's first and last battle and Paroissien's baptism of fire. Already employed as an army surgeon and in superintending the hospital services, at Huaquí he served as an aide to one of the divisional commanders,[2] and then, as in confusion and disorder the army melted away, he joined Castelli and Balcarce in precipitate retreat. For Castelli this was the end. Deprived of his post and ordered to Buenos Aires, he arrived there late in November, to be arrested and tried. Less than a year later he died, poor and in disgrace. But only Moreno—who had also fallen into disfavour, had been sent 'in honourable banishment' on

---

[1] *Gaceta de Buenos Aires,* 27 Dec. 1810.
[2] A. P. Carranza, ed., *Archivo general de la república argentina* . . . second series, 14 vols. in 7 (Buenos Aires, 1894–9), vi. 136; Representation to the Government of Buenos Aires, 24 Dec. 1825. P.P.

a mission to England, and had died at sea—and, perhaps, Belgrano, can compare with him as an intellectual force in the leadership of the revolution, and for Paroissien the memory of his friend and defender was always dear.[1]

Paroissien, meanwhile, had been ordered to Potosí, where the man whom the Junta had appointed as its own President of Charcas hastened to assume command and attempted to retain control. This was Juan Martín de Pueyrredón, who had already served Buenos Aires both at the time of the British invasions and later on a mission to Spain. But Pueyrredón's position was hopeless. Potosí, like other cities of Upper Perú, turned on its former liberators, and on the 26th August, taking with him the contents of the royal mint, Pueyrredón, with forty-five men, of whom Paroissien was one, and with mules loaded with silver, began his difficult retreat down the mountain passes to Salta. Harried by the enemy, often hungry, but with the silver secure, the ragged little band reached Salta and safety by October; and there Paroissien, whom Pueyrredón doubly commended both as a physician and as one who had shown that 'bravery is not confined to the military profession',[2] received the reward to which his services entitled him. On the 25th November he was granted letters of naturalization[3]—the first ever to be issued by the Government of Buenos Aires, apart from an honorary citizenship offered to Lord Strangford—and, shortly afterwards, the new 'citizen of South America' was appointed physician-in-chief to the Auxiliary Army of Perú at a salary of one hundred pesos a month.[4]

He remained at Salta, where a demoralized army attempted to regroup and to re-form, for some weeks more, and in January 1812 again took the northern route to meet a further contingent of retreating and defeated men fleeing from the highlands, every object reminding him of the journey made more than a year earlier with 'my poor friend Castelli'.[5] In the desert region of Humahuaca, nine thousand feet up, he found his wounded, 'mounted on mules and horses, many of them

[1] Journal, 22 Jan., 13 March 1812.
[2] *Gaceta de Buenos Aires*, 31 Oct. 1811.
[3] Ibid., 27 Dec. 1811. The decree, dated 25 Nov. 1811, was enclosed in a letter to Paroissien at Salta. P.P.
[4] Representation to the Government of Buenos Aires, 24 Dec. 1825. P.P.
[5] Journal, 22 Jan. 1812.

with fractures, many with balls pass'd thro' their bodies, arms and thighs, enduring wet and cold thro' the day and at night sleeping upon the bare ground . . . without medical aid . . . and even upon most occasions without bread . . . and swarming with vermin and filth'.[1] Paroissien led them to Jujuy, and then, with a party of wounded on horseback and muleback and in waggons, he took, in March, the road to Tucumán.[2]

A new sphere was opening to his talents. At Córdoba the directorship of the gunpowder factory, which the Junta, with sound foresight, had established, was vacant. Paroissien, a dabbler in many things, seems himself to have made proposals on the proper mode of manufacture,[3] and he was now appointed to the vacant post at a salary, this time, of two thousand pesos a year.[4] Leaving Tucumán early in April in the company of a young army officer, and reflecting, as he entered the plains, on the isolation of 'these fertile provinces which at present cannot export their produce on account of the enormous expence of land carriage', and on the 'opportunity now presented' of destroying the 'little narrow policy which has ever distinguished the conduct of the Spaniards in the new world',[5] he paused for a few days at Santiago del Estero, where the weather was bad and saltpetre abundant, to conduct experiments, and then made a vast detour through the western towns of Catamarca and La Rioja. Córdoba itself he seems to have reached early in May, only to leave at once for Buenos Aires, there to give evidence before the tribunal which was investigating the causes of Castelli's defeat in Upper Perú.[6] Not till the end of July did he return to Córdoba to take up his post,[7] and in this delightful city he was to make his home for the next three years.

So ended Paroissien's connexion with the Auxiliary Army of Perú. The expedition to Upper Perú had been a failure, and Upper Perú, like Paraguay and like Montevideo, was lost to the Provinces of the Río de

---

[1] Ibid., 25 Jan. 1812.     [2] Ibid., 4 March 1812.     [3] Ibid., 18 April 1812.
[4] The appointment, dated 6 June 1812, took effect from 1st March. P.P.
[5] Journal, 3 April 1812. Paroissien refers to his companion as 'Alvarez', possibly his future friend, José Alvarez de Condarco, but possibly also his future assistant, Ildefonso Antonio Alvarez. For the confusion between them see E. U. Bischoff, *La primera fábrica argentina de pólvora* (Córdoba, 1951), pp. 103–7.     [6] Carranza, *Archivo general*, vi. 135–42. See also ibid., x. 224.
[7] Bischoff, op. cit., pp. 84–6.

la Plata, though it was long before the *porteños* could reconcile themselves to that fact. Twice again, in 1813 and 1815, an Argentine army
advanced to Potosí. Each time it struggled back defeated. But if 'la
gente de abajo', 'the people below', could never hold the heights,
neither could the royalist forces from the mountains penetrate the
plains. In 1812, after the defeat of Castelli's army, their counter-
offensive carried them to Tucumán. But this was the limit of royalist
advance, and though the region north of Salta was to be for many years
the scene of frontier war, nature as well as men divided Upper Perú
from the Provinces of the Río de la Plata.

In 1812, however, this issue was far from clear, and, in the struggle
for Upper Perú, the *porteños* and the royalists each had a further aim.
The royalists' object was Buenos Aires itself. The *porteños* hoped to
carry the revolution to Lima, three thousand miles or more away.[1] It
remained for a comparatively unknown soldier, who arrived at Buenos
Aires in this very year, José de San Martín, to realize that the long road
through Upper Perú was 'not the true strategical line of the South
American revolution',[2] and that though Perú must indeed be liberated
from the Spaniards before Buenos Aires could be safe and South America
free, it must be invaded by a different route, and invaded by sea.

San Martín, with whom Paroissien's life was soon to be closely
linked, and who was some six or seven years his senior, had been born
on a remote mission station high up on the banks of the Uruguay river.
He was educated in Spain and, having served the Spanish Crown for
twenty-two years first as a cadet and then as an officer, returned to
Buenos Aires in March 1812 a professional soldier, a strategist and a
tactician. Here his first assignment was to raise and train a corps of
mounted grenadiers, whose virtues were soon demonstrated in a brush
with a detachment of royalist troops from Montevideo. His second, in
January 1814, was to take command of that Army of the North which
had, for a second time, advanced to Potosí, only to be completely
crushed; and at Tucumán, where his headquarters were established,
San Martín seems to have formulated the plan which, in conception and

---

[1] F. A. Kirkpatrick, *A History of the Argentine Republic* (Cambridge, 1931),
pp. 90–1.

[2] Bartolomé Mitre, *Historia de San Martín y de la emancipación sud-
americana*, 4 vols. (2nd edn., Buenos Aires, 1890), i. 283.

execution alike, was to win him undying fame. In April he resigned his post and retired, in poor health, to Córdoba, where he and Paroissien certainly met.[1] Then, appointed at his own request Governor of Cuyo, he left in August for Mendoza, the provincial capital. His task now, secret and self-imposed, was to raise in Cuyo an army to pass into Chile: 'Mendoza was the door to Chile; Chile was the door to Perú.'[2]

'Tall, erect, well-proportioned', with a deep olive complexion and piercing jet-black eyes, simple in his manners, 'irresistible' in address, his whole appearance 'highly military',[3] San Martín is an enigmatic figure, taciturn, stoic, very much the soldier, and very much also the Castilian gentleman. His health was precarious and for many years he resorted to the use of opium. But he was yet capable of the most vigorous exertions; and though secretive, sometimes even devious in his ways, in resolve he was inflexible. Cautious and austere, but possessed of deep human sympathies, a born leader—but not always a good judge—of men, he was to reveal at Mendoza an infinite capacity for taking pains; and here, for the first time, his organizing genius was fully displayed.

The task which he had set himself while governing Cuyo took two years to accomplish. Funds were raised, despite the poverty of the province. Its mines and fields were exploited to supply foodstuffs and raw materials. An arsenal, a gunpowder factory, a cloth mill, were created. Spies were sent to Chile and false rumours disseminated. Chilean refugees, troops from Buenos Aires, volunteers and conscripts from Cuyo, negro slaves, all were welcomed and rigidly trained. Cuyo, under San Martín, became an armed camp, a world of its own, its resources concentrated on one end.

Yet San Martín needed more help than Cuyo could afford, if his great undertaking was to succeed. He needed the full support of the Government at Buenos Aires; and until the middle of 1816, when his army still numbered under two thousand men, that support was doubtful. The enterprise of the Andes in the circumstances of the times seemed little but a fantastic dream. For, even were the Government convinced

[1] San Martín to Paroissien, 27 Sept. 1814. P.P.

[2] J. P. Otero, *Historia del libertador Don José de San Martín*, 4 vols. (Buenos Aires, 1932), i. 278.

[3] Basil Hall, *Extracts from a Journal, written on the coasts of Chili, Peru, and Mexico, in the years 1820, 1821, 1822*, 2 vols. (3rd edn., Edinburgh, 1824), i. 213.

of the soundness of San Martín's plans—and it still looked to Upper Perú—the times were not propitious. At the beginning of 1815 a *porteño* army had been driven from the Banda Oriental. At its end yet a third expedition to Upper Perú met disaster. And in 1815 itself the affairs of the Provinces of the Río de la Plata reached a crisis.

Buenos Aires, it is true, was growing, and there was no doubt of what the revolution had meant to the capital. Visitors noted that 'everybody was dressed better, everybody lived better than before'.[1] In the surrounding country the value of hides and the prices of cattle were rising. The capital of the creole merchants was increasing. The *estancieros*, as a class, were gaining in importance, and the small community of British traders was flourishing. In 1816 alone eighty ships docked at the port.[2] But there was no doubt also what the revolution had meant to the other provinces of the old viceroyalty of La Plata. Across the river, in the Banda Oriental and its adjoining territory, 'desolation was spread over the face of the country', and the herds of cattle were diminishing.[3] The trade of the interior provinces with Chile and Perú had been cut off; even with Paraguay it was nearly extinguished. The north-western provinces had experienced the devastating transit of armies. All were reduced to poverty. And while economic dislocation and social disintegration proceeded hand in hand, five years after the May revolution at Buenos Aires the Provinces of the Río de la Plata had utterly failed to solve a problem vital to their welfare—the problem of their political organization.

In 1810 itself this problem had been shelved. It was shelved by the simple expedient of incorporating within the Junta set up by the May revolution those provincial deputies whom the Junta had invited to the capital. This step, which brought to a head the divergences between the more conservative and the more radical members of the Junta and precipitated the resignation of Mariano Moreno himself, certainly associated provincials with *porteños* in the work of government. But it did so at the cost of postponing the meeting of a congress to consider

---

[1] J. P. and W. P. Robertson, *Letters on South America*, 3 vols. (London, 1843), ii. 67.

[2] Ibid., ii. 67–8; Burgin, op. cit., p. 30; Humphreys, *British Consular Reports*, pp. 42, 47.

[3] Humphreys, op. cit., p. 40.

the problem of political organization *à fond*, and at the cost also of creating an unwieldy executive 'jarring in principle, desultory in debate, tardy in council' and 'wavering in action'.[1] Some months later the Junta was transformed into a rudimentary legislature and a triple executive was established in its place. But this also was no solution. The triumvirs, all *porteños*, dissolved the Junta, affronted the provincial cities by expelling their deputies from the capital, and inaugurated what was in fact a *porteño* dictatorship. Nor was it till the triumvirs had been themselves removed and replaced that a 'constituent assembly' of the 'United Provinces of the Río de la Plata' at last met.

The 'Assembly of 1813' is justly celebrated in Argentine history. Notable administrative, judicial and other reforms had already been instituted by the original Junta and the first of the triumvirates, but the Assembly went much further. Abolishing the Inquisition, titles of nobility, royal symbols, and judicial torture, initiating the gradual abolition of slavery, prohibiting forced labour, it took every step to make Argentine independence plain to the world except that of explicitly declaring it. Later in its career, it unified the national government in the hands of a Supreme Director, and thus at last did away with government by committee. But it failed to adopt a constitution, and it took the fateful step of refusing to admit deputies who, representing those rural areas of the Banda Oriental which acknowledged the sway of the great guerrilla leader of the *orientales*, José Gervasio Artigas, brought with them instructions to demand, not only an immediate declaration of independence, but the establishment of a federal system of government in which each province should retain its own autonomy.

Provincial autonomy within a federal system, or a centralized government based on *porteño* supremacy, here at last was the constitutional problem fully stated. Since the Assembly evaded it, since, moreover, the Government at Buenos Aires showed itself plainly determined to enforce its own authority in the Banda Oriental, Artigas went his own way. It was in June 1814 that the royalists in Montevideo at last capitulated to a *porteño* army. Seven months later the city as well as the province fell under the control of Artigas. As the 'Protector of the Free Peoples', the champion of the rude democracy of the rural masses

[1] Robertson, *Letters on South America*, ii. 133.

and of provincial as against *porteño* interests, he dominated, in 1815, not only the Banda Oriental but the adjoining provinces of Corrientes, Entre Ríos and Santa Fe also. And while what had been the territory of the old viceroyalty of La Plata seemed about to suffer yet further dismemberment, in Buenos Aires itself the 'national' government was overthrown by rebellion and mutiny. The United Provinces of the Río de la Plata had become in 1815 no more than a loose confederation of semi-independent, imperfectly organized, and even semi-hostile states. No wonder that many, Belgrano among them, had turned their thoughts once again to the erection of a constitutional monarchy under a European prince as the sole solution to the problems of the new state.

In 1816, however, the tide of disunity and anarchy was temporarily arrested. Through the action of the local government at Buenos Aires, the meeting of a new Congress was arranged, this time in an interior province. It assembled at Tucumán in March 1816, and though the regions which Artigas controlled, and, of course, Paraguay, were not represented, all the other provinces sent delegates, and there were even representatives-in-exile from Upper Perú. On the 3rd May it restored 'national' government by appointing Juan Martín de Pueyrredón as Supreme Director of the State, and on the 9th July, partly through the pressure which San Martín and Belgrano both exercised upon the assembly from without, it formally proclaimed the independence of the 'United Provinces of South America'. Ferdinand VII had been restored in Spain. No other part of Spanish America was free. But the step was taken, and the movement begun at Buenos Aires on 25 May 1810 was, at Tucumán on 9 July 1816, at last completed.

For San Martín, building up his army at Mendoza for the invasion of Chile and the subsequent liberation of Perú, these events were all-important. In mid-July he hastened to Córdoba to meet Pueyrredón, and gained a valuable ally. Henceforth, the Supreme Director, completely won over to the support of San Martín's plans, assisted them by every means in his power. On the 1st August, three days after Pueyrredón had assumed the reins of government in Buenos Aires, San Martín was appointed commander-in-chief of the Army of the Andes, and on the 3rd October, still further to enhance his prestige, he was invested with the character of captain-general. The enterprise of the Andes had moved from the realm of fantasy to that of fact.

It was at this point that Paroissien prepared to join San Martín. For four years his life had been divorced from the main currents of affairs. Three of them had been spent in charge of the gunpowder factory at Córdoba; and though the powder he made seems not to have been of the best quality, he had displayed great energy in difficult circumstances[1]—money was short, workmen were troublesome—and his services had not gone unnoticed. The General Assembly, in 1813, formally renewed his certificate of naturalization.[2] He was invited to assist in compiling an inventory of the State mineral collections,[3] and he was promoted in 1814 to the rank of lieutenant-colonel of artillery.[4] But, alas, in April 1815, the gunpowder factory blew up, and Paroissien, though he escaped uninjured, was out of a job. 'You will be apprised', he wrote to his sister, 'of the Providential escape I had from being blown up in the Powder works. . . . For various reasons I determined on leaving Cordova, but the principal one was my want of health.'[5] Relieved of his post by the local governor, by July he was back in Buenos Aires, prepared, if necessary, to open 'an apothecaries shop'. But, treated 'with every consideration', he remained, instead, attached to the General Staff[6] until, on 24 September 1816, he was gazetted chief surgeon to the Army of the Andes.[7] In October he was ordered to join a battalion which the Government was preparing to send to Mendoza,[8] and in November the troops began their march.

The convoy, wrote Paroissien, consisting of '160 waggons to draw which there were near 2,000 oxen employed', and occupying 'near a league in length', was like 'the cavalcades of the antient patriarchs'. Travelling by night, in order to avoid the burning heat of the plains by day, it skirted what was, in effect, the southern frontier of the United

[1] Bischoff, op. cit., pp. 87 ff.; Emilio Loza, 'Breve noticia sobre la fábrica de pólvora de Córdoba', *Boletín del instituto de investigaciones históricas*, xix (Buenos Aires, 1935), pp. 83–93.

[2] Dated 13 Feb. 1813. P.P.

[3] M. J. García to Paroissien, 23 Aug. 1813. P.P.

[4] *Gaceta ministerial del gobierno de Buenos Aires*, 16 April 1814.

[5] Paroissien to Mrs. Beuzeville, 17 July 1815. P.P.          [P.P.

[6] Ibid.; Representation to the Government of Buenos Aires, 24 Dec. 1825.

[7] Archivo de la Nación Argentina, *Documentos referentes a la guerra de la independencia y emancipación política de la república argentina*, 3 vols. (Buenos Aires, 1914–26), vol. ii, *Paso de los Andes*, pp. 441, 496.

[8] Ibid., p. 496.

Provinces, following a line of forts established 'to protect the people from the incursions of the Indians'.[1] It reached Mendoza in the middle of December, and Paroissien at once took his place at the head of the medical and hospital services.

His resources were small. Three doctors, five Bethlehemite monks, and seven assistants,[2] this was all the staff he could get together for an army which, at the end of the year, consisted of 4,000 regular troops and an auxiliary militia of 1,400 more. But it had to suffice. In December Pueyrredón signed the instructions for the invasion of Chile, and by the middle of January the army was ready to march. It is one of the great coincidences of South American history that at the moment when San Martín was preparing to move, another great soldier, Simón Bolívar, landing in Venezuela after long exile from his native land, was launching the emancipation of northern South America; and Bolívar, like San Martín, took the long and distant view. 'Yes, yes,' he told his companions, 'you shall fly with me to rich Perú. Our destinies call us to the uttermost parts of the American world.'[3]

[1] Journal, under 25 Nov. 1816.
[2] *Documentos referentes*, ii. 468, 471; vol. iii, *En campaña*, p. 117.
[3] Vicente Lecuna, *Cartas del libertador*, 11 vols. (Caracas, 1929–30; vol. xi, New York, 1948), i. 258–9.

VIEW OF THE GREAT CHAIN OF THE ANDES

taken from the Plain of the Maypu.

THE MINT OF SANTIAGO.

# CHAPTER V

## THE LIBERATION OF CHILE, 1817–20

THE Spanish captaincy-general of Chile was, at the beginning of the nineteenth century, an island country. To the east stood the Andes; to the west was the sea; to the north the desert of Atacama, 'one of the most unredeemable deserts on the face of the earth', where 'for years at a time no rain falls',[1] presented as formidable a barrier to the passage of man as the mountains themselves; to the south lay the Indian land of Araucania, and, beyond that, forest. As Copiapó, in its desert oasis, marked the limit of settlement to the north, so Valdivia and Osorno were outposts of civilization in the south. But, within these frontiers, the real Chile was smaller still. Between the desert's rim and the lovely Bío-Bío river, which marked the edge of Araucania, it was a region smaller, indeed, than England and Scotland, and, with its Mediterranean climate, its deep ravines and rushing streams, its smiling central valley flanked by the glittering chain of the Andes and the wooded slopes of coastal hills, it was as fair to see as any country in the world.

At the time of the revolution in Buenos Aires, in 1810, the captaincy-general contained between half and three-quarters of a million people,[2] apart, that is, from the Indian tribes of Araucania. Santiago, the simple but dignified capital, with its great square and unfinished cathedral, was much the largest town: it counted at least thirty thousand souls. Next came Concepción, Santiago's former rival in the south, on the banks of the Bío-Bío river, and, at an almost equal distance to the north, the ancient city of La Serena. But these counted no more than six thousand each. As for Valparaíso, the chief commercial port, it

[1] G. M. McBride, *Chile: Land and Society* (New York, 1936), p. 351.
[2] Cf. F. A. Encina, *Historia de Chile* (Santiago, 1940–), v. 161, 168; Rosenblat, *Población indígena de América*, p. 149.

F

hardly deserved the name of city at all. It was a large and straggling fortified village, and even the road which linked it to the capital had not long been finished.

For society in Chile was rural, not urban. Agriculture and stock-raising were the chief occupations, and provided, with the mining of copper and the coining of money, for what had been a limited though increasing trade with Perú and Buenos Aires and Spain, and even, by contraband channels, with other parts of the world. The mestizo peasantry, who tilled the fields and tended the herds, formed the major part of the rural population. But the peasantry, the *inquilinos* of the *haciendas* and the wandering labourers, were either not far removed from serfdom or sunk in poverty. In the countryside the landed gentry ruled. They lacked political power, for in Chile as in all other Spanish dominions the higher posts in Church and State were in general filled by officials sent out from Spain, by Spaniards native-born, by that Peninsular bureaucracy which formed the civil service of the empire. But to the creole landed gentry almost all else belonged. Sometimes merchants and mine-owners, as well as land-owners, they formed at their apex a native aristocracy. Even at their base they were far removed from the class that served them; and with the colonial officials, with the Spanish emigrés, and with their hangers-on, they constituted a society which was conservative by instinct, habit and conviction.

Yet the history of Chile was now to be both turbulent and violent. Loyal to the Spanish Crown, the native aristocracy nevertheless bitterly resented the rule of Spaniards. It aspired to govern itself, and in the critical year 1810 when established institutions were falling both in Spain and in America, it took the first steps to this end, culminating, on the 18th September, in the establishment of a Junta at Santiago, after the manner of the Junta at Buenos Aires, to govern the country during the captivity, and in the name, of Ferdinand VII. Composed of creoles, Chilean or at least American by birth, it was dominated by a distinguished lawyer, born at Mendoza but long resident at Concepción, Juan Martínez de Rozas, who was to form an effective link between the revolutionary movement in Buenos Aires and that in Chile; and, like the Junta at Buenos Aires, the Junta at Santiago acted with vigour and independence, organized an army, dissolved the royal *audiencia*,

invited the provinces to send deputies to the capital, and opened the ports of the country to foreign trade.

So far, events had been orderly enough. But not only was the Chilean aristocracy conservative, it was divided within itself by regional and family rivalries. A Congress, meeting in 1811, amply revealed both the confusion of mind and the struggle for power within the aristocracy's ranks, and while the Congress was torn by dissension, a twenty-six-year-old creole officer, recently returned from Spain, José Miguel Carrera, took matters into his own hands. Handsome, popular, arrogant and ambitious, Carrera, with the support of his two brothers and the battalions of creole troops, first purged and then dissolved the Congress, succeeded in eliminating Rozas, and established, by July 1812, a military dictatorship which equated independence with his own personal rule.

The Viceroy of Perú, however, now turned his attention to the rebellious colony, as he had already turned it to the provinces of the Río de la Plata, and within a year the south of the country had succumbed to royalist insurrection and Spanish invasion. Within another, Carrera, whose military and political incapacity had alike been proved, had been deposed by the Chileans and captured by the Spaniards. At last, in May 1814, at a time when the country longed for peace, the warfare was halted and a truce signed, under which, with whatever reservations on either side, the royalist troops were to be withdrawn and Chile, again recognizing Spanish sovereignty, was to send deputies to Spain. And, with this, the final tragedy of the 'old fatherland'—so it is termed in Chile—began.

To Carrera's military command there had succeeded Bernardo O'Higgins, whose father, an Irishman in the service of Spain, had been both Captain-General of Chile and Viceroy of Perú. Half-Irish, half-Chilean, Bernardo had been born in Chile but educated abroad. In England, as a youth, he had fallen under the spell of that great precursor of Spanish American independence, the exiled Venezuelan adventurer, Francisco de Miranda.[1] In Chile Martínez de Rozas had been his mentor, and with Carrera his relations had always been strained. But Carrera, deliberately allowed to escape by the Spaniards

---

[1] Above, p. 3; Ernesto de la Cruz, *Epistolario de D. Bernardo O'Higgins*; 2 vols. (Madrid, 1920), i. 31.

in the reasonable expectation that he would embarrass the patriot cause, again seized supreme power. O'Higgins refused to recognize him, and while the lovely central valley of Chile was plunged in civil war, a fresh expedition, sent by the Viceroy of Perú to reduce the country to submission, landed near Concepción. Outwardly composing their differences but ill co-ordinating their plans, the rivals turned to meet the common enemy, and at Rancagua, fifty miles south of Santiago, O'Higgins's army was annihilated.

So ended the first republic of Chile, and such had been its troubled history. It fell on 2 October 1814. Across the Andes, at Mendoza, the capital of Cuyo, San Martín had only just arrived as governor, expecting 'day by day' the action that would 'decide the fate' of Chile.[1] His great design—to raise an army in Cuyo, to cross the Andes, to pacify Chile, and, with Chile as his base, to move onwards to Perú, was instantly made more difficult, for Chile must now be liberated before Perú could be freed. But San Martín was unmoved, and even in disaster there were compensations. As the refugees from Chile, Carrera and O'Higgins among them, streamed across the mountains, San Martín took their measure. Arrogant as ever, Carrera was packed off to San Luis and then to Buenos Aires. There he did his best to undermine San Martín's own position and then sailed to the United States. But in O'Higgins, who also went to Buenos Aires, San Martín found both a loyal friend and a staunch, if impetuous, ally; and when in 1817 the Army of the Andes was at last ready to move, O'Higgins was in its ranks, not only as an Argentine general and San Martín's deputy, but already marked out as the future 'President or Provisional Director of Chile'.

There have been few more spectacular operations in military history than the invasion which now began, and none more carefully prepared. The difficulties were formidable. Behind Mendoza the wall of the Andes rises to its loftiest heights in the great peaks of Aconcagua and Tupungato. Between these giants lies the desolate pass which had long formed the main line of communication between Buenos Aires and Santiago. From the little plain of Uspallata the route lies upwards through the grim gorge of the Mendoza river, strange and terrible indeed, to the wild and windswept Paso de la Cumbre, 12,600 feet

[1] San Martín to Paroissien, 27 Sept. 1814. P.P.

above the level of the sea, then to fall with fearful steepness down the
mountain slopes of Chile. It leads to the great ravine of the Aconcagua
river. To the north of Aconcagua, a second route, the Los Patos route,
longer, equally difficult, but less well known, also led, by the gorge of
the Putaendo, to the valley of the Aconcagua; and these were the routes
chosen by San Martín for his main attack. The troops emerging from
these deep defiles would unite in a small and level plain, and then,
seizing those heights which wall in the northern end of the Central Vale
of Chile, would move on Santiago. While they marched, two southern expeditions, both small, were to confuse and mislead the enemy;
and, simultaneously, two other detachments, crossing from the northern towns of San Juan and La Rioja, were to secure the north of Chile.

Each route had been carefully surveyed. Great pains and ingenuity
had been taken to conceal San Martín's real intentions and his true line
of march. A timetable had been minutely laid down. Emergency
supplies, mountain equipment, every detail, had been carefully calculated; and on 9 January 1817, when the first of the flanking detachments left Mendoza, the campaign began. Nine days later, the smaller
of the two main forces, under the command of Juan Gregorio de Las
Heras, who had himself fought in Chile, began its march, followed by
the artillery. His was the Uspallata route. On the 19th the vanguard
of the principal army, commanded by another *porteño* soldier, Miguel
Estanislao de Soler, broke camp. With him was Paroissien,[1] and theirs
was the Los Patos route. Some way behind them came the reserve
under O'Higgins, and San Martín.

Of more than 9,000 mules which left Mendoza with the troops, less
than a half reached Chile. Of 1,600 horses, less than a third survived.
Many of the men succumbed. But despite the terrible nature of the
terrain, the fierce cold of the nights, mountain sickness, and skirmishes
with parties of the enemy, the whole operation, conducted over a front
of some five hundred miles, proceeded with clockwork precision. Early
in February each commander arrived precisely where he was intended
to arrive and at precisely the right time. On the 9th the two main
bodies joined forces at no great distance from the present terminus of

[1] Representation to the Government of Buenos Aires, 24 Dec. 1825. P.P.;
*Documentos referentes a la guerra de la independencia*, vol. iii, *En campaña*,
p. 81.

the Transandine Railway—Santa Rosa de los Andes; and on the 12th, at Chacabuco, the royalist troops, taken by surprise, outnumbered and outgeneralled, were put to flight. Two days later the triumphant army entered Santiago, to be received, by a people which had suffered much from royalist repression, with delirious enthusiasm. The government was at once offered to San Martín, but San Martín wisely and properly declining the honour, on the 16th February, at an open meeting of the Santiago *cabildo*, O'Higgins was elected Supreme Director *ad interim* of the country which his father had once ruled as captain-general.

Chacabuco was Paroissien's second great battle. Acting, by permission of the commander-in-chief, as an aide-de-camp to Soler,[1] he was commended by San Martín for his efficient organization of the hospital services and for his 'humanity and devotion' to the wounded, and O'Higgins, soon creating the Legion of Merit of Chile, enrolled him among its first members.[2] And to have crossed the Andes with San Martín and to have fought at Chacabuco (as well as scaling the table-land of Upper Perú with Castelli and fighting at Huaquí) was, for an Englishman, no mean claim to distinction. For Chacabuco was one of the great battles of South America. Defeat at Chacabuco would have postponed indefinitely both the liberation of Chile and the emancipation of Perú; it would have imperilled the future of the United Provinces of the Río de la Plata themselves; it might well have changed the entire course of South American history.

And yet the battle was not decisive. Intent on his great strategic design, seeking the road to Lima,[3] San Martín, after a momentary hesitation, hurried back from Santiago across the Andes to Buenos Aires. From Pueyrredón and the Government of the United Provinces he wanted fresh supplies, money, munitions, and, above all, naval support in the Pacific—for Perú must be invaded by sea; and while from Buenos Aires an agent was sent to buy ships and munitions in the United States, from Santiago Paroissien's intimate friend[4] and old acquaintance in his Córdoba days, José Álvarez Condarco, was sent on a similar mission to England. Incidentally, at Buenos Aires San Martín

---

[1] Journal, 10 Feb. 1819; Representation to the Government of Buenos Aires, 24 Dec. 1825. P.P.

[2] *Documentos referentes a la guerra de la independencia*, iii. 116, 113.

[3] Mitre, *Historia de San Martín*, ii. 83.

[4] Paroissien to Mrs. Beuzeville, 24 Dec. 1818. P.P.

again met Carrera, who had now returned from the United States and, with ships that he had managed to procure, proposed to sail to Chile. His presence would have dispelled all unity in the patriot ranks; his reconciliation with O'Higgins was impossible; and the Government of the United Provinces very wisely detained him. His ships—only two of them arrived—turned out to be useless, and he himself, fleeing to Montevideo, was to prove as troublesome a figure in the politics of the United Provinces as he had previously been in those of Chile.

But San Martín was absent from Santiago for two months, and he had committed a grave tactical error. He had failed, after Chacabuco, to pursue the defeated Spanish army, and many of the royalist troops were allowed to escape by sea from Valparaíso. Still worse, while he lingered in Santiago and then left for Buenos Aires, the royalist forces in the south of the country were given time to entrench themselves in what is today the Chilean naval base of Talcahuano, six miles from Concepción. Las Heras, it is true, had been ordered to the south, but, with weary troops, he moved slowly. Not till early April did he reach Concepción, and he was there joined by O'Higgins in besieging Talcahuano. Once again Paroissien—now surgeon-general of the Army of Chile—was in charge of the hospital services (with a 'gratification' of forty pesos a month);[1] and here there was a disagreeable episode. He was accused by an ex-Napoleonic general, Michel Brayer, who had enlisted with the patriot forces, not only of inefficiency but of dishonesty.[2] But the charges were not proved; Brayer's career in Chile was, to say the least, uniformly unsuccessful; he later vented his rage in a violent personal attack on San Martín himself; and the epithets which he applied to Paroissien—'wretch', 'insufferable vampire' (whom he had 'prevented from devouring the blood of the soldiers')—scarcely proclaimed a calm and dispassionate mind.[3]

[1] His appointment was dated 26 August but took effect from 8 July 1817. P.P. See also *Documentos referentes a la guerra de la independencia*, iii. 175, 179.

[2] Diego Barros Arana, *Historia jeneral de Chile*, 16 vols. (Santiago, 1884–1902), xi. 275 note.

[3] *Exposición de la conducta del teniente general Brayer durante el tiempo que ha estado en la América del Sud. La pública el General San Martín, con su contestación* (Buenos Aires, 1818), pp. 13, 22. Reprinted in Museo Mitre, *Documentos del archivo de San Martín*, 12 vols. (Buenos Aires, 1910–11), xi. 71–91.

For more than six months the rival armies faced each other in Concepción and Talcahuano. But a direct assault on Talcahuano failing in December, and the news arriving that a fresh Spanish expedition was approaching by sea from Perú, O'Higgins, early in January 1818, raised the siege and made a strategic retreat northwards. Meanwhile, Chile had still not declared her independence, and since no Congress existed to give weight to such a declaration, the people had been invited to express their own opinions. Registers were opened in Santiago and the other cities, in which partisans of independence, and its opponents, could each sign their names. Not surprisingly, no contrary signatures appeared; and, a suitable document having been drafted, at last, on 12 February 1818, the anniversary of Chacabuco, the independence of Chile was formally proclaimed. Exactly five weeks later, the joint forces of San Martín and O'Higgins were surprised and dispersed by the new royalist commander, General Osorio, at Cancha Rayada, half-way between Concepción and Santiago.

The news filled Santiago with wild dismay. 'All the patriots of property and political importance began to prepare for flight across the Cordilleras, and, packing up their plate and valuables, they marched towards the mountains. The streets were filled with cargo-mules, and carriages, conveying the emigrants, with their wives and families, from the city. The number that left the town for Mendoza was very great, and persons holding high situations under government were the first to depart.'[1] San Martín and O'Higgins were reported killed, captured, fled; and O'Higgins was indeed wounded. Paroissien, who dressed his wounds, attempted to cheer him with the reflection that, even should further disaster overtake the patriot troops, it would still be possible to retire to Mendoza and to raise another army there. 'No,' replied O'Higgins, 'while I live and there is a Chilean to follow me, I shall fight in Chile. No more emigration.'[2] Nor was it necessary. Cancha Rayada was a negative action, and San Martín quickly recovered. On the 5th April he met Osorio again at Maipú, where the guns could be heard in Santiago itself. Their forces were almost equal—about 5,000 men a side—and when the battle ended more than 2,500 lay dead. Of

[1] Samuel Haigh, *Sketches of Buenos Ayres, Chile, and Peru* (London, 1831), pp. 194–5. Cf. *Memoirs of General Miller*, i. 178.
[2] Barros Arana, op. cit., xi. 388 note.

the royalists nearly as many were captured. Only a ragged remnant escaped, and though in the south of Chile, beyond the Bío-Bío river, it was long before the royalist cause was completely extinguished, Maipú was the decisive battle of the war. It sealed the independence of Chile. It foreshadowed the independence of Perú.

An English merchant and traveller, present on the field, has left a picture of Paroissien at Maipú, in the mill 'half a mile from the rear of the army', which he had converted into a temporary hospital, its 'front yard' filled 'with wounded, chiefly blacks', and himself engaged 'in the act of amputating the leg of an officer'. There, his hands stained with blood, he wrote a brief dispatch to O'Higgins in Santiago, and though San Martín had already sent a laconic note, it was Paroissien's messenger who first revealed to the waiting crowds in the streets of the capital the news of the victory.[1] As for his own services at Maipú, they were, once again, recognized by San Martín in dispatches, and, promoted to the rank of colonel in June, he was awarded the Gold Medal of Maipú in December.[2] 'The Govt.', he wrote in that month, 'has been very liberal to me, and besides my pay and allowances as Colonel of Artillery (all which in horses, servants and the devil knows what I am obliged to spend) I have been presented with a landed estate of a league and a half square in the vicinity of the City of Mendoza, to which place our excellent General and many of our officers mean to retire after the General Pacification, and the acknowledgment of the Independence of this Country, an event which will doubtless soon take place . . . the horizon looks at present very well. God knows if it will again become cloudy. The only thing that can effect it is the failure of the Expedition to Lima.'[3]

The expedition to Lima! This was still San Martín's consuming ambition. Scarcely giving himself time to rest, after Maipú, as after Chacabuco, he again hurried across the mountains to Buenos Aires to solicit fresh financial aid—an embarrassing request to an impecunious government—and this time he was absent six months. Not till the end of October, after anxious negotiations and much delay at Mendoza,

[1] Haigh, op. cit., pp. 228–9.
[2] *Documentos referentes a la guerra de la independencia*, iii. 263, 268 c.; Representation to the Government of Buenos Aires, 24 Dec. 1825. P.P.
[3] Paroissien to Mrs. Beuzeville, 24 Dec. 1818. P.P.

caused by the winter storms which raged in the Andes, was he back in Santiago, ready for a new command. O'Higgins, for his part, looked with equal ardour to 'our enterprise against Lima'.[1] He fully realized, no one better, that on the Pacific command of the sea gave command of the land; that without such command, and so long as Perú remained in Spanish hands, the independence of Chile was insecure. And from the day that Chacabuco had been fought O'Higgins had turned his thoughts and bent his energies to building up not only the army but, above all, a navy.

The creation of the Chilean navy was O'Higgins's most distinguished achievement. His financial resources were scanty. He himself was not popular, at least in the upper ranks of the Chilean aristocracy. His liberal views were disliked. Argentine influence in his government was suspected and resented. The friends of the Carreras were united against him, more particularly after Carrera's two brothers, irregularly tried, had been executed at Mendoza for their subversive activities. A dictator *malgré lui*, he early reached the conclusion that it was 'impracticable to form a constitution, and dangerous to convene a congress'.[2] He could do no more than create, in the constitutional statute of 1818, a legislative senate of five, establish certain constitutional guarantees, and promise to summon a constituent assembly at a later date.

But the navy grew. The first acquisition was the *Águila*, an ex-English merchantman, condemned by the Spaniards for engaging in contraband trade. She was seized in Valparaíso harbour a few days after the battle of Chacabuco and was later to be known as the *Pueyrredón*. In 1817 also, letters of marque were issued to a number of American and English vessels, and some prizes brought in. But these were little ships. Chile, as yet, had no substantial ship of war, and, though the future admiral, Manuel Blanco Encalada, had served in the Spanish navy, she had few trained sailors.

In March 1818, however, arrived the *Windham*, an ex-East Indiaman of 820 tons, built in 1801, and sent out from London by Alvarez Condarco to be paid for in Chile. The purchase price was 180,000

[1] O'Higgins to San Martín, 12 June 1818. De la Cruz, op. cit., i. 182.
[2] Manning, *Diplomatic Correspondence of the United States concerning the Independence of the Latin-American Nations*, ii. 948.

dollars, and O'Higgins emptied his treasury, as well as calling on private individuals, to buy and arm her. But, commanded by a former British naval officer, with English officers and a mixed crew of English-men and Chileans, she promptly won fame as the *Lautaro* and more than covered her costs by her first prize. A second East Indiaman, also commissioned by Alvarez Condarco, followed in May—the *Cumberland*, 1,200 tons and built in 1802. She is best known to history as the *San Martín*. Two other vessels, the *Chacabuco*, an ex-American privateer, and the *Araucano*, sold to the Government by her American captain, were acquired in the Chilean winter of 1818; and these four, officered and manned, for the most part, by Britons and Americans, and commanded by Blanco Encalada, achieved the brilliant feat of capturing in October the 1,200-ton Spanish frigate, *María Isabel*, together with a number of transports bearing troops from Spain to Perú. Where four ships had left Valparaíso in October, thirteen returned in November,[1] and the *María Isabel* took her place at the side of the *Lautaro* and the *San Martín* as the *O'Higgins*.

Such were the proud beginnings of Chilean naval traditions. The squadron had already been joined by the *Intrépido*, sent to its aid from Buenos Aires, and by the *Galvarino*, a former British sloop of war, brought out from England by two British naval officers; and other ships were acquired in 1819, notably the *Independencia*, an American-built corvette, commissioned from the United States, and the *Monte-zuma*, a merchant prize.[2] And while arms and munitions arrived from the United States, procured with the aid of British and American merchants,[3] and the ranks of the infant navy were swelled by British and American seamen, on the 28th November there landed at Val-paraíso one of the most daring and distinguished, as he was also one of the most incalculable, of British naval officers, Thomas Cochrane, the future Earl of Dundonald. Dismissed by the British Admiralty, expelled

[1] *Memoirs of General Miller*, i. 198.

[2] Cf. Antonio García Reyes, 'Primera escuadra nacional', in B. Vicuña Mackenna, *Historia jeneral de la república de Chile*, iv (Santiago, 1868); Gonzalo Búlnes, *Historia de la espedición libertadora del Perú*, 2 vols. (Santiago, 1887–8), i, passim; W. H. Neumann, 'United States Aid to the Chilean Wars of Independence', *Hispanic American Historical Review*, xxvii (1947), pp. 204–19; and Encina, op. cit., vii. 569 ff.

[3] Cf. Eugenio Pereira Salas, *Henry Hill, comerciante, vice-consul y misionero* (Santiago, 1940), pp. 7–30; Neumann, op. cit., pp. 216–18.

from Parliament, and engaged in a private war with the British Government, Cochrane had been persuaded by Alvarez Condarco to undertake the command of the Chilean navy, and, received with enthusiasm, he quickly added to his reputation. In two expeditions in 1819 he ranged the Pacific coast as far north as Guayaquil, appeared in Callao harbour, struck as much terror into the hearts of the Spaniards as Drake himself, and, finally, in February 1820, achieved the almost incredible feat of capturing the royalist stronghold of Valdivia in southern Chile, an exploit which completed the liberation of mainland Chile and confined the royalist troops thereafter to the island of Chiloé.

With the sailors and the marines, the naval officers on half-pay, the seamen discharged after the close of the Napoleonic wars, came the merchants and commission agents, both British and American; and they were, in their way, equally important. Frigates from New York and New England, Nantucket whalers, South Sea sealers, had touched at Chilean ports in colonial times for the sake of contraband trade. In 1807 and 1808 the same eager expectation which had taken the British merchant to Montevideo and Rio de Janeiro had turned his thoughts to Chile,[1] and the opening of the ports by the Junta at Santiago in 1811 had at once been answered by the arrival of the foreign merchant. But the adventurers were as yet few. Chile was far distant. Britons and Americans ran in common danger from the Spaniards. They themselves went to war in 1812, and off the coast of Chile the United States frigate, *Essex*, arriving in 1813, terrorized British shipping till her capture in the following year.[2] In any event, the Spanish reconquest of the country again closed its ports, and it was not till 1817 that they were finally and permanently opened.

But from that moment foreign merchant vessels came in numbers. The markets were 'quite glutted with every description of goods and wares'.[3] Chile, in 1817, for the first time figured in the British customs

[1] E. Pereira Salas, *Buques norteamericanos en Chile a fines de la era colonial* (Santiago, 1936), p. 11; Humphreys, *British Consular Reports*, p. 127 note.

[2] J. J. Barnard to Commanding Officer, H.M. Naval Force, Río de la Plata, 22 Jan. 1814, F.O. 72/171; Neumann, op. cit., pp. 206–9; D. Amunátegui Solar, 'Origen del comercio inglés en Chile', *Revista chilena de historia y geografía*, No. 103 (1943), pp. 82–95.

[3] Haigh, op. cit., p. 253. Cf. Manning, op. cit., ii. 984, and C. W. Centner, 'Relaciones comerciales de Gran Bretaña con Chile, 1810–1830', *Revista chilena de historia y geografía*, No. 103 (1943), pp. 96–107.

records. Paroissien, two years later, could report that 'we have constant communication with Calcutta'.[1] Valparaíso, according to British visitors, was transformed into a 'coast town' of Great Britain, where English 'tailors, shoemakers, saddlers, and inn-keepers' hung out their signs in every street.[2] And though some of these immigrants proved to be 'of the lowest description, and of the worst characters',[3] nevertheless the aid which the larger commission agents and merchants in Santiago and Valparaíso were able to afford to the infant state both in money and supplies was invaluable.

Commercial penetration from overseas had already begun, and military and naval preparedness had proceeded far when, in October 1818, six months after the battle of Maipú, San Martín returned to Santiago from his visit to Buenos Aires. 'We have an army in Chile', wrote Paroissien in December, 'of 10,000 men' (he greatly exaggerated its number), 'and 50,000 stand of arms and a powerfull fleet which has just gained an important victory over the Spaniards.'[4] And though in the south of the country, beyond the Bío-Bío river, royalist resistance had yet to be overcome, O'Higgins and San Martín were in agreement that the moment was approaching when the last stage of San Martín's great design—the invasion and liberation of Perú—could be put into execution. The general details of the expedition were discussed and approved;[5] a formal treaty of alliance between Chile and Buenos Aires was proposed and prepared; and at this seemingly eleventh hour the plans were shattered on the rock of finance. The Government of the United Provinces was unable to supply all the financial aid which it had promised, and the Government of Chile, its resources stretched to the limit, could not make up the deficiency.

For San Martín the blow was bitter. It was in vain that he represented to the Government at Buenos Aires the extreme penury of Chile: Buenos Aires could do no more. It was in vain that he heaped reproaches on the Government of Chile: O'Higgins's hands were tied.

---

[1] Paroissien to Mrs. Beuzeville, 20 Oct. 1819. P.P.

[2] Maria Graham, *Journal of a Residence in Chile, during the year 1822* (London, 1824), p. 131.

[3] Robert Proctor, *Narrative of a Journey across the Cordillera of the Andes. and of a Residence in Lima* (London, 1825), p. 109.

[4] Paroissien to Mrs. Beuzeville, 24 Dec. 1818. P.P.

[5] Barros Arana, op. cit., xii. 55.

He took an extraordinary step. He proposed that the Army of the Andes should be recalled before it dissolved in misery and discontent, as dissolve, he declared, it would, though some troops, he was careful to insinuate, should remain in Chile. Next, he suggested that a pretext for this recall might be found in the reported preparations at Cádiz of an expedition to be directed against the Río de la Plata. And finally, on 14 February 1819, calling together his army commanders, he announced that he must leave Chile at once for Santa Fe in order, Paroissien reported, to settle 'the disputes between Artigas and B.ˢ Ayres', which had 'arrived at a height to threaten the destruction of the Gov.ᵗ' and paralysed 'completely all S.ⁿ Martin's operations'.[1] On the next day he once again took the weary road across the Andes to Mendoza. He was followed in May by a part of the army, and he was not to return for close on a year.

It is difficult to deduce with certainty the workings of San Martín's mind from the apparent contradictions, the recommendations, the counter-recommendations, the complaints, the reassurances, that his correspondence with the Government at Buenos Aires at this time contained.[2] Probably enough he hoped by the threat of the withdrawal of his army and by his own retirement to intimidate the Chilean Government into compliance with his will, while, at the same time, he was anxious to restrain the Buenos Aires Government from withdrawing the army completely.[3] Probably also he hoped, with one foot in Chile and the other in Mendoza, to be ready for any emergency, to lead the expedition to Perú on the one hand, to contain the rising tide of anarchy in the United Provinces on the other. But whatever his purpose, and whatever the justice or the falsity of his reasoning, two inevitable consequences followed: he exposed his army to dispersion and desertion;[4] and he himself was caught on the horns of a dilemma.

For in the United Provinces the domestic situation had daily grown graver. The national government, re-established by the Congress of

[1] Journal, 14 Feb. 1819.

[2] *Archivo de San Martín*, iv. 384–99; Mitre, *Historia de San Martín*, iv. 503–15.

[3] Mitre, *Historia de San Martín*, ii. 335–6; Ricardo Levene, ed., *Historia de la nación argentina* (Buenos Aires, 1936–), vi, *segunda sección*, p. 630.

[4] Cf. Encina, op. cit., vii. 652–6.

Tucumán in 1816, was again in jeopardy. The Congress, moving to Buenos Aires, had early lost its transient popularity. José Artigas, the *Jefe de los Orientales* and the Protector of the Free Peoples, driven out of the Banda Oriental by the invasion of the Portuguese from Brazil,[1] was now the irreconcilable enemy of Buenos Aires and the Portuguese alike. In the adjoining provinces where his influence ran, and even beyond them, the rude *gauchos* of the plains, recognizing no other authority than that of local *caudillos*, guerrilla chieftains, plunged the unhappy country into continuous strife. And in Buenos Aires, San Martín's friend and ally, Pueyrredón, the Supreme Director, was helpless. He himself resigned in June 1819, and the successor Government, first genuinely perturbed by the threat—which proved to be illusory—of Spanish invasion, and then menaced with its own dissolution by the tide of civil war, summoned San Martín, with his troops, to the defence of the capital.

While Pueyrredón had remained at the head of affairs in Buenos Aires, no undue pressure had been put upon San Martín, and Pueyrredón's loyalty to him was beyond all praise. But what saved the liberating expedition to Perú was the loyalty of O'Higgins, supported by that semi-masonic and secret organization of military and political leaders known as the *Logia Lautaro*, which, with its declared object of the 'independence and happiness of America', had first made its appearance in Buenos Aires in 1812 and had subsequently been introduced into Chile. O'Higgins did not falter. The plans for the expedition were modified, but its preparations were pushed forward, and, in 1819, while the prospects of the United Provinces continued to deteriorate, those of Chile continued to improve. San Martín, in painful perplexity, still lingered at Mendoza, but in December, forced at last to choose between Buenos Aires and America, he sacrificed the lesser to the larger loyalty. Disobeying the orders to return to Buenos Aires, he resigned his command, and in January 1820 once more crossed the Andes to Santiago.

Ill and distressed, San Martín rested from late February to early March at the thermal springs of Cauquenes, picturesquely situated in a narrow ravine at no great distance from Rancagua—the scene of O'Higgins's great defeat in 1814. And here Paroissien (he has left two

[1] Above, pp. 53, 61.

pleasing sketches of the place)[1] attended him. His life, during the months of San Martín's absence, had been full of variety. He had lived for a time at army headquarters with General Antonio González Balcarce,[2] whom he had first known in Upper Perú in 1810 and 1811, and who, though stricken with mortal illness, had been acting as San Martín's deputy. As in the United Provinces in 1812, so in Chile in 1819, he had been placed in charge of the manufacture of explosives,[3] and he retained his rank as surgeon-general. But Santiago, enlivened by the society of soldiers and sailors and the ubiquitous English adventurer, was a gay capital,[4] and the world was still young. The 'Order of Buffers'—to which Paroissien belonged, together with the future General William Miller, two young merchants, J. J. Barnard (who had first arrived in 1811) and John Begg, both of whom were to become well known in Chile, and, still more generally known on account of his book of travels, Samuel Haigh—seems to have had its share of young men's follies; and there were other, and familiar enough, temptations besides. But Paroissien could also find his diversions in reading Gibbon and sketching in the streets of the capital, and the face which looks out from the clever portrait by the distinguished mulatto artist, Gil de Castro—amiable, not strong, but full of sensibility—is probably a fair index to the man.

Possibly tempted by the thought of commercial speculations,[5] in March 1820, on the plea of ill-health, Paroissien threw up his military career altogether.[6] But his retirement was of short duration. On the 2nd April, at Rancagua, at a time when the national government in Buenos Aires had ceased to exist, the commanders of the Army of the Andes (now much reduced in size) solemnly affirmed their loyalty to San Martín. In May he was formally appointed commander-in-chief of the liberating expedition to Perú, which was to sail under Chilean auspices alone. Shortly afterwards the officers of Argentina were con-

[1] Reproduced in Peter Schmidtmeyer, *Travels into Chile, over the Andes, in the years 1820 and 1821* (London, 1824).

[2] Journal, 2 April 1819.

[3] Order of Supreme Director of Chile, 9 Sept. 1819. P.P.; Cf. Barros Arana, op. cit., xii. 478.

[4] Haigh, op. cit., p. 253.

[5] John Begg to Paroissien, 28 Jan. 1820. P.P.

[6] Order of San Martín, 24 March 1820; J. I. Zenteno to Paroissien, 29 March 1820. P.P.

BERNARDO O'HIGGINS

THE CANADA. SANTIAGO.

firmed in their respective ranks in the army of Chile, and on the 4th June Paroissien was gazetted as one of San Martín's principal aides-de-camp.[1] Eleven weeks later, on August 20th, the liberating expedition was ready to sail.

[1] Order of San Martín, 4 June 1820. P.P.

G

# CHAPTER VI

## THE LIBERATING EXPEDITION TO PERÚ, 1820–1

THE liberating expedition to Perú which began to embark at Valparaíso on 18 August 1820, with bands playing and colours flying, every avenue crowded with spectators,[1] was some 4,400 or 4,500 strong. It was well armed and well equipped. The greater number of the troops were Chilean, though there was a strong contingent of Argentine veterans both among the officers and the men. Las Heras was chief of staff, and of the two divisional generals, Toribio de Luzuriaga, a Peruvian by birth, had succeeded San Martín as Governor of Cuyo, and Juan Antonio Alvarez de Arenales, though born in Spain, had long identified himself with the cause of the United Provinces. The navy—eighteen transports and seven ships of war, proudly afloat in Valparaíso Bay—was commanded by Lord Cochrane. Of the sailors and marines, perhaps a third, including nearly all the officers, came from England, Ireland, Scotland and the United States. The rest were Chileans. The transports were under the charge of an American, Captain Paul Delano, of Massachusetts.

As a principal aide-de-camp, San Martín took, besides Paroissien, Tomás Guido, a loyal and devoted friend who had long ago visited England and who had been Argentine representative in Chile. He was accompanied also by a civil staff quite as important as the military. One of its members, Juan García del Río, a young man of considerable literary abilities who had arrived in Chile from New Granada by way of England, was soon to be Paroissien's intimate friend and colleague. He sailed as Secretary of Government. A second, Bernardo Monteagudo, Paroissien had first met in Upper Perú in 1810, when the two

[1] *Memoirs of General Miller*, i. 266.

had struck up a fairly close friendship.[1] Utterly amoral, Monteagudo, in the course of his varied career—as a tribune of the revolution at Buenos Aires, in exile abroad, later attached to San Martín's army in Chile, and then banished to San Luis (where he consoled himself with the *Letters of Junius* and petitioned Paroissien for the poems of Ossian[2])—had acquired a sinister reputation, and was to exercise a fateful influence. He sailed as Secretary of War. With him in the *San Martín* were Guido, García del Río, Paroissien, and San Martín himself. Cochrane, whose relations with the Government of Chile had recently been greatly strained (his relations with any government were usually greatly strained) sailed in the *O'Higgins*.

The afternoon of the 20th August, when the squadron and transports weighed, was fine and calm, but it was not till the evening of the next day that all the ships, as Paroissien remarked, could get into the offing.[3] A further transport was picked up at Chile's most northerly port, Coquimbo, on the 25th, and on the 8th September, after a voyage of more than a thousand miles, which had given rise to some alarm through the disappearance of two of the transports, and some criticisms also of the Admiral's handling of the convoy, the expedition landed on Peruvian soil near the town of Pisco. That same evening Pisco was occupied. Two days later the disembarkation of the army was completed, by which time one of the missing transports had made her appearance, having been navigated, wrote Paroissien, with the aid of 'a small compass the surgeon happened to have appended to his watch';[4] and to the joy of the army her arrival was followed, some days later, by that of the other. Advance guards were thrown out, and, that done, San Martín, much to Cochrane's disgust, settled down at Pisco for the next six weeks.

Pisco, a green oasis on a barren coast, and well known for its brandies, was within two to three days' sail of Callao, the port of Lima, and three to five days' march of Lima itself. The sugar plantations and vineyards in its agricultural hinterland, worked by slave labour, yielded, as San Martín anticipated, great supplies of sugar, brandy, fresh meat and provisions. Several hundred negroes, tempted by the

[1] Monteagudo to Paroissien, 25 Nov., 10, 26 Dec. 1811; 10, 24 Jan., 10 March 1812. P.P.        [2] Monteagudo to Paroissien, 7 May 1819. P.P.

[3] R. A. Humphreys, ed., 'James Paroissien's Notes on the Liberating Expedition to Perú', *Hispanic American Historical Review*, xxxi (1951), p. 254.

[4] Ibid., p. 257.

prospects of freedom, joined the invaders' ranks,[1] though San Martín was careful to promise compensation to their owners. And at Pisco the 'revolutionizing' of Perú began.

To add to his resources and to sow the seeds of revolution were San Martín's primary objects in landing at Pisco; and the broad lines of his strategy, as they here revealed themselves, were simple enough. A flying column was to march into the mountains and along the longitudinal valleys parallel to the coast, thus cutting off the supplies of Lima from the interior. The main body of the troops would be transferred to the north of the capital, thus severing its connexions with the northern agricultural provinces. A general insurrection would be promoted; and while, as Paroissien expressed it, 'a line of circumvallation' would be drawn 'completely round Lima', the city, blockaded both by land and sea, would be forced to capitulate.[2]

But San Martín had no intention of attacking Lima itself or of fighting a general action.[3] Cochrane, it is true, was all impatience. His own highly characteristic design was to land as near to Callao as possible 'and forthwith to obtain possession of the capital; an object', he observed in his famous justification of his conduct, 'by no means difficult of execution, and certain of success'.[4] This was a bold plan and a bold surmise. The royalist forces in Perú may, or may not, have amounted to some 23,000 men.[5] But in Lima alone there was an army of between 6,000 and 7,000 regular troops, quite apart from the city militia and the Callao garrison;[6] and reinforcements could be summoned. Cochrane may have been right, but the risks were great, and San Martín, always a cautious commander, was not prepared to run them. Too much was at stake for a hazard of this kind.

[1] Ibid., pp. 258, 268.

[2] Ibid., pp. 265, 268; Historia de la nación argentina, vi, 2da. sección, pp. 655, 659–60.

[3] Museo Histórico Nacional, San Martín. Su correspondencia, 1823–1850 (2nd edn., Madrid, 1910), p. 103; Humphreys, loc. cit., pp. 265, 268.

[4] Thomas Cochrane, Earl of Dundonald, Memoranda of Naval Services in the Liberation of Chili and Peru from Spanish Domination (London, 1858), p. 79.

[5] Memoirs of General Miller, i. 263. This estimate, often quoted, is given 'on the authority' of the Manifiesto en que el virey del Perú Don Joaquín de la Pezuela refiere el hecho y circunstancias de su separación del mando . . . (Madrid, 1821). But the Manifiesto nowhere confirms it. The matter is much disputed.

[6] Cf. V. Rodríguez Casado and G. Lohmann Villena, eds., Memoria de gobierno del virrey Joaquín de la Pezuela, 1816–1821 (Seville, 1947), p. 777, and Búlnes, Historia de la espedición libertadora, i. 405–14.

For Perú was the fortress of Spain in America. The viceroyalty (excluding the provinces of Upper Perú, which had only been annexed after the outbreak of the revolution in Buenos Aires) contained in 1820 rather less than a million and a half people, and in social structure it was as different from Chile as society in Chile differed from that in Buenos Aires. It was a land of contrasts and of castes. The inhabitants of the coastal plain, its aridity relieved by fertile valleys, dwelt in a world apart from those of the high sierras; distance and deserts divided the north from the south. Pure-blooded Indians, or, in smaller proportion, mestizos, formed the majority of the population, and while at the bottom of the social scale the negro slaves and the humble Indians were the hewers of wood and the drawers of water, at its top the Spaniards and creoles were the favoured of fortune and of Spain. No other city in South America rivalled the wealth and magnificence of Lima, with its stone gateways, its walls ten feet thick, its convents and colleges, its cathedral and university, its multitude of churches, and its population of not less than 64,000 persons.[1] Nowhere else was there so powerful an army, so numerous a nobility, so wealthy a body of merchants allied to the great commercial houses of Seville and Cádiz, or so large a number of ecclesiastics. And, 'till the enemy came and knocked at the "silver gates of the city of the kings" ',[2] society in Lima had been comparatively undisturbed by the currents of revolution that swept the continent from north to south and from east to west.

But even in Perú, where the rivalry between Spaniards and creoles, despite their common fear of the classes beneath them, was no less acute than in Chile or Buenos Aires, there had been 'intimations of independence'; and from the moment when in 1816 that scourge of revolution and last of the great viceroys, José Fernando de Abascal, departed, Perú was exposed both externally and internally to increasing danger. In 1816 the revolution in South America had seemed to be dead or dying. Only in the United Provinces and, at the other end of the continent, in the more easterly parts of Venezuela, was it still flickeringly alive. Yet it was now to revive with redoubled force. As, in

[1] W. B. Stevenson, *A Historical and Descriptive Narrative of Twenty Years' Residence in South America*, 3 vols. (London, 1825–9), i. 211, 289; Rosenblat, *Población indígena*, p. 146.

[2] Hall, *Extracts from a Journal written on the Coasts of Chili, Peru, and Mexico*, i. 92.

1817, San Martín crossed the Andes to establish the independence of Chile, so, in 1819, by an equally heroic march, Simón Bolívar led his ragged army from the plains of the Orinoco to the capital of the viceroyalty of New Granada to found the Republic of Colombia. And while in the north and in the south the skies thus darkened, Perú, her lines of communication cut both by sea and land, was increasingly isolated. Her revenues diminished; her commerce decayed; and, in the very home of monopoly, the Viceroy was compelled to connive at the trade of foreigners, and despairing merchants were constrained to employ their services.[1]

But it was events in Spain, combined with the operations of Lord Cochrane's squadron and the approach of San Martín's army, that completed the demoralization of Perú. In Spain, in January 1820, the army at Cádiz mutinied. In March, Ferdinand VII, who had been restored to his throne and despotism six years earlier, was forced to accept that liberal constitution, first promulgated in 1812, which he had himself suppressed; and while all plans of military reinforcements to the royalist armies in America were abandoned, the Viceroy of Perú, Joaquín de la Pezuela, found himself instructed to promote a pacification of the colonies or, at the least, to procure a suspension of hostilities during which grievances and differences might be rationally discussed.

On the 11th September the news of San Martín's invasion reached Lima. The Viceroy, who had already published the resuscitated Spanish constitution and was preparing, according to his instructions, to send commissioners to Chile, instantly invited San Martín to enter into negotiations; and San Martín, with equal alacrity, accepted the offer. Time, he thought, was on his side. The whole of his army, when the Viceroy's flag of truce arrived, had not yet assembled at Pisco, for one of the transports, with several hundred men on board, was still missing; and the opportunity to obtain a more precise knowledge of the Viceroy's intentions and of the state of feeling in Lima was too good to be lost. He offered, therefore, to send his own commissioners to the capital, and these, Guido and García del Río, meeting the Viceroy's representatives at the pleasant seaside village of Miraflores, signed, on the 26th September, an armistice which was to last for eight days.

The subsequent discussions revealed that even between a constitu-

[1] Humphreys, *British Consular Reports*, p. 127 note.

tionalist Spain and independent South America the gulf was impass-. able. Nor could agreement be reached on the terms which should govern any longer suspension of hostilities. But before Guido and García del Río left Miraflores, on the collapse of the negotiations, they met the Viceroy himself at the neighbouring village of Magdalena;[1] and it was probably here that they made the remarkable suggestion that a measure of reconciliation might yet be found in the establishment in Perú of an independent monarchy under a prince of the Spanish royal house. 'The general', recorded Paroissien, in an account which may well have been derived from Guido and García del Río themselves, 'has proposed to the Viceroy to allow the Peruvians free and complete liberty to elect the form of Government they please, even if they should wish to crown a King of the Spanish Branch of the Bourbons, but he insists upon the seat of Government's being in America. This the Viceroy says he has not authority to agree to, and I suppose we must go to Loggerheads.'[2]

Superficially the idea was attractive. Its prototype was the plan proposed by Saturnino Rodríguez Peña in 1808 for the establishment of a constitutional monarchy in the Río de la Plata, under the Princess Carlota. In the United Provinces San Martín's friend, Manuel Belgrano, had favoured the coronation first of Carlota, then of Francisco de Paula, a younger brother of Ferdinand VII, and finally of an Indian 'prince' of Inca descent! Pueyrredón, the Supreme Director, had proposed to crown the Duke of Orleans, and the Congress at Buenos Aires in 1819 had secretly supported the young Duke of Lucca, Ferdinand's nephew. As for San Martín, he seems to have formed the opinion soon after his arrival in Chile that that country was more suited to a monarchical than a republican form of government. Experience had merely confirmed his view,[3] and if he now believed that in countries less than half-literate,

[1] Pezuela, *Memoria de gobierno*, p. 772.

[2] Humphreys, 'James Paroissien's Notes . . .', p. 265. See also *Manifiesto de las sesiones tenidas en el pueblo de Miraflores para las transaciones intentadas con el general San Martín* . . . (Lima, 1820), doc. núm. 33, and Mitre, *Historia de San Martín*, ii. 551–3.

[3] Staples to Hamilton, 25 May 1817. C. K. Webster, ed., *Britain and the Independence of Latin America, 1812–1830. Select Documents from the Foreign Office Archives*, 2 vols. (London, 1938), i. 553; Bowles to Croker, 14 Feb. 1818, Ad. 1/23.

and wholly lacking in the traditions of self-government, monarchy was the form best suited to contemporary needs and conditions, the conclusion was not unreasonable. What vitiated all such schemes (and some of them were ridiculous enough) was the character of the Spanish princes, the jealousies of the Spanish Crown, and the passions, the prejudices and the ambitions which the revolution had unleashed. But the negotiations at Miraflores revealed the direction in which San Martín's mind was tending, and they foreshadowed more definite proposals to come.

Once the negotiations had ended, and the armistice had expired, San Martín acted with decision. He was satisfied with his prospects. The revolutionizing of Perú, he believed, had already begun; the enemy faced destruction from within; and the time had come to take further measures. Accordingly, on the 4th October, Arenales, in command of a force of some 1,200 or 1,400 men, was dispatched inland to the town of Ica, some fifty miles distant from Pisco. He was to penetrate the mountains, stimulate insurrection among the Indian inhabitants of the highlands, and march to the north by that ancient and famous route of Andean history, the central Jauja Valley.[1] Meanwhile, the main body of the troops was to be transported to the north of Lima; and on the 25th October, five days after Arenales's campaign could properly be said to have begun, San Martín moved.

Once again Lord Cochrane's handling of the squadron and the convoy caused uneasiness. 'It really is requisite', wrote Paroissien, in language which may well have reflected the feelings of the General and is certainly an index to the relations between the military and the naval arms, 'to have more than the patience of an angel with Lord C. He is the most careless, unmethodical man I ever knew, promises everything and performs nothing. He appears only to be anxious about making money. Avarice and selfishness do certainly appear to form the groundwork of his character and from his speculative disposition he is often in great want of money to obtain which he is not so scrupulously exact in his word as every man ought to be, particularly a man of his rank and station. Not a day passes but brings some proof of this unfortunate

---

[1] Humphreys, 'James Paroissien's Notes . . .', pp. 264–5, 268; *Archivo de San Martín*, vii. 223; *Historia de la nación argentina*, vi, 2ᵈᵃ· sección, pp. 659–60.

selfish disposition and there is not a man in the fleet who does not lament his carelessness in keeping the convoy together, altho we are within a few miles of the enemies port . . .'[1]

All, however, went well. On the 29th the fleet boldly anchored in the Bay of Callao—to the consternation of the inhabitants of Lima—and while the squadron stayed to blockade the port, the transports, escorted by the *San Martín*, sailed twenty-five miles farther on to the miserable hamlet of Ancón, isolated amid sandy deserts and barren hills but possessed—its only merit—of a respectable anchorage.

Here San Martín received excellent news of the spread of revolution. Far to the north, Guayaquil, after Callao the most important port on the Pacific, the seat of a ship-building industry and equipped with dock-yards, had joined the patriot cause. The garrison had risen on the morning of the 9th October. The people joined the soldiers. A junta was established under the presidency of a poet, and the news was at once sent to San Martín in Perú and to Bolívar in New Granada. The Governor and other officials were packed off by sea to San Martín, who immediately offered to exchange them for patriot prisoners held in Callao. The exchange was entrusted to Paroissien. Leaving Ancón on the 5th November he could hear that night the distant cannonading which heralded Cochrane's brilliant capture of the Spanish frigate, *Esmeralda*, in Callao harbour.[2] He boarded the captured ship on the following day, to witness 'a sight too horrible to describe', and, taking off the wounded Spanish officers, delivered them, with his other prisoners, to the Viceroy's representative.[3] He was not, however, allowed on shore, and so enraged were the soldiers in Callao at the capture of the *Esmeralda* that they massacred the crew of the market boat of a United States frigate, then in harbour, under the impression that the Americans had assisted Cochrane in his exploit.

Two days later the whole convoy sailed to the small port of Huacho, seventy miles to the north of Callao and commanding the entry to the fertile Huaura Valley. Here, on the 10th November, the final dis-embarkation began, and first at Huacho, and then near the little village of Huaura, San Martín established his headquarters for the next six months.

So placed, the liberating army isolated Lima from that northern

[1] Journal, 27 Oct. 1820.      [2] Ibid., 6 Nov. 1820.      [3] Ibid., 7 Nov. 1820.

region of Perú from which she drew much of her supplies, and, despite Cochrane's contempt for such 'incomparable prudence',[1] San Martín was still determined to rely on blockade and insurrection. He was resolved, in Paroissien's words, 'not by any means' to 'risk a general action';[2] and events seemed to confirm his judgment. At Huacho supplies, recruits, and deserters from the viceregal forces flowed in. A whole battalion, the famous *Numancia*, composed almost entirely of creoles recruited in Venezuela or New Granada, passed over on the 2nd December, an event, thought Paroissien, likely to give a 'decisive blow to the before tottering power of Pezuela'.[3] At the end of the month the walled city of Trujillo, the most important place between Lima and Guayaquil, pronounced for independence. In the interior the expedition sent from Pisco under Arenales was crowned with success when at Pasco it severely defeated a royalist army dispatched from Lima to contain it; and on the coast Spanish naval power had been practically destroyed; Cochrane was master of the sea, and Callao and Lima were subjected to all the rigours of blockade.

The consternation produced in the royalist camp by this accumulation of disasters fully equalled San Martín's expectations. Civil and military counsels were alike divided. The prestige and authority of the Viceroy were undermined. So violent was the irritation caused by his irresolution and uncertainty that at the end of January 1821 he was compelled by his own troops to surrender his powers to one of his generals, José de La Serna; and in Lima itself 'all was doubt and despair'. 'From the highest to the lowest person in society', wrote a British naval officer, Captain Basil Hall, who visited the city in February, 'every one felt the increasing evils that crowded round the sinking state. Actual want had already begun to pinch the poor; the loss of almost every comfort affected the next in rank; and luxuries of all kinds were discarded from the tables of the highest class. Military contributions were heavily exacted from the monied men; the merchants lost their commerce; the shopkeepers their wonted supplies.'[4]

But there was another side to this picture. Lima was not Perú. Though the north of the country had risen, the south had been left to its

---

[1] Stevenson, op. cit., iii. 306. Stevenson, it should be noted, was Cochrane's secretary.
[2] Journal, 17 Nov. 1820.
[3] Ibid., 4 Dec. 1820.
[4] Hall, op. cit., i. 96, 115.

fate: Pisco and Ica were reoccupied. Though Arenales had spread disaffection in the highlands, nevertheless the highlands were all but abandoned, for in January, whether through a confusion of orders or not, Arenales came down from the sierras and joined San Martín. In Lima, in the same month, the royalist army was reinforced by a division of close on 1,000 men which had marched on the heels of Arenales from Arequipa and Cuzco.[1] And though San Martín, at the end of the year, had moved his troops forward, apparently 'to close in upon Lima',[2] within a few days he again hastily withdrew to Huaura, where the fevers and agues which lurked in that smiling valley attacked both himself and his men. By the end of February nearly nine hundred men lay in hospital.[3]

As, also, week after week passed in apparent inaction, other evils made their appearance. On the one hand, the blockade of the capital was not complete. Some supplies could be brought by land, and more than one merchantman slipped past Lord Cochrane's squadron into Callao, for as Cochrane himself observed: 'The few vessels we have cannot be everywhere.'[4] On the other, the foreign merchants, inclined to object to any blockade of the coast of Perú at all, certainly objected to a prolonged one. From Chile, before the liberating expedition sailed and blockade was proclaimed, they had enjoyed a profitable contraband trade at one or another of the viceregal ports.[5] British vessels, moreover, had sailed to Perú—such were viceregal necessities—under Spanish licence. And while Cochrane, detaining ships and seizing cargoes, was involved in disputes with the British naval commanders who had assumed the defence of British interests in the Pacific,[6] the merchants, who had at first eagerly looked forward to the liberation of Perú, were filled with exasperation by San Martín's Fabian tactics.

The state of mind of Paroissien's two friends in Chile, Begg and Barnard, illustrates the effect on outside opinion. 'I look every day', wrote John Begg from Santiago in November 1820, 'for a namesake of

[1] Pezuela, *Memoria de gobierno*, p. 821.  [2] Journal, 4, 31 Dec. 1820.
[3] Ibid., 26 Feb. 1821. Cf. Encina, *Historia de Chile*, viii. 181.
[4] Cochrane to Paroissien, 19 April 1821. P.P.
[5] Begg to Paroissien, 28 Jan. 1820, and Barnard to Paroissien, 17 Nov. 1820, P.P., on the voyages of the *Caledonia* and the *Thais*.
[6] Sir Thomas Hardy to Croker, 12 Nov. 1821, enclosing a list of vessels seized by Cochrane. F.O. 72/264; Humphreys, *British Consular Reports*, p. 127 note.

mine from Liverpool with a cargo of some $200,000 and I hope (if you fight well) there will be no just cause or impediment to my embarking on board of her and visiting the new conquered capital.' But by January, Begg, who had begun his voyage, was complaining: 'I am almost at a stand, such an uncertainty appears to hang over your operations.' Reaching Guayaquil in February, he found the port open indeed, but under prohibitive duties on foreign trade, and by May he was almost in despair. 'The system your head man has adopted of procrastinating the war', he wrote to Paroissien, 'has not been attended with the great results expected'; and in July, back in Valparaíso, he added tartly: 'Had not this blockade of the Coast been abandoned you would ere this have seen a British squadron in front of Callao and the port open to even contraband of war.'[1]

Barnard, less irritated, was still more gloomy. 'If you dont do something very soon', he told Paroissien in March, 'here we shall all assuredly be ruined, for ships will be coming out upon ships, cargoes upon cargoes. . . . By and bye we shall have a grand squadron of embargo breakers. . . .' 'Trade is very bad . . .', he declared in April, 'and unless we are speedily relieved by some successes on your part, we shall all be ruined together.'[2] And in the same month a third British merchant, recently arrived in Chile, summed the matter up. 'The utmost anxiety', he wrote, 'prevails to hear from San Martín who is besieging Lima; no doubt is entertained of its ultimate fall; but the poverty of the Treasury here and the large stocks of goods in the hands of the merchants, make the Government impatient and the English uneasy about the delay.'[3]

Finally, in the liberating expedition itself, Lord Cochrane was just as exasperated and impatient. He could not bear doing nothing. He was convinced that Lima was ready to fall into San Martín's, or his own outstretched hand. 'Were the army here *now*', he wrote to Paroissien from his flagship on a visit to Callao Bay in April, 'we could drink our champaign this very night in your room over the great entrance of the Palacio.'[4] Only an 'insane jealousy', he later asserted, had prevented

[1] Begg to Paroissien, 15 Nov. 1820, 19 Jan., 10 Feb., 11 May, 3 July 1821. P.P.

[2] Barnard to Paroissien, 24 March, 13 April 1821. P.P.

[3] J. P. Robertson to John Parish, 17 April 1821 [copy]. P.P.

[4] Cochrane to Paroissien, 3 March [April] 1821. P.P.

San Martín from putting an adequate force at his disposal to capture the place.[1] This was fantasy. But the lack of confidence between the two men had been obvious from the first. At army headquarters there had been a constant undercurrent of criticism of the Admiral, who was felt to be over-zealous for prize-money, reckless, and negligent. 'What a pity', commented Paroissien, 'this man, who certainly does possess the elements of a hero, is so extremely avaricious!'[2] On the Admiral's flagship, resentment at San Martín's authority, contempt for his plans, and pride in the navy's achievements, held to be insufficiently recognized or even deliberately obscured, were still more marked; and the relations between the two commanders, never cordial, grew steadily worse. Cochrane despised a caution that he could not understand, and the General saw in the Admiral not so much the qualities that made for his spectacular success as the flaws by which it was disfigured.

San Martín, however, was unmoved by the clamour for action. In April he sent Arenales on a second expedition into the highlands. He allowed Cochrane to harass the southern shores of the viceroyalty in expeditions to Pisco, and, still further south, to Arica, with a landing party under the command of Paroissien's friend, William Miller. But he maintained his original plan. His forces were still outnumbered. Rather than run the risk of a pitched battle before the walls of Lima, it had been decided in January—so Paroissien recorded—to cut off the Viceroy's resources 'by small flying parties, so as to induce him to dismember his army by sending part of it to the Sierra', or to compel him, if he dared, to attack San Martín in his own 'strong position of Huaura'.[3] And the decision still held. Lima, San Martín knew, must ultimately be starved into surrender; and there was, also, another thought in his mind. He had 'no ambition', as he somewhat later explained, 'to be the conqueror of Peru'. 'I want solely to liberate the country from oppression . . .' he declared. 'I wish to have all men thinking with me, and do not choose to advance a step beyond the gradual march of public opinion.'[4] And in May, for a second time, he agreed to an armistice with the royalists.

Already in February, almost immediately after Pezuela had been

[1] Dundonald, op. cit., p. 106.
[2] Journal, 25 Nov. 1820, also 27 Oct., 22, 26 Nov. 1820.
[3] Journal, 14 Jan. 1821.          [4] Hall, op. cit., i. 215.

deposed from the viceregency, there had been an exchange of views between the royalist and the patriot camps, and in March there had arrived at San Martín's headquarters a royal commissioner, Manuel Abreu, sent out from Spain, as Paroissien reported, in the role of 'pacificator',[1] just as, at this time, other commissioners had been sent to other parts of the revolted colonies. Well received by San Martín, and much impressed, he was allowed to proceed to Lima, and, on the 4th May, formal conversations were opened at the *hacienda* of Punchauca, not far from the capital. On the 23rd a provisional armistice was signed, to last for twenty days, and on the 2nd June, San Martín, accompanied, incidentally, by Paroissien, met the new Viceroy, La Serna, himself.

Eight months had passed since, at the time of the armistice of Miraflores, San Martín's representatives had first hinted at the establishment of an independent monarchy in Perú, and, for San Martín, the idea had lost nothing of its attraction. In his talks with Abreu he had frankly confessed his opinion that the countries of America were quite unfitted for republican government;[2] the idea of a monarchy had been privately canvassed in correspondence with the royalists;[3] and now, in the presence of the generals of both armies, San Martín explicitly and formally proposed that Perú should be erected into an independent and constitutional monarchy under a prince of the Spanish royal house. Pending the arrival of the prince, a triple regency should be created, with La Serna as its president, and a provisional constitution drafted with the assistance of provincial representatives. Envoys should be sent to Spain to obtain the approbation of the Spanish Crown; and it is even possible that San Martín offered to form a part of this embassy himself.[4]

Many years later San Martín asserted that he was well aware that these proposals would never be accepted at Madrid, and that his object at Punchauca was to compromise the Spanish commanders by inducing them to recognize the independence of Perú. That the Court of Madrid would have accepted them is, indeed, extremely improbable. But it is

---

[1] Journal, 19 March 1821.
[2] Abreu's diary, cited by Otero, *Historia del libertador*, iii. 265.
[3] Barros Arana, op. cit., xiii. 251–2.
[4] Otero, op. cit., iii. 289–90; Mitre, *Historia de San Martín*, ii. 653–5; *San Martín. Su correspondencia*, p. 109; J. A. de la Puente Candamo, *San Martín y el Perú. Planteamiento doctrinario* (Lima, 1948), pp. 316–17.

idle to deny that San Martín seriously hoped for the establishment of a constitutional monarchy in Perú, whether in this form or some other. This was not the first, it was not the last evidence, of the workings of his mind. Equally, it is useless to speculate whether, by the reconciliation of royalists and patriots in the promotion of some such plan, Perú could, or could not, have been saved years of anguish. The plan was doomed. La Serna could not agree on terms acceptable to San Martín. Discussions were continued and the armistice, twice renewed, was prolonged until the end of June. Then, a few days after it had finally expired, the royalist army, on the 6th July, at long last evacuated Lima, retired to the mountains, but left a strong garrison in the fortress of Callao.

Quietly, almost surreptitiously, San Martín entered the capital on the 10th July. On the 28th the independence of Perú was solemnly proclaimed, and on the 3rd August San Martín assumed the title of Protector, uniting in his own person both civil and military powers. He had, he confessed to that sympathetic English observer, Captain Basil Hall, some thoughts of Oliver Cromwell when the title was proposed to him, and 'hoped to imitate his good points';[1] and, as Hall himself observed, 'Under whatever name he might have chosen to mask his authority, he must still have been the prime mover of everything. . . . It was more creditable to assume the full authority in a manly and open manner, than to mock the people with the semblance of a Republic, and, at the same time, to visit them with the reality of a despotism.'[2] On the same day he appointed García del Río as his Foreign Minister, Bernardo Monteagudo as his Minister of War, and Hipólito Unánue, a distinguished Peruvian economist, physician and philosopher, as his Minister of Finance. The constitutional framework was completed in October by a provisional statute of government which established a council of state and provided both for municipal and departmental government and for the administration of justice.

Yet, while San Martín occupied Lima, the royalists had continued to hold Callao, eight miles away. When the Viceroy had abandoned the capital, no attempt had been made to pursue his dispirited and hungry men. Part of the viceregal forces, under General José Canterac, a Frenchman who had been Pezuela's chief of staff, had already been sent away into the highlands, where Arenales was operating. But no attempt

---

[1] Basil Hall to Paroissien, 22 Dec. 1823. P.P.      [2] Hall, op. cit., i. 277–8.

was made to engage Canterac either. Instead, at a time when the royalist forces were divided and weakened, Arenales was recalled, and, early in September, Canterac reappeared to relieve Callao. San Martín, taken by surprise, drew up his troops to defend Lima but allowed the enemy, unmolested, to take shelter under the guns of Callao. Everyone now expected a general action. Paroissien made his will. 'As there is very great probability', he wrote to a friend, 'that the action which may take place today or tomorro' between the Patriot forces and the Spanish army will be bloody, and as from my situation I shall necessarily be much exposed, I may perhaps lose my life.'[1] But no battle took place. Canterac, faced with starvation at Callao, was allowed to retreat, if not so quietly as he had arrived, at least with no attempt to destroy him. Callao, on the other hand, its supplies exhausted and all hopes abandoned, on the 21st September surrendered.

'The slightest military reverse at that moment', wrote Hall, in explanation of San Martín's tactics, 'must at once have turned the tide; the Spaniards would have retaken Lima; and the independence of the country might have been indefinitely retarded.'[2] All of this was true. What was more, San Martín had gained Callao, as he had gained Lima, without a battle, and Canterac arrived back in the highlands with his army a good deal depleted both by desertion and by rearguard actions. But the results of this extraordinary episode did not end there. San Martín's reputation was severely damaged. His 'loss of popularity', in Hall's opinion, dated from this hour, and however justified his tactics, the fact remained that the royalist armies in Perú had not been destroyed. San Martín had redeemed the coast but not the interior. The war had still to continue, and in the end it was to be not San Martín but Bolívar who would complete the country's liberation.

The fall of Callao, eleven weeks after the evacuation of Lima, was, however, a matter for rejoicing. The port was immediately opened to the trade of all friendly nations. Its harbour was soon 'crowded with ships unloading rich cargoes; while the bay, to the distance of a mile from the harbour, was covered with others waiting for room to land their merchandise',[3] and the first arrivals alone contained more goods

[1] Paroissien to S. Price, 11 Sept. 1821. P.P.
[2] Hall, op. cit., ii. 72.
[3] Ibid., ii. 65.

VALPARAISO BAY.

THE CUTTING OUT OF THE SPANISH FRIGATE *ESMERALDA*

than the country, in its depressed condition, could possibly consume.[1] Representatives of the British mercantile houses in Chile and elsewhere—Paroissien's friend, Begg, among them—quickly arrived. The news, seeming to herald the final fall of the Spanish empire in South America, ran like wildfire through America and Europe—and it was followed by a resounding scandal.

For with the occupation of Lima the relations between Cochrane and San Martín reached breaking-point. Cochrane believed that he and his officers 'had been mainly instrumental in establishing the independence of Peru'. His vanity was offended by an 'extraordinary assumption of power' on San Martín's part in which he 'had not been at all consulted', and which, in any event, he disapproved. San Martín's conduct, he thought, fully revealed that the army had 'been kept inert for the purpose of preserving it entire to further the ambitious views of the General'.[2] He had a particular and quite genuine cause of grievance in that arrears of pay were due to his crews and promises of bounty money were unfulfilled; and he suspected, not altogether unjustly, that the new Government would have liked to acquire the ships of the Chilean navy, or certainly the seamen, for itself. In August, after a stormy interview with San Martín, he attempted, without success, to induce the Governor of Callao to surrender the fortress, not to San Martín, but to himself, offering him permission to depart with two-thirds of the property contained in the fort, on condition of the remainder, together with the fort, being given up to the squadron. There was a last and very frigid meeting in September when he begged San Martín to attack Canterac's troops as they passed to Callao. Then, learning that a quantity of treasure belonging partly to the Government of Perú and partly to private individuals had been placed for safety's sake on board a number of vessels at Ancón lest Lima should again fall into royalist hands, Cochrane deliberately sailed to Ancón and on the 14th September seized the treasure to pay his men.

San Martín was outraged, and though some of this property was returned, the rupture was complete. On the 26th September the Admiral was peremptorily ordered to leave Peruvian waters, and that same night Paroissien, in company with one of Cochrane's former

[1] J. Henderson, 'A Commercial and Statistical Sketch of the Republic of Peru', F.O. 18/2.     [2] Dundonald, op. cit., pp. 124–6.

H

officers, undertook the highly invidious task of visiting the vessels of the
fleet in order to induce the foreign seamen to throw in their lot with the
General rather than the Admiral. He even, in what must have been an
exceedingly embarrassing interview, saw Cochrane himself—'telling
me', wrote Cochrane, 'how much better it would be for me to be First
Admiral of a rich country like Peru, than Vice-Admiral of a poor
province like Chili'.[1] But of this interview only Cochrane's account
survives. In the event, twenty-three officers abandoned the fleet and a
number of the foreign seamen remained on shore. The Admiral, when
on the 6th October he left Perú, sailed with a squadron 'half un-
manned'.

San Martín never forgave the man whom he was wont to call the
'metálico Lord', and the damage done to the reputation of both commanders was enormous. But San Martín's decline had already begun.
As the year drew to its close there were signs of disaffection within his
own ranks. In his own army there was a conspiracy against his authority and possibly against his life. His old companion, Las Heras, resigned.
And while the troops entered upon a winter of discontents, among the
civilians the persecution of the Spaniards, which Monteagudo, always a
terrorist, had begun, roused fear and hatred. Perú was to owe to San
Martín her first attempts at constitutional organization, the beginnings
of her navy, the first steps towards the emancipation of the slaves, the
abolition of forced labour, and the establishment of her national library.
But the population of Lima quickly tired of its liberators, and, while the
army proved a burden and the country was still not free, San Martín
was accused, both at home and abroad, of an insensate ambition which
would be contented only with a crown.

This suspicion was unjust. San Martín sought a crown, but not for
himself. For him the protectorate was Dead Sea fruit. He had no
Napoleonic ambitions, no desire to perpetuate his power.[2] But he was
convinced that under a monarchy lay Perú's best hope of salvation. His
ministers, García del Río, Monteagudo, and Unánue shared his views.
They could count upon a measure of support among the Peruvian
aristocracy, who were, significantly enough, allowed to retain their

[1] Ibid., pp. 161–2; Stevenson, op. cit., iii. 391–4.
[2] For the contrary opinion see J. M. Yrarrázaval Larraín, *San Martín y sus
enigmas*, 2 vols. (Santiago, 1949), ii. 57, 71, 79, 138.

Spanish titles of nobility. And in November San Martín resolved to send García del Río and Paroissien to Europe, not only to secure European recognition of Peruvian independence, but to offer a crown to a European prince.[1] On the 24th December the instructions for the two envoys were drawn up by the Council of State. On the 29th the commodore in charge of the British South American station, who happened, at that moment, to be in Callao Bay, was notified of their appointment, and on the last day of the year the two envoys set sail.[2]

[1] Puente Candamo, op. cit., p. 74.
[2] Monteagudo to Hardy, 29 Dec. 1821; Hardy to Croker, 25 Jan. 1822, F.O. 72/264.

# CHAPTER VII

## POLITICS AND DIPLOMACY IN
## SOUTH AMERICA, 1822

WHEN on 31 December 1821 Paroissien left Callao for Valparaíso on the first stage of his journey to Europe, he had reached the summit of his career. He was still only thirty-seven. He was an Officer of the Legion of Merit of Chile, a Founder of San Martín's new Order of the Sun, an Honorary Councillor of State, and a Brigadier-General of the Armies of Perú, to which rank he had just been promoted;[1] and, with García del Río, he had now been entrusted with the conduct of the first Peruvian diplomatic mission to Europe.

He was not a rich man. But he was certainly not a poor one. The life of a soldier of fortune has its rewards. His private savings probably amounted to no more than £2,000, part invested in commercial speculations, part sent to England, and part held by his friend and banker, John Begg. They must have been acquired mainly in the past two or three years. His salary as an envoy, however, was £3,000 a year, and he had been presented by the municipality of Lima with a share, valued at $25,000 (roughly £5,000), in a large *hacienda* near Pisco, known as the Caucato estate,[2] the sequestrated property of an old Spaniard. He joined with the other nine shareholders in appointing an administrator of this estate and left John Begg in charge of his interests. The administrator, however, went over to the enemy,[3] the *hacienda* went to rack and ruin, and Paroissien received nothing. As for the estate which, according to his own account, had been given to him three years earlier at Mendoza, of that also no more was heard. The life of a soldier of fortune has its disappointments. But, with a handsome sum paid down for the

---

[1] Appointment dated 22 Dec. 1821. P.P.

[2] The grant was ratified by San Martín on 19 Dec. 1821. P.P. See also M. F. Paz Soldán, *Historia del Perú independiente, primer período, 1819–1822* (Lima, 1868), p. 224.    [3] Miller to Paroissien, 10 May 1822. P.P.

expenses of his journey and an advance of one year's salary, Paroissien, certainly, had no cause for financial anxiety.

The instructions, secret and in cipher, which the envoys carried with them stated that to secure order at home and respect abroad Perú needed a strong government, the recognition of her independence, and the alliance or protection of one of the principal European powers. Britain, because of her maritime strength, her financial might and vast resources, and the excellence of her political institutions, and Russia, because of her political influence and power, were the most desirable allies. Accordingly, the envoys should accept as Emperor of Perú either the Prince of Saxe-Coburg (presumably Leopold, the future king of the Belgians, who had been married to the late Princess Charlotte and still lived in England) or, failing him, a member of the British royal house, preferably the Duke of Sussex—certainly one of the less disreputable sons of George III, but hardly qualified by his mild literary tastes to reign in Perú. The new Emperor would be required to embrace the Roman Catholic faith and to swear to uphold the constitution which would be presented to him. If neither the Prince Leopold nor the Duke of Sussex was available, a German or an Austrian prince, provided he was assured of British support, would suffice. If Britain raised insuperable difficulties, the envoys should then address themselves to the Emperor of Russia to secure a prince who would enjoy Russian protection. Failing that, they might have recourse to France or Portugal, and, as a last desperate expedient, there was always the young Duke of Lucca.[1]

This was a comprehensive list. But the envoys' powers extended far beyond this imperial mission. By further instructions they were enabled as envoys extraordinary and ministers plenipotentiary to enter into treaties of alliance, amity and commerce, nor would these treaties require to be ratified in Perú; they were to raise in Europe a loan of six million dollars; and they were empowered to concede special privileges to mining companies which might be tempted to operate in Peruvian territory.[2]

[1] For the instructions see B. Vicuña Mackenna, *El ostracismo del jeneral D. Bernardo O'Higgins* (Valparaíso, 1860), pp. 372–4; Paz Soldán, op. cit., pp. 272–3; and De la Cruz, *Epistolario de D. Bernardo O'Higgins*, ii. 143–9, who prints the cipher as well as the deciphered text.

[2] For these powers see *A Report of the Trial of Kinder versus Everett and Others, in the Court of King's Bench, Dec. 20, 1823, before Lord Chief Justice Abbott and a Special Jury* (London, 1824), pp. 56–8. See also Paz Soldán, op. cit., p. 271.

Their journey to Europe, moreover, was to be made by way of Chile and the United Provinces, and they were given special missions to the Governments of both these countries. In Chile they were to secure the adhesion of O'Higgins to San Martín's monarchical designs. San Martín hoped, indeed, that Chile would embrace the plan with enthusiasm, would join in the search for a crowned head, and would appoint envoys of her own to accompany Paroissien and García del Río to Europe. Quite apart from this, however, the two ministers were to make strong representations against the conduct of the Vice-Admiral of Chile, Lord Cochrane, and to demand satisfaction for it. They were to solicit Chilean recognition of Peruvian independence, and they were to beg the Chilean Government, in order to bring the war to a rapid end, to send an expedition against the royalists in the southern parts of the old vice-royalty. In Buenos Aires, similarly, they were to point out the necessity of exterminating royalist opposition in Upper Perú and to ask for the help of the United Provinces in this enterprise, and, as in Chile, they were to discuss with the Government their secret instructions.[1]

Accompanied by their secretary, a German who had recently taken out naturalization papers in Perú, Pedro Creutzer by name, Paroissien and García del Río reached Valparaíso early in February and remained in Chile rather more than six weeks. Here Paroissien visited old friends and inspected the Lancastrian schools which James Thomson, of the British and Foreign Bible Society, had recently established in Santiago and which San Martín proposed to introduce into Perú.[2] He met, also, Jeremy Robinson, a semi-official agent of the United States, to whom he made some severe reflections on the conduct of American commanders in Peruvian waters,[3] and who gave him a letter of introduction to the American Minister in London. But the atmosphere, he found, was far from favourable for the promotion either of the more general purpose of his mission or of its particular objects in Chile. Chilean

---

[1] See the *Justificación de la conducta pública seguida por D. Juan García del Río i D. Diego Paroissien* (London, 1825), pp. 2–3, reprinted in *Archivo de San Martín*, xii. 454 ff.; Paz Soldán, op. cit., p. 270; Búlnes, *Historia de la espedición libertadora*, ii. 378–81.

[2] Journal, 9 March 1822.

[3] Robinson to Richard Rush, 6 March 1822, enclosing Paroissien to Robinson, 3 March 1822. National Archives, Washington, State Department Records, Special Agents series, vol. v.

opinion was hostile to the idea of a monarchy. It was hostile to San Martín. Cochrane's complaints and accusations, and what had been interpreted as the strange lassitude, even the ineptitude, of San Martín in the conduct of the war, had done their work, and not all the eloquence which García del Río could muster in a public allocution could stem the tide of feeling. Nor were matters at all improved by the rude treatment which Monteagudo, now San Martín's Minister of Foreign Affairs, accorded to a Chilean envoy sent to Perú to ask for some financial return for the expenses which Chile had incurred in fitting out the liberating expedition to that country.[1]

The envoys first saw O'Higgins on the 21st February, when they asked that Chile should 'crown the work so happily begun under her auspices' by sending an expedition of 1,000 men to defeat the royalists in southern Perú, that the 'scandalous conduct' of Lord Cochrane should be punished, and that diplomatic relations between Chile and Perú should at once be established. And they found O'Higgins friendly but evasive. So far as further military aid to Perú was concerned, he pointed out that a rebellion had occurred in the south of Chile, in Valdivia, which made it necessary to dispatch a force of five hundred men there, lest the Spaniards (who still held the island of Chiloé) should attempt to get possession of the mainland; and, secondly, that the Chilean treasury was exhausted. As for Cochrane, he was no doubt 'the most perverse man in the world' and a 'criminal and impostor' to boot, but it was essential not to exasperate him and so to precipitate his departure, perhaps with the whole squadron. And finally, if diplomatic relations were to be established and Chile was to appoint a minister to Perú, Perú must first modify an existing law which infringed the principle of diplomatic immunity.[2]

Despite this discouraging reception, Paroissien and García del Río, in a formal letter to O'Higgins's Foreign Minister, persisted in their request for military assistance, only to be told that in the present state of Chilean finances it could not be given; and the Minister, when Paroissien saw him, did not conceal his resentment at the brusque

[1] Journal, 4 March 1822; Paroissien and García del Río to Monteagudo, 18 March 1822, in M. F. Paz Soldán, *Historia del Perú independiente, 1822–1827*, 2 vols. (Lima, 1870–4), i. 23, 370.

[2] Minute of 21 Feb. 1822. Puente Candamo, *San Martín y el Perú*, pp. 241–4.

manner in which Chile's own request for financial recompense had been rejected.[1] A further letter, in which the envoys complained in bitter terms of Lord Cochrane's conduct, of the evils to which his negligence had exposed the liberating expedition from the moment of its sailing, of his avarice, his indecorous references to the Government of Chile, his libellous accounts of San Martín, his private negotiations with the Governor of Callao, and his seizure of the treasure at Ancón, met with a worse fate. A copy fell into Cochrane's own hands. The incensed Admiral indicted a still more violent reply—'negras e infames inposturas' was San Martín's description of it[2]—and published the whole.[3]

To complete their disillusionment, when, in a final interview with O'Higgins, Paroissien and García del Río approached the heart of their mission, the proposal to establish monarchy in America, they met with an equally unsympathetic reception. A monarchy in Perú, said O'Higgins, would no doubt do very well. But so far as Chile was concerned, things had better stay as they were; and the envoys left the palace convinced, for their part, that O'Higgins intended to cling to power and that it was useless to pursue the matter further.[4]

No good, therefore, came out of the mission to Chile. This was not an auspicious beginning, and it was an additional omen of ill that the envoys had already had occasion to complain of the 'cruel silence' of Lima and of the lack of continuing instructions or information. 'God grant', wrote García del Río, 'that the same method will not be pursued when we are further away and in greater need of news.'[5] And with this uneasy feeling, on the 23rd March they left Santiago. Paroissien had been joined by a schoolboy whom he had agreed to take to England to complete his education, and García del Río by a young countryman of his own recently arrived from Europe.[6] Crossing the

---

[1] Journal, 4 March 1822; Puente Candamo, op. cit., pp. 244–6.

[2] San Martín to Paroissien, 15 Oct. 1823. P.P.

[3] *Manifiesto de las acusaciones que a nombre del general San Martín hicieron sus legados ante el gobierno de Chile contra el vice-almirante Lord-Cochrane y vindicación de este dirigida al mismo San Martín* (Lima, 1823).

[4] Puente Candamo, op. cit., p. 244, gives the date of this conference as 22 February, but it probably took place on 19 March. See De la Cruz, op. cit., ii. 142.

[5] García del Río to San Martín, 21 March 1822. *Archivo de San Martín*, vii. 455–60.

[6] Domingo Santiago Toro and Agustín Gutíerrez de Moreno.

Andes by the Uspallata route, they rested for a week at Mendoza and reached Buenos Aires on the 23rd April. They had been a month on the road and it was already nearly three months since they had left Perú.

Buenos Aires in 1822 presented a remarkable spectacle. Two years earlier, at a time when San Martín, wisely declining to embroil himself in the civil wars of the United Provinces, had refused to go with his troops to the defence of the city, then threatened by the *montoneras*—the half-wild, mounted *gauchos* of the countryside—and had assumed, instead, the command of the liberating expedition to Perú, Buenos Aires had been made to feel 'that imperious law from her rebellious children of the provinces, which she for ten years had so liberally dealt out to them'.[1] In that 'terrible year' of anarchy, 1820, the national government of the United Provinces had collapsed; its Congress and its Supreme Directorate vanished; the provinces each became autonomous; and, while only the shadow of a federation remained, Buenos Aires, in one year, knew at least twenty-four governors and, on one June day, no fewer than three.

Yet, though the unity of the United Provinces was shattered, though the interior provinces suffered convulsive disorder, Buenos Aires recovered her stability and prosperity with astounding resilience. Already in September 1820, a Junta of Representatives, established in the name of the city and its province, called to the governorship Martín Rodríguez, who, ten years earlier, had played a prominent part in the overthrow of Spanish colonial rule. In July 1821, Rodríguez appointed as his Minister of Government and Foreign Affairs a forty-one-year-old *porteño* statesman, Bernardino Rivadavia, recently returned from long residence abroad; and within three years, Rivadavia, in the opinion of the first British consul-general to Argentina, was to do more for the amelioration of Buenos Aires than all his predecessors put together.[2]

'Universally admired for his talents, integrity and energy', remarked Paroissien, but with 'scarcely any friends from his repugnant manner',[3] Rivadavia had already shown his abilities as Secretary to the Governing Junta—known as the first Triumvirate—set up in 1811,

---

[1] Robertson, *Letters on South America*, iii. 300–1. See above, pp. 78–80.
[2] Parish to Canning, 27 April 1824, F.O. 6/3.
[3] Journal, 23 April 1822.

and later as a member of the Junta itself. Sent to Europe in December 1814 to propose the establishment of a monarchy in the Río de la Plata under the rule of a European prince, he had engaged in various chimerical negotiations to that end, but, what was more important, had fallen strongly under the influence of that 'Newton of Legislation', as he called him, Jeremy Bentham, whose works he began to translate.[1] He had read widely and well, and, back in Buenos Aires, he attempted to bring Europe to America 'and to accomplish in ten years', it has been remarked, 'a work which had formerly required the passage of centuries'.[2]

In 1822 the 'bold and enterprising Rivadavia'[3] was in the middle of his labours. 'The Executive', wrote a British merchant of long experience in South American affairs, 'has been busily engaged in carrying on reforms in every shape, and into every branch: and truly it is wonderful to observe the different aspect which affairs in general have taken. Everything breathes activity and public spirit: and public prosperity is the natural result . . . there is something like a regularly organized Government here at last; and if they do but continue a year or two longer in the path which they have chosen, we shall in all probability see the Spanish Colonies generally recognized as free and independent nations.'

What above all impressed the writer of this letter—it was that canny but adventurous Scotsman, William Parish Robertson—was the funding of the public debt and the restoration of public credit. When Rivadavia and his fellow Minister of Finance, José Manuel García, came in, wrote Robertson, 'they found public credit at the very lowest ebb. . . . They first of all entirely suspended the issue of Bills receivable at the Custom House, and those in circulation they so arranged as to have all paid off by the end of last year. Then all the transactions of the Government were cash ones. They received cash at the Custom House, or good bills, and paid and still continued to pay all demands with as much punctuality as is observed in the English Treasury. . . . In the meantime a Commission was named to take an account of all the

---

[1] J[eremy] B[entham] to Bolívar, 24 Jan. 1820. Bentham MSS., x. 5–6, University College, London; Rivadavia to Bentham, 25 Aug. 1818, Brit. Mus., Add. MSS., 33,545, f. 312.

[2] D. F. Sarmiento, *Civilización y barbarie* (Buenos Aires, 1889), p. 100.

[3] W. P. Robertson to John Parish, 20 July 1822 [copy]. P.P.

claims on Government from the very Commencement of the Revolution, and even indeed of those existing against the old Spanish Government. These being all called in, they were classed into two kinds for debts contracted with the Buenos Ayres Government, or its dependencies', and funded.[1] And Robertson might have added also that measures were taken to secure the inviolability of private property, that a representative assembly was established, that a university was founded and the Lancastrian school system introduced, and that the judiciary and the police were reformed.

Such was the situation when Paroissien and García del Río arrived at Buenos Aires. But from Rivadavia, thus preoccupied with his work of regeneration, they had nothing to hope. He entertained no friendly feelings towards San Martín, who had helped to overthrow the Government of which Rivadavia was a member in 1812 and whose conduct in Perú he seems thoroughly to have distrusted.[2] (So strained did their relations become that at a later date San Martín was only with difficulty prevented from challenging Rivadavia to a duel.[3]) He could not, even if he would, have sent troops, as San Martín wished, to Upper Perú; the *porteño* army was small, and over the provincial forces Buenos Aires, in 1822, had no control. As for monarchical projects, Rivadavia had done with them once and for all.

Rivadavia, therefore, when the envoys called upon him on the 23rd April, received them 'in a most cool, distant manner'.[4] A further interview, on the following day, when Rivadavia explained how impossible it was for him to send an army to Upper Perú, was rather more friendly, and the governor, Rodríguez, received García del Río and Paroissien 'very well'.[5] But the impression of veiled hostility was never eradicated. Rivadavia made difficulties about receiving a communication from the Peruvian Foreign Minister, Bernardo Monteagudo, on the ground that it was improperly addressed. The envoys, although at the last they parted from him 'under the appearance of friendship', discovered among the members of the Government a

---

[1] W. P. Robertson to John Parish, 7 May 1822 [copy]. P.P. On Rivadavia's achievements see Burgin, *The Economic Aspects of Argentine Federalism*, pp. 87 ff., and Humphreys, *British Consular Reports*, pp. 9 ff.

[2] Webster, *Britain and the Independence of Latin America*, i. 110–13.

[3] Journal, 23 March 1825.

[4] Ibid., 23 April 1822.

[5] Ibid., 24 April 1822.

positive ill-will 'towards anything that comes from Perú'. They found reason to complain of the tone of the Press, particularly of *El Argos de Buenos Aires*, which, though Rivadavia assured them it was quite independent of the Government, they were convinced was not.[1] And when, indeed, the *Argos* reported Rivadavia as saying, in an address to the House of Representatives (to which the envoys listened), that Perú should show herself worthy of the co-operation she solicited, though these were not Rivadavia's words, they may well have been his sentiments.[2]

The mission in Buenos Aires, therefore, like the mission in Chile, was a failure. The envoys did not discuss their secret instructions relating to the establishment of a monarchy at all: it would obviously have been futile and unwise to do so. Paroissien had renewed old acquaintances and taken charge of a second schoolboy[3] who was to be educated in England. But it could have been in no very cordial frame of mind that he and García del Río left Buenos Aires on the 26th May, to arrive, on the 18th June, at Rio de Janeiro.

Here there was no official business to transact. The envoys refrained from calling either on the Brazilian Minister of Foreign Affairs or on the Austrian and French *chargés*. They dined, however, with the British consul-general, Henry Chamberlain, and with the naval commander on the South American station, Sir Thomas Hardy (Nelson's old flag-captain in the *Victory*), and made a good impression. 'Don Juan', wrote Chamberlain of García del Río, 'appears to be of a more sedate character than the generality of his countrymen, and I understand from Sir Thomas Hardy that he is held in general estimation, as an able and good man. . . . Brigadier General Paroissien is a British subject. . . . His knowledge of . . . Buenos Ayres, Chile, and Peru, is very extensive, and I do not think that any other man can give more correct information respecting them than himself. . . . His character is good; he is much respected; and he has, upon all occasions, shewn an anxious wish to be useful to his countrymen. . . . They have, both, told me that their first and greatest object is to conciliate the good will

---

[1] Journal, 25 April 1822; García del Río and Paroissien to Monteagudo, 13 May 1822, in Puente Candamo, op. cit., pp. 246–9; *El Argos de Buenos Aires*, 24, 27 April, 4 May 1822.

[2] *El Argos de Buenos Aires*, 4 May 1822. For the official version see H. Mabragaña, *Los mensajes*, 6 vols. (Buenos Aires, 1910), i. 188–9.

[3] Bernardo Galup.

of the British Government, and that every other is insignificant compared with this.'[1]

Thus free from diplomatic duties, Paroissien, while arranging passage to England by the monthly packet which now ran between Rio de Janeiro and Falmouth, could devote himself wholeheartedly to sightseeing. Rio de Janeiro was much changed since his first visit, fourteen years earlier. There was a 'wonderfull increase in the number of houses'. The police of the city, though not its sanitation, was enormously improved. He was greatly impressed by the Exchange and Museum, and the Powder Factory (he had an especial interest in gunpowder factories) was 'infinitely superior' to anything he had seen elsewhere in America.[2] He still thought, however, as in 1808, that the Portuguese lagged behind the 'American Spaniards' in civilization, and noted, with a sardonic eye, their love of orders and decorations, which spread even to the 'retail shopkeepers', few of whom were 'without their little cross'.[3]

But the greatest change was political. Gone were Dom João and his tiresome wife, Carlota Joaquina, who had worked so much harm to Paroissien. Dom João, after extreme vacillation, had returned to Portugal rather more than a year earlier, taking with him a crowd of Portuguese nobles and almost the entire contents of the Bank of Brazil. His son, Dom Pedro, the 'fine promising boy' of 1808, had remained behind as regent, and with Dom João's departure the intention of Portugal to reduce Brazil to her former colonial status had been made all too plain. The rule of Rio was to be overthrown, the provinces were to be freed from its jurisdiction, and the central tribunals and institutions which Dom João had established were to be abolished. Dom Pedro himself was ordered home, and the young, impetuous, ardent prince, with his dissolute habits and easy manners, who would play tennis with the country people, saddle his own mule, and trim his own horse,[4] at once became the symbol of the unity of Brazil and the hope of the native aristocracy. On the 9th January, in response to pressure both within and without the capital, he gave the historic promise, 'I will remain'. He accepted in May the title of Perpetual Defender of Brazil and agreed in

---

[1] Chamberlain to Castlereagh, 3 July 1822, F.O. 63/246.
[2] Journal, 22, 27, 29 June 1822.
[3] Ibid., 23, 30 June 1822.
[4] Ibid., 1 July 1822.

June to summon a constituent assembly. It would not be long, as Paroissien noted on July 1st, before Brazil declared her independence, and on the 7th September, when Pedro received dispatches conveying the news of the determination of Portugal to compel Brazil to obedience, he raised the famous cry 'Independence or Death'. On the 12th October he was proclaimed Constitutional Emperor and on the 1st December was crowned; and the throne thus peacefully established was to survive for more than sixty-five years.

When, therefore, on the 4th July, Paroissien and García del Río set sail from Rio de Janeiro in the *Salisbury Packet* bound for Falmouth, great events were impending in Brazil. And though they did not know it, events of much more moment to themselves were also pending in Perú. They had been six months on their road, and those months had witnessed in Perú a continued loosening of morale both in Lima and in the liberating army, a continued decline in the prestige of San Martín, and a revival of hope among the royalists. Already in April, even before Paroissien and García del Río had reached Buenos Aires, a patriot division sent to the south of Lima, to the neighbourhood of Pisco, had been surprised and severely defeated by a royalist column coming down from the mountains, and though the military consequences were bad enough, the effect on Peruvian opinion was even worse. Nevertheless, the disaster was not irremediable. 'Although we have lost much', wrote Paroissien's friend, General William Miller, 'I cannot but anticipate speedy success and an early conclusion of the war and of Spanish dominion in this country. My political spirits never were higher than at present.' In May he wrote equally cheerfully, to announce the arrival of an envoy, 'a gentlemanly and clever fellow', Joaquín Mosquera by name, from the new state of Colombia which Bolívar had created on the ruins of the viceroyalty of New Granada, to negotiate a treaty between Colombia and Perú;[1] and in a secret dispatch, written two days before Paroissien and García del Río left Rio de Janeiro, García del Río's successor at the Peruvian Foreign Office, Bernardo Monteagudo, was more reassuring still.

The negotiations between Perú and Colombia, wrote Monteagudo, were on the point of conclusion and would terminate in 'the formation of a general alliance between the five sections of America—Perú,

[1] Miller to Paroissien, 18 April, 10 May 1822. P.P.

Colombia, Mexico, Chile and the Provinces of Buenos Aires'—and in
the establishment of an 'august assembly' or 'amphictyonic council'
with deputies from each. This, indeed, was Bolívar's own dream. 'How
wonderful', he had once written, 'if the isthmus of Panamá should be
for us what Corinth was to the Greeks. Oh that we may one day have
the good fortune to instal there an august congress of the representatives of the republics. . . .'[1] And plans for such a congress were in fact
being discussed. But, more than this, the secret ideas of the Government of Colombia and those of the Government of Perú, wrote
Monteagudo, were in substantial accord. They looked to the establishment of constitutional monarchy in the countries of America. This,
it was true, could not instantly be achieved. The *'furor republicano'*
must be allowed to die down. Mexico, however, had already shown
her inclination for this form of government. Chile knew nothing of
republicanism but the name, and the Provinces of Buenos Aires would
soon weary of the 'horrors of anarchy' and the 'farce of democracy'.
Everything, therefore, conspired to favour that monarchical mission
with which García del Río and Paroissien had been entrusted, and,
because of its extreme importance, the two envoys should be the more
careful in their selection of the prince who was to occupy the throne of
Perú. On the other hand, since the Peruvian treasury was empty, it
would be wise to defer negotiations until the credit of the Government
had been consolidated and to raise, in the first instance, as large a loan
as possible in the shortest possible time.[2]

A fortnight after Monteagudo had written this remarkable dispatch,
which moved so easily from the realm of fact into that of fantasy, San
Martín set sail from Callao for the port of Guayaquil, nearly eight
hundred miles to the north. His purpose was to meet Bolívar, the great
liberator of northern South America. He was away from Perú for rather
more than five weeks, and on the day on which he arrived off Guayaquil—July 25th—a conspiracy in Lima compelled Monteagudo to
resign and, shortly afterwards, to flee the country. Paroissien, when the
news reached him many months later, heard of it without surprise.
'This', he wrote, 'is what I expected to happen but not so soon', for, he
observed, although Monteagudo had plenty of talent, 'his morality'

[1] Lecuna, *Cartas del libertador*, i. 202.
[2] Monteagudo to García del Río and Paroissien, 2 July 1822. P.P.

was 'not by any means sound' and he was 'far too tyrannical'.[1] And Monteagudo's persecution of the Spaniards, his scandalous private life, and his arrogant public conduct, had made him generally odious. His fall was lamented by none.

So far as Paroissien and García del Río were concerned, Monteagudo's fall was of small importance. What was important, and overwhelmingly so, was the resolution which San Martín formed, while his envoys were still on the high seas between South America and England, to lay down his command and himself to retire from Perú. The thought had been present in his mind even before he left Callao—San Martín was not a happy man—and at Guayaquil, in those secret interviews with Bolívar at which no third person was present, and in which, as Bolívar recorded, San Martín complained bitterly of the burden and penalties of office, his resolve was taken. For whatever the hopes that had sustained him, amid the increasing difficulties of his position, when he landed at Guayaquil on the 26th July, none remained when forty hours later he again set sail for Callao.

Disillusionment had awaited him at the very moment of his arrival. Guayaquil was the port of the old Spanish presidency of Quito—the modern Ecuador—which lay between the former viceroyalty of Perú and that of New Granada. 'I hope that San Martín is fully alive to the importance of this place', an English merchant had written soon after the city, in 1820, had risen in revolt against its Spanish governors. 'It is the arsenal of the Pacific. . . . It will no doubt be the object of the Govert. of New Columbia to get possession of so important a key to its southern provinces.'[2] And the prognostication was correct. Guayaquil, in Bolívar's view, belonged to Colombia, since the presidency of Quito had been a dependency of the old viceroyalty of New Granada, and a province had 'no right to separate itself from the association' to which it belonged![3] San Martín, on the other hand, hoping for the incorporation of Guayaquil in the territory of Perú, nevertheless sustained the right of the *guayaquileños* to decide their own destinies; and until

[1] Journal, 1 Jan. 1823.

[2] Begg to Paroissien, 10 Feb. 1821. P.P.

[3] D. F. O'Leary, *Bolívar y la emancipación de Sur-América. Memorias del general O'Leary*, 2 vols. (Madrid, n.d.), ii. 139. See also W. H. Gray, 'Bolívar's Conquest of Guayaquil', *Hispanic American Historical Review*, xxvii (1947), p. 615.

DOM PEDRO I OF BRAZIL
AS HE APPEARED ON THE DAY OF HIS CORONATION

SIMÓN BOLÍVAR

July 1822 they did in fact govern themselves. The Spaniards still held the mountain capital of Quito. Not till May 1822 were they defeated, on the slopes of Mount Pichincha, by an army commanded by Bolívar's greatest lieutenant, the twenty-nine-year-old Antonio José de Sucre; and Sucre's victory was won with the aid of troops supplied by San Martín from Perú as well as by Bolívar from Colombia. It decided, however, the fate of Guayaquil. Bolívar, reaching the capital, hurried to the port, and from that moment self-determination, so far as the *guayaquileños* were concerned, was an academic question. When San Martín, who believed that Bolívar was still in Quito, arrived at Guayaquil, Bolívar was already there to welcome him to 'Colombian soil'.

There can be no doubt but that the seizure of Guayaquil—for it was little less—was an unpleasant surprise to San Martín, and on his return to Perú he addressed to Bolívar a dignified rebuke.[1] But the meeting with his northern rival was, in any event, doomed to failure. The two men were poles apart in character and temperament. They differed not only in their political ideas—San Martín's monarchical plans met with no sympathetic response from Bolívar—but in almost every other respect. The younger man—Bolívar had been born at Caracas in 1783 —was by far the more brilliant. He had come to Guayaquil after a series of resounding triumphs. He was the liberator of Venezuela and Colombia; he had just consolidated his position in Quito; and his head was full of grandiose plans. In him the romantic and the realist were curiously combined. Seer as well as soldier, and endowed with an immense vitality, he lived for America. But he lived, also, for fame. He was enamoured of 'glory', prone to jealousy. Neither man was likely to understand the other, and while Bolívar's star was still ·waxing, San Martín's had already begun to wane.

The two men met as equals. But in fact San Martín was the petitioner, and a petitioner whom Bolívar might still admire but whose ideas, strategy and leadership it may well be supposed that he had begun to distrust. It was San Martín, not Bolívar, who needed help; and whatever problems San Martín may have wished to discuss with Bolívar, whether concerning the future relations of Colombia and Perú or American affairs in general, there seems no reason to doubt that one

---

[1] San Martín to Bolívar, 29 Aug. 1822. The authenticity of this letter is debated. I incline to accept it. See the following footnote.

I

of the principal objects of his journey was to secure Bolívar's co-operation in bringing the war in Perú to a speedy end. His expectations were disappointed. The offer which he made, with much self-abnegation, to serve under Bolívar if the great northern liberator would come with his troops to Perú, Bolívar understandably rejected—for this was both to offer, and to ask, too much; and the aid which Bolívar was ready, for his part, to furnish, San Martín found inadequate.[1]

For San Martín this was the end. He returned to Callao a bitterly disappointed man. He had reaped in Perú nothing but ingratitude and misunderstanding. He was ill and weary, and if, as he seems to have believed, his presence in Perú was an obstacle to the appearance of Bolívar, it could soon be removed. His mind was made up. On the 20th September, the day on which a Constituent Congress, whose meeting had long been contemplated, for the first time assembled, the Protector resigned his command. That night he left Lima and the next day sailed for Chile. 'My promises to the countries for which I have fought are fulfilled', he declared in his famous farewell address—'to secure their independence and to leave them to select their own governments. The presence of a fortunate soldier, however disinterested he may be, is dangerous to newly constituted states.'

Thus left to its own devices the Congress appointed a junta of three of its members to govern in San Martín's place, and what followed was summed up for Paroissien, now in England, by his friend John Begg. 'From the sentiments existing against the Government of San Martín', wrote Begg in October, 'I fear that your deputation will not be reconnoised [sic] by the Congress. The instructions given you were the other day laid before a Secret Committee and as far as I can learn your mission was not approved of. . . . Every act of San Martín's administration is reprobated and it is enough to deprive his officers of the consideration due to their services the mere supposition that they are his friends.'[2]

---

[1] The opposing views on this celebrated interview are set out in Vicente Lecuna, *La entrevista de Guayaquil* (Caracas, 1948), Ricardo Levene, *La authenticidad de la carta de San Martín a Bolívar de 29 Agosto de 1822* (Buenos Aires, 1950), and Ernesto de la Cruz and others, *La entrevista de Guayaquil* (Madrid, 1917). See also G. Masur, 'The Conference of Guayaquil', *Hispanic American Historical Review*, xxxi (1951), pp. 189–229, and Ricardo Rojas in *Historia de la nación argentina*, vi, 2ᵈᵃ sección, pp. 813–925.

[2] Begg to Paroissien, 17 Oct. 1822. P.P.

John Begg was right. On the 22nd November the Congress resolved that the powers and instructions given to the diplomatic agents of Perú in Europe were opposed to the public will and detrimental to the true interests of the country. It revoked those powers 'in everything that relates to the form of government and in so far as they exceed the precise objects of consolidating the national independence and liberty'. The Executive Junta was to name new agents with new powers and instructions. But whether Congress intended to revoke the whole of the powers given to Paroissien and García del Río, or only that part of them which related to their mission to find in Europe a prince to reign in Perú, was not made plain; nor did the dispatch which communicated this decree to the envoys throw light upon the matter.[1]

As for the envoys themselves, they had arrived in England on the 29th August, just three weeks before San Martín, in Perú, had laid down his powers. Not till February 1823 did they learn of San Martín's retirement, and not till the following June did the news reach them of the action taken by Congress in November 1822.

[1] *Gaceta del gobierno* [of Lima], 23 Nov. 1822; Francisco Valdivieso to García del Río and Paroissien, 24 Nov. 1822. P.P.

# CHAPTER VIII

## THE MISSION TO ENGLAND, 1822-3

WHEN, early in September 1822, Paroissien and García del Río
arrived in London to establish, at 21 Grosvenor Street, the
first Peruvian legation in England, the tide of public feeling
was running strongly in favour of Spanish America.

For twelve years Spain and her colonies had been at war, and from
the first, but more particularly after the despotic Ferdinand VII had
been restored in Spain, the independent cause had aroused warm sympathies in England. British soldiers had served in the revolutionary
armies and British sailors in the revolutionary navies. The *Edinburgh
Review* had early championed the cause of freedom. The *Morning
Chronicle* and, eventually, *The Times*, were on its side. It moved the
Protestants and Whigs. It appealed to the growing liberal movement.
And it solidly engaged the interests of those British merchants and
manufacturers who had so long seen in Spanish America a new and
apparently fertile field for the expansion of British trade. Any contest
carried on in the name of freedom, observed *The Times* in 1817, must
always be looked at with emotion by a free people, and every step
towards the overthrow of a mercantile monopoly must always animate
the hopes of a commercial nation;[1] and as the charmed circle which
Spain had drawn round her empire in America had been broken, as the
ports of Spanish America had been opened, British brokers and British
commercial agents had moved from one liberated area to another;
British trade had increased by leaps and bounds; and by the 1820's
there were few centres in the southern continent with which the
British merchants had not begun to establish some connexion.

No British statesman could afford to ignore the interests of British
trade, or of British shipping. None would forgo the trade of Spanish

---

[1] *The Times*, 1 Dec. 1817.

America. Should 'the future system of Spain for South America' be 'commercial exclusion as heretofore', wrote Lord Castlereagh, who for so long and so ably conducted British foreign policy, then the separation of Spain and her colonies might 'secretly' be the British Government's wish and interest.[1] This was in 1812. 'No exertion compatible with national honour', he declared four years later, 'should be wanting to cherish' the commercial connexion between Britain and Spanish America;[2] and in the Latin-American policy of Great Britain the interests of British trade remained a permanent factor.

But they were not the only factor. If policy was ceasing to control trade, trade did not control policy. Whatever the hopes which 'animated' a commercial nation, so long as the Napoleonic wars lasted the British Government, far from desiring the disintegration of the Spanish empire, would have preferred to see the concentration of its entire strength and resources against a common enemy. Castlereagh, like his predecessor at the Foreign Office, Richard Wellesley, was willing, even eager, to mediate between Spain and her colonies and to promote their reconciliation, and though his efforts failed, once the war was ended his policy did not radically change. Britain was still by treaty bound to Spain. She had no special love of republics. What was more, she was a member of that 'great experiment in international organization', the European Alliance. And while the issue between Spain and her colonies remained in doubt, while, moreover, the European powers could be brought to act in concert, neutrality in the struggle between Spain and Spanish America was, she held, a duty.

Yet Castlereagh had seen, no one more clearly, that unless Spain was prepared to place 'the inhabitants of America upon a commercial footing of corresponding advantage with the inhabitants of European Spain', unless she realized that 'provinces of such magnitude' would no longer 'submit to be treated as mere colonies', their 'separation from the Parent State' was 'inevitable and at hand'. From this reasoning he never departed. On these conditions alone, conditions which amounted to 'virtual self-government and free trade with the rest of the world,' he was prepared to mediate.[3] And he not only refused, in this

[1] Webster, *Britain and the Independence of Latin America*, ii. 312.
[2] 9 April 1816. *Parliamentary Debates*, xxxiii. 1129.
[3] Webster, op. cit., ii. 311; i. 13.

conviction, to assist Spain by force of arms, he took care that no other European power should do so either.[1] He kept the arena free, and by 1820 he was himself convinced that the independence of large parts of Spanish America was an accomplished fact and that European recognition of this independence was merely a question of time and method.[2]

His conviction was soon strengthened. In July 1821, Dom João of Portugal, still at Rio de Janeiro, recognized the independence of Buenos Aires. In March 1822, the United States announced her intention to recognize not only Buenos Aires but Chile, Perú, Colombia and Mexico as well. In South America the interests of British trade now demanded greater protection than the British naval commanders in South American waters could afford. In England, merchants and shipowners, fearful not only of what Brougham had once somewhat ludicrously described as the 'indefatigable activity and vast commercial resources' of the United States,[3] but also of the possibility of discrimination against British interests by the new South American countries themselves, agitatedly laid their complaints before Parliament; and Castlereagh, seizing his opportunity, took advantage of the revision of the Navigation Acts at this moment in progress to recognize the flags of South American vessels and to permit South American ships to enter British ports with the produce of their own countries.

This was in June 1822, and it constituted *de facto* recognition. 'Every right of real value', so far as shipping and commerce were concerned, Castlereagh argued, 'had been conceded.'[4] Formal diplomatic relations with the new South American countries were another question, and this he proposed to discuss at a coming European conference. 'He desired recognition to be made by Europe, and he wished it to be accompanied by an effort to get the Colonists to accept Bourbon Princes as the heads of the independent States.'[5] But what Castlereagh could have achieved remains in doubt. On the 12th August he died by his own hand, and a month later George Canning took office. In Europe British foreign policy was to be revolutionized. In Spanish America it was to

[1] Webster, op. cit., i. 14; ii. 352–8.
[2] Ibid., i. 15.
[3] 9 April 1816. *Parliamentary Debates*, xxxiii. 1119.
[4] 23 July 1822. Ibid., n.s., vii. 1734.
[5] Webster, op. cit., i. 16–17, 31.

enter a new phase. But British recognition of the new states of Spanish America was not thereby hastened. Possibly, indeed, it was delayed.[1] For Canning, whatever the hopes of immediate action he may at first have entertained, lacked, in 1822, that commanding influence both with the king, who had strong prejudices against revolution, and with the cabinet, that Castlereagh had enjoyed. He could do no more than again offer British mediation to Spain and resolve to send out consuls to those ports and places in Spanish America where British interests were most extensive; and even this step he postponed.

It was between Castlereagh's death and the advent of Canning, that 'baleful meteor hurled on Europe', that Paroissien and García del Río reached England. They notified the Foreign Office of their credentials as envoys extraordinary and ministers plenipotentiary of Perú on the 9th September,[2] and then immediately left for Liverpool, where they had private business to transact. And at Liverpool, naturally enough, all, so far as Paroissien could judge, 'appeared unanimous in support' of the independent cause, though he was forced to confess that in general the 'darkest ignorance' of South American affairs prevailed and that interest rose and fell as trade was 'augmented or diminish'd'.[3] But the visit was short, and, back in London by the end of September, the envoys were received privately first by the Under-Secretary for Foreign Affairs and then, on the 7th October, by Canning himself.

This, perhaps, was not the moment for the two agents to reveal the full purport of their mission to Europe, and certainly they did not do so. They limited themselves to expressing their hope of negotiating a treaty of friendship and commerce between Perú and Great Britain; and Canning, for his part, was equally reserved. Polite as always, he asked many questions, but seemed, thought Paroissien, 'to know little about S. Amc[n] affairs', and the envoys, though satisfied with their reception, gained little expectation of a speedy recognition of Peruvian independence by Great Britain.[4] They promised, however, to supply

<hr/>

[1] Ibid., i. 17–18, and the same author's The Foreign Policy of Castlereagh, 1815–1822 (2nd edn., London, 1934), pp. 435–6, 488–9.

[2] García del Río and Paroissien to Foreign Office, 9 Sept. 1822, F.O. 72/265.

[3] Journal, 21, 17 Sept. 1822.

[4] Ibid., 7 Oct. 1822; Minute of Conference, Puente Candamo, San Martín y el Perú, pp. 288–9; Manning, Diplomatic Correspondence of the United States concerning the Independence of the Latin-American Nations, iii. 1474.

the Foreign Office with a detailed report on Perú—an enormous document which they forwarded some weeks later and which closed with the cryptic statement that, provided Britain were willing to use her influence to overcome the reluctance of Spain to acknowledge the independence of Perú, they themselves would gladly submit a plan whereby Spain would be able to retain substantial advantages for herself.[1] And visiting on the next day the American Minister, Richard Rush, a 'remarkably gentlemanly man', they were given the assurance of all the help which he, at least, could afford to them in promoting British recognition of Peruvian independence.[2]

But here their diplomatic negotiations both began and ended. This first interview with Canning was also their last. The secret object of their mission to Europe was never to be revealed. Neither Prince Leopold nor the Duke of Sussex was ever to know the honour which had been reserved for the one or the other of them. The envoys concluded no treaties. Their adventures in European diplomacy were strictly limited, and their rôle as diplomats was, indeed, to be confined to that of observers, propagandists, reporters, and commercial and financial agents.

Their duties in these capacities, however, while they waited on events in Europe and instructions from Perú, Paroissien and García del Río took seriously enough. Dispatches, copies of official documents, newspapers, books, poured out of 21 Grosvenor Street for Perú in unending stream, and so great were the labours of the legation's secretary that Paroissien's nephew, a young man of the name of Charles John Myles, was engaged to help him. A secret agent was sent to Spain to investigate the state of affairs there.[3] William Walton—a hack journalist, well known for his books and articles on South America, who worked for the *Morning Chronicle* and received 'gratifications' from various American Governments—was given a retaining fee to sustain the Peruvian case in England,[4] and García del Río himself compiled and published, in March 1823, a *Peruvian Pamphlet*,

---

[1] Memoir on the Present State of Perú, 5 Nov. 1822, F.O. 72/266.
[2] Journal, 8 Oct. 1822; Manning, op. cit., iii. 1474.
[3] Item under 20 Nov. 1822. Cuenta Jeneral, 6 April 1825. P.P.
[4] Item under 12 Dec. 1822, ibid.; Legation Dispatch, no. 182, 27 April 1825. P.P. For Walton see also A. P. Whitaker, *The United States and the Independence of Latin America, 1800–1830* (Baltimore, 1941), pp. 169–70.

which contained, incidentally, the first biography of San Martín (translated by Walton) to appear in English.[1]

The envoys maintained, moreover, fairly close relations with the agents of other South American countries in England, and once, in May 1823, their interest was a good deal excited when a merchant who had already been of some slight assistance to Paroissien, Simon Cock, proposed both to them and to other of these agents that he should enter into negotiations with Spain for the recognition of Spanish American independence on the basis of a monetary compensation to Spain, the free entry of Spanish produce into Spanish American ports for a stated period, and an equality of treatment in Spanish America between Spaniards and Spanish Americans. Paroissien and García del Río were the more inclined to pay attention to this dubious proposal because Cock had just returned from Spain (where he had been privately engaged in the difficult business of trying to secure an adjustment of claims against the Spanish Government on account of the seizure, by Spanish commanders, of British ships and property in South American waters), and because he was believed by Paroissien to be an old friend of Canning's. But they ventured to do no more than report the offer to the Peruvian Government,[2] and nothing further was heard of it.

But however exacting these labours, the chief interests of the two envoys lay not in the field of diplomacy or even of propaganda, but in that of finance. Neither of them, it is true, was a financier. But this technical disqualification hardly mattered. They had been instructed to raise a loan on behalf of Perú, and in England, in 1822, nothing could be easier. 'He must indeed be more than temperate, he must be a cold reasoner', Brougham had said in 1817, 'who can glance at those regions', of South America, 'and not grow warm.'[3] And in 1822 reasoning was at a discount and warmth was at a premium. Already in March, Francisco Zea, the agent of the republic of Colombia, Bolívar's own creation, had negotiated a loan of £2,000,000 on behalf of that country with the firm of Herring, Graham and Powles, who had

[1] *Peruvian Pamphlet; being an exposition of the Administrative Labours of the Peruvian Government* . . . (London, 1823).

[2] Legation Dispatches, Abstracts, nos. 108 and 109, 31 May, 2 June 1823. P.P.; Puente Candamo, op. cit., pp. 100–3, 256; Ricardo Donoso, ed., *Archivo de don Bernardo O'Higgins* (Santiago, 1946–), iv. 45–50.

[3] 13 March 1817. *Parliamentary Debates*, xxxv. 1026.

extensive interests in the trade of the Caribbean area. In May Antonio José de Irisarri, a Central American untroubled by scruples or morals, who was acting as the representative of Chile, floated with the firm of Hullett Brothers, the financial agents of the Government of Buenos Aires, a Chilean loan of £1,000,000, which certainly benefited Irisarri, however much it was to damage the credit of Chile. And it was even possible to put on the market in October a loan for £200,000 on behalf of the ludicrous 'Kingdom of Poyais' allegedly existing on the Mosquito Shore of Central America.

When, therefore, so soon as they were settled in London, Paroissien and García del Río let it be known that the Government of Perú was prepared to pledge the revenues from its mint and customs house against a London loan, they had no difficulty in finding a contractor, and on the 11th October an agreement was signed with Thomas Kinder, the younger, 'of Basinghall-street, in the City of London, Merchant, for raising a Loan of One Million two hundred thousand pounds', estimated to be 'of the value of six million dollars of Spanish currency, or thereabouts', for 'the service of the State of Peru'. Bearer bonds were to be issued paying interest at the rate of six per cent. The contractor's price for each £100 bond was £75, and he was to be given two pounds per cent on all dividends paid through him. The Government of Perú was to receive the proceeds of the loan in six instalments. Its revenues were pledged to meet both principal and interest, and the bonds were to be paid off at par in equal portions each year during thirty years, beginning in 1826.[1]

Such was the Peruvian loan. Its value to the Government of Perú was obviously considerably less than £900,000, but its terms compared very favourably with those of other foreign loans, and when on Saturday, the 12th October, the loan was put on the market 'a scene of extreme confusion took place on the Royal Exchange, caused by the excessive competition to obtain shares'. On account of the immense profits realized by the two previous American loans, wrote a hostile witness, the greatest anxiety had prevailed to subscribe to the Peruvian loan, and when the contractor and his agents presented themselves they were 'immediately surrounded by a crowd of brokers and others' anxious to

[1] See *A Report of the Trial of Kinder versus Everett and Others* . . . pp. 143–50.

know his terms. 'The confusion and pressure was so great, that nothing for some time could be distinctly heard', but at length the price of 88 was named, soon raised to 89. 'Meantime the crowd, having received a large accession from the Stock Exchange, increased round the contractor and his agents; and the confusion rose to such a height, that the possibility of transacting business was out of the question . . . he and his agents were forced by the multitude surrounding them from the Dutch walk, where the confusion began, to the opposite corner of the Exchange, where the Swedish merchants assemble. Here the brokers became so highly exasperated, being still unable to come to terms with. the agents, that they forced the whole party off the Exchange, out at the north gate, opposite to Bartholomew-lane. They succeeded, however, after a desperate struggle, in re-entering the Exchange; and having at length, with some further effort, effected a lodgment on one of the seats of the Exchange, they became once more visible, if not audible, to the brokers, who surrounded them. They were then tumultuously called on to name a price, and one of the agents at last named 90 as the *minimum* of the contractor. . . .' Subsequently the price dropped to $87\frac{1}{2}$ or 88, and at this point the launching ended of what, in the opinion of the writer, was one of the most 'adventurous' speculations ever brought into the market.[1]

For the next three or four weeks all went well. The contractors for the Colombian loan, who had been anxious to take the Peruvian loan also, but whose terms had been rejected, did their best both in newspaper paragraphs and by private report to damage the new speculation, but Paroissien and García del Río, who complained bitterly of the venality of the Press, managed to reply, as they hoped, to 'a very good effect'.[2] Seven days after the loan had been issued Kinder paid into the account of the Government of Perú at his bankers, Messrs. Everett, Walker, Maltby and Ellis, a first instalment of £120,000,[3] and to make these and future funds more easily available in Lima, as also to carry out the loan contract for ratification, it was decided to send a special agent to Perú, one Robert Proctor. Kinder was in partnership with Robert Ponsonby Staples, a merchant who had had long experience of South

---

[1] *The Times,* 14 Oct. 1822. See also *Annual Register,* 1822, p. 193.
[2] *The Times,* 14 Oct. 1822; *The Morning Chronicle,* 14, 15 Oct. 1822; Journal, 14, 15 Oct. 1822.     [3] Journal, 19 Oct. 1822.

American affairs at Buenos Aires and who was later to become a British
consul (he was soon dismissed) in Mexico; and Proctor was to establish
in Lima the firm of Robert Ponsonby Staples and Co., which would be
empowered to draw either on Kinder or on Everett, Walker and Co. for
such sums as the envoys might wish to remit to Perú. He was to
receive the moneys which the British merchants in Perú wanted to send
to England, pay them into the Peruvian Treasury, and draw bills for
the appropriate amounts, duly certified by the Peruvian Government,
which would, of course, be honoured in England, though Paroissien and
García del Río were careful to insist that Proctor's credit should be
limited to £700,000, the remaining portion of the loan to be retained
in England to cover interest payments and also legation and other
expenses.[1]

At the end of October, however, an alarming report reached England
from Colombia. It seemed that the validity of the Colombian loan was
questionable, since the authority of the agent of the Colombian Government to contract a loan at all had been impugned by that Government
itself.[2] The agent, a dying man, stoutly defended himself. But,
naturally enough, the holders of Colombian scrip were thrown into a
panic. Naturally, also, confidence in the credit of other South American
countries and their agents was severely shaken;[3] and the position of
Paroissien and García del Río was the more embarrassed because they
themselves had been left in complete ignorance of the state of affairs in
Perú. 'No news for us from Lima—all uncertainty', complained
Paroissien. 'Tis strange the heads of that Govt. do not see their interest
in letting us have details of everything—but so it is.'[4] And so it continued to be. The complaint was only too often, and with too much
justice, to be repeated, and while rumours—unpleasant rumours, such
as that Lima had been recaptured by the Spaniards—abounded, the
envoys were quite unable to contradict them with authority. To make
matters worse, a London merchant, who had suffered the loss of his

[1] Legation Dispatches, Abstracts, nos. 60 and 68, 10, 24 Nov. 1822. P.P.
*Kinder versus Everett*, pp. 5, 21–6, 39. For Staples see Humphreys, *British
Consular Reports*, p. 331 note.
[2] *The Times*, 22 Oct. 1822; Herring, Graham and Powles to Canning, 9 Jan.
1823, F.O. 18/2.
[3] Legation Dispatches, Abstracts, no. 57, 6 Nov. 1822. P.P.
[4] Journal, 15 Nov. 1822.

property through the condemnation at Lima of a British vessel which had attempted to run a blockade of that part of the coast of Perú still in Spanish hands, tried to attach a portion of the funds of the Peruvian loan in the possession of Everett and Walker and began an action for recovery in the Lord Mayor's court. The defence, of course, denied the competence of the court to deal with this matter, and the action in any event failed.[1] But in this unfortunate combination of circumstances, and at a time when Peruvian scrip had fallen precipitately in price, both Kinder and his bankers took alarm. They proposed, and the envoys agreed, that the payment of the second instalment of the loan, due on the 25th November, should be postponed till the following May, by which time, it was hoped, the loan contract would have been ratified in Perú.[2]

This step seems to have allayed public anxiety, at least temporarily.[3] Nor were García del Río and Paroissien themselves seriously disturbed. The arrangements for Proctor's departure were hurried on, and on the 8th December he sailed. But still there was no news from Perú. Not even the fact that the Foreign Minister, Monteagudo, had fallen was communicated to the envoys officially; they learnt it on the 1st January by common report. And in January, when the third instalment of the loan became due, not only were more unpleasant rumours in circulation about the state of affairs in Perú, but it was obvious that the 'fright all the holders of foreign securities' were in as a result of the doubts cast upon the Colombian loan had by no means diminished.[4] There was nothing for it but to agree that the payment of the third instalment, like that of the second, should be deferred, though the envoys insisted that Kinder pay £50,000 on account.[5]

By February 1823, therefore, the total sum which had been paid into the account of the Government of Perú with Messrs. Everett and

[1] Hodgson v. San Martín and others, The Morning Chronicle, 19 Nov. 1822; Legation Dispatches, Abstracts, 13, 20 Nov. 1822, both numbered 67. P.P.
[2] The Morning Chronicle, 8, 9, 13 Nov. 1822; Journal, 12 Nov. 1822; Legation Dispatches, Abstracts, no. 67, 13 Nov. 1822, P.P., printed, but wrongly dated in Paz Soldán, Historia del Perú independiente, 1822–1827, i. 367.
[3] The Morning Chronicle, 14 Nov. 1822.
[4] Journal, 6 Jan. 1823.
[5] Ibid., 4 Jan. 1823; Legation Dispatches, Abstracts, no. 79, 8 Jan. 1823. P.P.

Walker was £170,000, and of this sum rather more than a half had been drawn out.[1] This was a discouraging result after the high expectations raised when the Peruvian loan had been floated rather more than three months earlier. And yet it was only now that the real difficulties of Paroissien and García del Río were to begin. For on the 3rd February they learnt to their horror, though again only from public report,[2] not only that San Martín had ceased to be Protector of Perú, but that he had left Perú even before his envoys in England had had time to call on Canning, even before the Peruvian loan had been floated; and what, since then, had happened in Perú the envoys could only dimly con- jecture. What was to happen in England was soon made plain. 'This is a most important day for us', wrote Paroissien on the 7th February. 'A Mr. Jenkin Jones and two others have filed a bill in Chancery, attach- ing our loan and praying for the dissolution of the funds already in the hands of Everett and Co. upon the grounds of our having defrauded them by false representations.'[3] And not content with obtaining an injunction forbidding these funds to be used, the three bondholders wrote to Canning to beg that no measure of recognition should be extended to Perú while their suit was pending.[4]

Even Paroissien's resilient temperament and García del Río's easy- going nature could not but be discomposed by blows such as these. For not only were the funds of the Peruvian loan frozen, and not only was the whole future of the loan imperilled, but the envoys were placed in a highly equivocal position. Their powers had been given to them by San Martín and the Peruvian Council of State, and these powers they must now consider to be invalidated, at least in so far as any future use could be made of them. In dispatch after dispatch, they begged that new powers should be sent to them. They explained that they had taken no steps to carry out their secret instructions relating to the establishment of a monarchy in Perú under a European prince, for the times had not seemed opportune and their first object had been the loan. They pointed out how essential it was, at a moment when a new crisis had

---

[1] *Kinder versus Everett*, pp. 3–5.

[2] Journal, 3, 5 Feb. 1823; Legation Dispatches, Abstracts, no. 83, 6 Feb. 1823, P.P., printed in Puente Candamo, op. cit., pp. 254–5.

[3] Journal, 7 Feb. 1823; Legation Dispatches, Abstracts, no. 92, 25 Feb. 1823, P.P., printed in Paz Soldán, op. cit., *1822–1827*, i. 218.

[4] Jenkin Jones to Canning, 21 March 1823, F.O. 61/1.

been reached in European affairs, when once again a French army was invading Spain—this time to destroy the constitutionalist cause in that country and to re-establish despotism—that Perú should be properly represented in Britain and Britain assured of the stability of Perú.[1] Did not Canning, in April, himself reveal his view that 'time and the course of events' had substantially decided the separation of Spain and her colonies? But they might have saved themselves their trouble, for they had reason to suspect later that their dispatches were never even opened;[2] and when, in June, they at last received a laconic communication from the Peruvian Foreign Office, it was merely to inform them of the decree passed by the Constituent Congress of Perú on 22 November 1822, depriving them of their powers in so far as these powers related 'to the form of government' and exceeded 'the precise objects of consolidating the national independence and liberty'.[3]

Their dilemma, therefore, was increased, for what meaning was to be attached to this decree? Did it refer only to their secret instructions? Or did it refer also to their powers to negotiate treaties and to raise a loan? To these questions there was no answer, and since their own good names and the good faith of Perú were bound up with the loan, only one course seemed to be open to them. They resolved to treat the decree as no more than a partial revocation of their powers, affecting their political instructions alone, to refrain from all such activities as might in any way compromise the Peruvian Government, but to remain in London till they should be recalled or superseded by such new agents as, according to the decree of Congress, were to be appointed, and, meanwhile, to take what measures they could to defend the loan and the sanctity of the contract into which they had entered.[4]

Exactly a fortnight before the terms of the decree of November 1822 became known, on the 6th June, to Paroissien and García del Río in London, the agent whom they had sent out to Perú, Robert Proctor,

---

[1] Legation Dispatches, Abstracts, nos. 83 and 84, both 6 Feb., no. 92, 25 Feb., nos. 98 and 101, 10, 16 April 1823. P.P. Nos. 83 and 101 are printed in Puente Candamo, op. cit., pp. 254-6.

[2] Legation Dispatches, Abstracts, no. 177, 22 Nov. 1824. P.P. Printed in Puente Candamo, op. cit., p. 301.

[3] Above, p. 115.

[4] Legation Dispatches, Abstracts, nos. 110 and 114, 7, 11 June 1823. No. 114 is printed in Puente Candamo, op. cit., p. 298.

reached Lima; and his arrival, he found, 'had been most anxiously looked for' both by 'the public authorities' and by the British and other merchants.[1] The 'public authorities' were not, it is true, united, for in place of the executive junta which had governed the country since the retirement of San Martín, the Peruvian Congress had recently been forced by the army to accept a President, not of its own choice, in the person of José de la Riva-Agüero, a popular, talented, energetic and ambitious lawyer who possessed a genius for intrigue. But whatever their mutual antagonism, President and Congress were agreed on the need for money; while the merchants, for their part, were anxious for security. They had previously been compelled to make forced loans to the Peruvian Treasury,[2] and, more recently, in view of the news from London, they had voluntarily been prepared to extend credit. Indeed, to a considerable extent, the funds of the loan had been spent in advance, primarily to meet the costs of military operations. For Perú was still divided between the patriots and the Spaniards; the war still continued; an expedition to the south of the country at the close of the previous year had failed disastrously; and at the very moment of Proctor's arrival a further expedition, fitted out by contract with various of the merchant houses, was about to sail.

Proctor, therefore, was assured of a hearty welcome, though in the opinion of Paroissien's old friend, John Begg, the credit which he was empowered to give was not sufficiently extensive.[3] Already in March, when the news of the loan had first arrived, Congress had hastened to approve it, and formal ratification of the contract which Proctor had brought with him presented no difficulties. It was endorsed on the 1st June and Proctor was at once engaged in drawing bills for the Government. Riva-Agüero, if his words are to be believed, had made an effort, also, to induce Congress to confirm Paroissien and García del Río in their posts.[4] But thankfulness for the loan did not include approval of San Martín's envoys. A new agent extraordinary, Congress insisted, should be appointed in their place, and on the 21st August the post of commercial agent was given to a British merchant who had

---

[1] Proctor, *Narrative of a Journey across the Cordillera of the Andes*, p. 132.
[2] Humphreys, *British Consular Reports*, pp. 128–9.
[3] Begg to Paroissien, 30 May 1823. P.P.
[4] Riva-Agüero to Paroissien, 22 July 1823. P.P.

LIMA WITH THE BRIDGE OVER THE RIMAC.

Scene in the Carnival at Potosi.

asked for it,[1] whom Paroissien knew, and with whom Proctor had taken up residence.

This was John Parish Robertson. Like Paroissien, he had first touched South American soil in 1807, and at the same place, Montevideo. During the course of a highly adventurous career he had built up, with his brother William (now in Buenos Aires), a lucrative commercial connexion with the United Provinces of the Río de la Plata, and, in 1821, after a few years' residence in England, he had returned to South America 'to lay the foundation of prosperous and extensive establishments' in Santiago and Lima.[2] Now appointed to supersede Paroissien and García del Río in everything that concerned the financial and commercial concerns of Perú in England, he set sail from Callao on the 22nd August.

But between the ratification of the loan by Congress on the 1st June and Robertson's departure a series of fantastic events had occurred in Perú. Riva-Agüero, like San Martín, had realized that Perú could not win her independence without further external aid. Like San Martín, he had sought the assistance of Bolívar, and Bolívar had already dispatched some troops under the command of his favourite general, Sucre. But suddenly, in mid-June, a royalist army, descending from the mountains, seized Lima, forcing the President and the Congress to take refuge in Callao. There, amidst violent dissensions, Congress insisted on appointing Sucre to the supreme command and deposed the President. The President, with a number of the deputies, fled to the northern town of Trujillo, where he dissolved the Congress; and the Congress, reconstituting itself in Lima when the royalists evacuated that city, as they soon did, elected a new President whom Riva-Agüero refused to recognize.

Such was the situation when Robertson, who drew his powers from the Government and Congress in Lima, left Perú towards the end of August. San Martín, watching the scene from his refuge in distant Mendoza, was bound to confess that Bolívar alone could save Perú, and that only with an iron hand;[3] and on the 2nd September, at the invitation of the Congress, Bolívar at last arrived in Lima. The country, as

---

[1] Paz Soldán, op. cit., *1822–1827*, i. 221; *Kinder versus Everett*, p. 68.

[2] Robertson, *Letters on South America*, iii. 232.

[3] San Martín to Paroissien, 15 Oct. 1823. P.P.

K

the final stages in its liberation now opened, had within its borders two presidents (each to be in turn eliminated), a liberator, and an undefeated viceroy.

News from South America to England travelled slowly in the days of the sailing ship, as Paroissien and García del Río had already discovered to their cost. Of events in Perú Englishmen had only the haziest knowledge. That the Congress had approved the London loan in March was, however, known in England by the end of August, and the formal ratification of the contract, which had taken place on the 1st June, was reported early in October. In October also, by the same ship which brought the news of the reoccupation of Lima by the royalists in June, there arrived Proctor's first drafts on the London loan—to the extent of some £200,000.[1]

Earlier in the year, in February, when a suit had been filed in Chancery on account of the loan and an injunction had been laid against the use of its funds, Paroissien and García del Río had been disconcerted but not seriously embarrassed, for they had had no immediate need of these funds, and after five months, in July, the injunction had been dissolved upon a point of form. It was true that a new bill in Chancery had at once been filed by an outraged bondholder, but to this a demurrer had been entered, and henceforward no legal prohibition against the use of the funds of the Peruvian loan existed.

On the day on which the injunction had been dissolved, however, the bankers who held these funds, Everett, Walker, Maltby and Ellis, had intimated that they themselves would not disburse a penny. They were, they declared, in the position of trustees on account of moneys whose ownership was uncertain and had yet to be determined; and until the whole question of the validity of the loan contract, of the authority of the contractor, and of the powers of the Peruvian envoys, had been cleared up, they would pay nothing either to the contractor, to the envoys, or to anyone else.[2]

The news of the formal ratification of the loan contract by the Peruvian Congress left Messrs. Everett and Walker quite unmoved. It

[1] Legation Dispatches, Abstracts, nos. 130, 131, 7, 9 Oct. 1823, P.P.; *Kinder versus Everett*, p. 75.

[2] Legation Dispatches, Abstracts, nos. 120, 123, 125, 16, 25, 27 July 1823, P.P.; *Kinder versus Everett*, pp. 6–7, 85–8, 102–4.

was, no doubt, reassuring that this formal step had been taken. It was reassuring also when Canning, in October, announced his intention of sending out consuls to Spanish America and appointed a consul-general for Perú (though Paroissien and García del Río advised their Government not to receive him, on the ground that his commission would imply no recognition of Peruvian independence).[1] But the terms of the decree of ratification made it quite plain that a new agent was to take the place of Paroissien and García del Río; their powers appeared to have been revoked; and it was doubtful whether their signatures on official documents had any legal validity. Moreover, from current reports, it might be questioned whether a Peruvian Government existed at all.

The dilemma in which the loan contractor, Kinder, and also Paroissien and García del Río, were placed when Proctor's drafts arrived from Perú was, therefore, acute, for how were the drafts to be honoured? The scripholders, moreover, their dividends unpaid, had become increasingly restive, particularly when Kinder, who needed more funds than existed, even in the hands of Everett and Walker, to meet his present and future obligations, had issued a new call on deposits. In desperation Paroissien and García del Río appealed to the agent of Chile in London, whom they knew well, to come to their aid with temporary accommodation.[2] But they appealed in vain, and, all efforts to reach an agreement with the bankers and the scripholders having failed, only one course remained. Kinder sued Everett and Walker for the recovery of the funds in their possession. He retained the services of Brougham, and the case, heard in the court of King's Bench on the 20th December, resulted, as Paroissien gleefully noted, in 'our complete triumph over Everett'.[3]

By now Robertson had arrived. The further conduct of the Peruvian loan and the financial and commercial representation of Perú in England lay with him; and from Robertson, also, Paroissien and García del Río learned that a new agent would soon arrive to take over their political functions.[4] Their mission was closing. They had already given

---

[1] Puente Candamo, op. cit., p. 259.
[2] *Archivo de don Bernardo O'Higgins*, iv. 64–5.
[3] Journal, 20 Dec. 1823; *Kinder versus Everett*, p. 142.
[4] Legation Dispatches, Abstracts, no. 151, 12 Dec. 1823. P.P.

up their house in Grosvenor Street, as well they might, since its rent was twenty-five guineas a week.[1] In January their secretary, Creutzer, sailed for Mexico, from whence he made his way back to Perú to become a mining agent. García del Río prepared to gratify a wish, long cherished, to see Paris before he should return to America, and Paroissien hastened to Derbyshire where, for the second time in his life, he had fallen in love.

As for Robertson, it was he who wound up the affairs of the first Peruvian loan and even succeeded in floating a second. Having realized a large fortune by his South American operations, he lost it in attempting to promote the emigration of Scotsmen to the Río de la Plata, became, in middle life, an undergraduate at Cambridge, and then retired to the Isle of Wight to write, in collaboration with his brother, his famous *Letters on Paraguay* and *Letters on South America*.

[1] Journal, 13 March 1823.

# CHAPTER IX

## EL DORADO, 1824–5

THOUGH Paroissien and García del Río had been superseded as the financial and commercial representatives of Perú in England in December 1823, and though their political powers had been revoked, certainly in part, possibly in whole, even earlier, they still regarded themselves as ministers and envoys. Their expected political successor failed to arrive; they received no letters of recall; and it was not till April 1825 that peremptory orders at last reached them to bring their activities to a close and to hand over the legation archives to Robertson.[1]

For another fifteen months, therefore, the two men continued to act as reporters and observers of the English and European scene, gathering information (though their reports continued to be ignored), entertaining the American Minister and the new envoy from Colombia (at the cost of £150),[2] sounding the French Ambassador,[3] and consulting with their South American colleagues. They were, from time to time, greatly exercised about the state of affairs in Perú, for there, despite the arrival of Bolívar, conditions moved from bad to worse. In February 1824, not only did the garrison of Callao mutiny and go over to the royalists, but Lima was again lost to the independent cause; and such was the consternation of García del Río and Paroissien when the news reached them, that they contemplated the immediate purchase of two ships of war, out of the funds of the Peruvian loan, which were to be at once sent to Perú. San Martín was now in England. He had arrived—

[1] Journal, 15 April 1825; Legation Dispatch, no. 181, 18 April 1825. Puente Candamo, *San Martín y el Perú*, p. 303.

[2] Journal, 22 June 1824.

[3] Conference of 25 May 1824. Puente Candamo, op. cit., p. 291. See also, for a fuller account, F.O. 6/5.

to Paroissien's great joy—in May, certainly with no thought that he was
to remain in Europe a permanent exile, but merely with the intention
of paying a brief visit and of providing for the education of his
daughter;[1] and the plan was discussed both with him and with Kinder,
Robertson, and the envoy from Colombia, who, being in a sense
Bolívar's own representative, was especially concerned. García del Río
was to purchase the ships in Stockholm and San Martín was to return
to America at once to seek support from the Governments of Buenos
Aires and Chile. Difficulties between Kinder and the Colombian envoy,
however, frustrated the plan,[2] and San Martín, having placed his
daughter at school in Hampstead,[3] retired to Brussels instead.

But this was merely an agitating interlude in the placid life which
the two envoys now led. García del Río, in 1824, comfortably divided
his time between London and Paris, and Paroissien had ample leisure
to indulge a liking for country life at Carnfield Hall, the home of the
young lady to whom he had become engaged in Derbyshire (what Mr.
Darcy of Pemberley would have made of him must be left to speculation), a passion for the theatre and the art galleries in London, and a
taste for foreign travel, in the Low Countries and in France. Money was
plentiful, for the envoys continued to credit themselves with their
salaries—and paid them out of the proceeds of the Peruvian loan. And
when, in April 1825, they wound up their accounts, it was to reach the
gratifying conclusion that the Government of Perú owed them some
£28,000. The expenses of their legation, including, of course, their own
salaries, during the past two and a half years amounted, they calculated, to over £23,000. To meet these expenses they had drawn on
the funds of the Peruvian loan for rather more than £19,000. This left
a deficit of £4,000; and, besides this £4,000, they claimed another
£24,000 as a commission of two per cent on the nominal value of
the loan itself. Other Latin American Governments, those of Mexico,
Colombia, Brazil and Buenos Aires, they argued, had all allowed such a
commission to the agents whom they also had sent to raise loans in
England; and so convinced were Paroissien and García del Río of the

---

[1] San Martín to Paroissien, 15 Oct., 13 Dec. 1823. P.P.
[2] Journal, 23, 28 July 1824; García del Río to Paroissien, c. 17 July 1824.
P.P. Cf. Otero, *Historia del libertador*, iv. 141–2.
[3] Journal, 2 Aug., 29 Nov. 1824, 18 March 1825.

reasonableness of their claim and the rectitude of their conduct that they published an account of both.[1]

Paroissien's political career, like his military career, was now ending. His talents awaited a new sphere, and when, in March 1825, he modestly took lodgings at 26 Charlotte Street, Bloomsbury,[2] it was soon to be found, and found, naturally enough, once again in South America. For in the England of 1825, as that experienced naval officer, traveller and writer, Captain Basil Hall, assured his publishers—he had only recently produced his *Extracts from a Journal written on the Coasts of Chili, Peru, and Mexico*, and Paroissien had supplied him with information[3]—South America was 'the great topic of the present hour'. 'Its interest', wrote Hall, 'is at the highest; and now or never (at least never so well) is the moment to strike the chord which vibrates with the same note over the whole kingdom.'[4] And while this chord vibrated, it was not likely that Paroissien, an Englishman with eighteen years' practical experience of South American affairs, and lately minister plenipotentiary of the state of Perú, would long be wanting occupation.

The chord had begun to vibrate many months earlier. In the winter of 1822–3, not long indeed after Paroissien and García del Río had comfortably settled themselves in London, public confidence and public interest in South America had temporarily declined. The embarrassments and uncertainties attending the course of the first South American loans, those of Colombia, Chile and Perú, and the war-clouds at this time gathering in Europe, had alike contributed to check the hopes and tighten the purse-strings of the British investor; and when, in April 1823, a French army once again crossed the Pyrenees to crush constitutionalism and restore autocracy in Spain, there was a genuine fear that intervention in Spain might be the prelude to intervention in Spanish America.

In the winter of 1823–4, however, these doubts and fears were cast

---

[1] Cuenta Jeneral, 6 April 1825; Legation Dispatch, no. 182, 27 April 1825. P.P.; *Justificación de la conducta pública seguida por D. Juan García del Río i D. Diego Paroissien* (London, 1825).

[2] Journal, 17 March 1825.

[3] Hall to Paroissien, 22 Dec. 1823. P.P.

[4] T. Constable, *Archibald Constable and his Literary Correspondents*, 3 vols. (Edinburgh, 1873), ii. 486–7.

aside. British commissioners had been sent to investigate conditions in Mexico and Colombia. British consuls, in January 1824, sailed for Buenos Aires, Montevideo, Chile and Perú. In the United States President Monroe had held up a hand in warning to Europe. Any European 'interposition' in Latin America for the purpose of oppressing the new Spanish American states, 'or controlling in any other manner their destiny', he had declared, in his famous message to Congress, could only be viewed as a 'manifestation of an unfriendly disposition' towards the United States. And though the United States lacked the physical strength to implement these words, in England Canning, supported by all the might of British naval power, had given a similar warning. That hostility to European interference in the affairs of Spanish America which the United States, skilfully availing herself of the divisions between Britain and Europe, had proclaimed loudly and in public, Canning, in private, had earlier made plain to Prince Jules de Polignac, the French Ambassador in London; and already in November 1823, Paroissien and García del Río had been able to record their conviction that France had no intention of contributing to the subjugation of the Spanish colonies, and that Britain, certainly, would tolerate no such enterprise.[1]

In 1824, therefore, all apprehension of European intervention in Spanish America—and perhaps the danger had never been more than imaginary—vanished; and, once the Monroe Doctrine had been proclaimed, Canning, for his part, lost no opportunity of revealing to the world 'how early and how anxiously Great Britain declared against any project of bringing back the late Spanish colonies under the dominion of the Mother Country by foreign aid'.[2] In March he made public not only the terms of his conversation with Polignac but also Britain's refusal to participate in another European Congress on Spanish American affairs; and in May, at the time of what Paroissien and García del Río described as 'the great crisis of the cause of America in Europe', the American Minister, Richard Rush, communicated to the two Peruvian envoys Canning's resolve to act without further reference to Madrid.[3]

[1] Legation Dispatch, 22 Nov. 1823. Puente Candamo, op. cit., p. 261.
[2] Planta to Woodbine Parish, 30 Dec. 1823, F.O. 118/1.
[3] Legation Dispatch, no. 163, 20 May 1824; Minute of Conference, 20 May 1824, Puente Candamo, op. cit., pp. 269, 289; Webster, *Britain and the Independence of Latin America*, ii. 427.

Public clamour for the recognition of the new Spanish American states had now reached its height. In the summer of 1824 petition after petition, from Liverpool, London, Manchester, Leeds, was laid before Parliament; and while the British merchants and manufacturers were in part moved by their fears of the commercial rivalry of the United States in Latin America, Canning was anxious to undermine such moral or political leadership as the United States might there have acquired. In July the cabinet secretly resolved on the negotiation of a commercial treaty with Buenos Aires, and ratification of this treaty would amount to diplomatic recognition. But it was not till December that Canning, who was anxious, by similar means, to extend the sphere of recognition more widely, finally overcame the opposition of his king and his colleagues. 'The deed is done', he wrote in mid-December. 'The nail is driven. Spanish America is free; and if we do not mismanage our affairs sadly, she is English. . . .' On the last day of the year the decision to recognize Buenos Aires, Mexico and Colombia was announced to Spain; on 11 January 1825, to the diplomatic corps; and on the 3rd February to Parliament, though the king, in dudgeon, refused to make the announcement himself; he had, he said, the gout, and his false teeth were lost.[1]

Paroissien and García del Río, in reporting the news, expressed their belief, or at least their hopes, that the recognition of Chile and Perú would soon follow and that with them, also, commercial treaties would be signed.[2] But of this there was no question. Of the state of affairs in Chile Canning was not well informed. But it was, in any event, highly unsettled. Discontented with the prolonged rule of Bernardo O'Higgins, disliking his social policy, and determined to preserve their own power and prestige, the Chilean aristocracy had risen against him. First the south of the country and then the north had revolted, and when the agitation spread to the centre, O'Higgins, in February 1823, was forced to resign. He sought refuge in Perú, where Paroissien's friend, General Miller, met him some months later, 'just the same honest, kind hearted, straightforward, unsuspecting character', wrote Miller, 'we

[1] H. W. V. Temperley, *The Foreign Policy of Canning, 1822–1827* (London, 1925), pp. 140–52; A. G. Stapleton, *George Canning and his Times* (London, 1859), p. 411.
[2] Legation Dispatch, 17 Jan. 1825. Puente Candamo, op. cit., p. 271.

always found him to be';[1] and to Chile he never returned. Nor was it till the 1830's that the Chilean state began to attain to that stability which characterized it for most of the nineteenth century; and Britain's recognition was deferred till 1839.

As for Perú, there the struggle was still maintained on behalf of Spain. In February 1824, Bolívar had been proclaimed dictator. But in the very month that the cabinet took its momentous decision to recognize Buenos Aires, the news arrived in England that Lima had once again been captured by the royalists, and Peruvian bonds fell by 15 per cent.[2] Not till the great battles of Junín and Ayacucho, in August and December, was the final seal set upon the independence of Perú, and not till January 1826 did the fortress of Callao at last surrender. In September of that year Bolívar himself withdrew, and Perú was left to Peruvians, but not to peace; and as with Chile, so with Perú, it was not till the late 1830's that Britain officially recognized the country's existence.

But if, in 1825, neither Chile nor Perú could fulfil those conditions, not only of independence in fact as well as in name, but also of internal security and stability, which Canning himself laid down as prerequisite to recognition,[3] this was of small moment. For Buenos Aires was to be recognized, and Colombia and Mexico. With 'a burst of satisfaction',[4] the 'manufacturing and commercial interest' saw its hopes confirmed, its fears removed, and, with faith refreshed, it turned with redoubled zeal to 'the absorbing theme, South American commerce and riches'. 'British merchants and manufacturers, British capitalists, in short, the whole British publick', wrote the American Minister, 'are eagerly turning their eyes . . . to the American hemisphere. They are endeavouring to link Britain to these new states, and these new states to Britain, by every tie that excited cupidity can devise, and enormous opulence carry into effect. Nothing was ever like it before, not even the days of the south sea scheme.'[5]

Already a year earlier, the Spanish American loan market had shown

---

[1] Miller to Paroissien, 29 Nov. 1823. P.P.
[2] Journal, 5 July 1824.
[3] Cf. Canning to Woodbine Parish, 23 Aug. 1824. Webster, op. cit., i. 114.
[4] The Times, 6 Jan. 1825.
[5] Manning, Diplomatic Correspondence of the United States concerning the Independence of the Latin-American Nations, iii. 1529.

signs of revival when the firm of B. A. Goldschmidt and Co. had floated a Mexican loan at the extremely low price of 58. In April 1824 came a second Colombian loan; this was issued at 88½, and the applications for subscriptions were ten times greater than the number of the shares.[1] A Brazilian loan followed in May, and Barings, a conservative house, themselves issued a Buenos Aires loan in July. Kinder and Robertson, meanwhile, marketed the balance of the Peruvian loan through the house of Frys and Chapman; and to these loans were added in 1825 further loans to Mexico, Brazil and even to Perú, and loans to Guatemala and the Mexican state of Guadalajara as well.

The face value of these speculations in 1824 and 1825 was close on £17,500,000,[2] though the amount which the borrowers themselves obtained was, of course, very much less. But the loans were not the only opportunities for profitable investment which dazzled the imagination of the British public. 'What a place London is for prospects!', wrote the young Robert Stephenson in March 1824,[3] himself on the point of leaving for South America, where he was to report on the cost of building a railway from La Guaira on the coast of Venezuela to Caracas, its capital. And 'prospects' abounded in 1824 and 1825. Britain was launched on the full tide of prosperity—and speculation. A mania for joint-stock enterprises swept the nation. Mining companies, insurance companies, gas companies, railway companies, dock and canal companies, were launched, one after the other, in rapid succession. 'A day now seldom passes', wrote The Times, in January 1825, 'without the arriving at maturity of some great project, requiring a large amount of capital.'[4] In two years more than six hundred and twenty such companies were founded or projected, of which only a sixth survived a year later.[5] 'It may be inferred', reported a parliamentary committee in the 1840's, 'that the Bubble Mania, carried into execution to its meditated extent, would have required, if it could

[1] The Times, 14 April 1824.
[2] J. F. Rippy, 'Latin America and the British Investment "Boom" of the 1820's', Journal of Modern History, xix (1947), pp. 122–9.
[3] J. C. Jeaffreson, Life of Robert Stephenson, 2 vols. (London, 1864), i. 73.
[4] The Times, 26 Jan. 1825.
[5] See Henry English, A Complete View of the Joint Stock Companies, formed during the years 1824 and 1825 (London, 1827), together with his A General Guide to the Companies formed for Working Foreign Mines . . . (London, 1825).

have been procured, a capital of three hundred and fifty millions sterling.'[1]

These companies, loans, schemes and 'bubbles' were not all, or even mainly, Spanish American. But it was Spanish American enterprises which excited the most eager expectations and which were, wrote Richard Rush, the 'great objects of attention with monied men'.[2] There was a company, launched in March 1825, with its shares at a premium of 4 per cent—Paroissien took a number and was almost persuaded to become a director—to join the Pacific and the Atlantic by a ship canal.[3] There were companies and plans to navigate the rivers of South America by steamboats, to fish for pearls in Colombia, to establish the 'unemployed poor' of Great Britain and Ireland as agricultural colonists in the United Provinces of the Río de la Plata. There were companies to promote emigration to Chile and Colombia. There was a company which proposed to export milkmaids to Buenos Aires in order to make butter, and a company was projected, its aims unspecified, to operate in Brazil, whose directors obligingly undertook to employ their capital in any profitable undertaking that might present itself.[4]

Some of these proposals were directly sponsored by the South American Governments concerned, or were actively canvassed by their agents or other South Americans in London. Mariano Egaña, the new agent from Chile, for example, was anxious to settle Irish peasants in the south of his country. His predecessor, Antonio José de Irisarri, was much interested, as also was Paroissien, in a plan to establish banks of discount, circulation and deposit in South America.[5] Rivadavia had recently arrived from Buenos Aires in the character of envoy extraordinary and minister plenipotentiary—it was at this time that San Martín, on a further visit to London from Brussels, was with difficulty

---

[1] 'First Report of the Select Committee on Joint Stock Companies . . .', *Parliamentary Papers*, 1844 [119] vii. 339.

[2] Manning, op. cit., iii. 1529.

[3] Journal, 25 Feb., 4, 5 March 1825.

[4] English, op. cit.; F. B. Head, *Rough Notes taken during some Rapid Journeys across the Pampas and among the Andes* (2nd edn., London, 1826), pp. 303–4; Humphreys, *British Consular Reports*, pp. 45 note 2, 168 note 3, 269–72.

[5] Journal, 20, 27 April, 2 May 1825.

restrained from challenging him to a duel[1]—and while Rivadavia fostered one colonization scheme in the Río de la Plata, John Parish Robertson fostered another.

But what, above all, excited the most sober imaginations were the glittering prospects of working the far-famed Spanish American mines, the source of fabulous riches, but many of them now abandoned through the flight of Spanish capital and capitalists, the disruption of the labour force, and the disorders which the Spanish American revolutions had brought in their train. The celebrated descriptions of Alexander von Humboldt, whose accounts of his travels and researches in Spanish America—he had spent nearly five years, from 1799 to 1804, exploring, collecting, indefatigably noting—had revealed a new world to an old, in part contributed to this excitement, for Humboldt's was a name to conjure with; and conjured with it was, very freely. The legend of El Dorado which, for nearly three centuries, had haunted western Europe, was born anew. Everyone knew, or thought he knew, that in Spanish America gold and silver were to be had for the taking. The Spaniards had reaped untold wealth. But Spanish methods of mining had been generally primitive; and what might not now be achieved by the introduction of modern machinery, by the experience of the miners of Cornwall or Germany, by the power of steam, the key to a new age? How the machinery would be transported to distant and lofty mountains, what might happen to Cornish miners in strange surroundings, whether the techniques of Europe were practicable in Spanish America, these were perfunctory questions which few stopped to answer.

The boom in Spanish American mines started, quietly enough, with the foundation in 1824 of three Mexican companies, all of which 'had some sort of basis for favourable expectations',[2] the Anglo-Mexican, the United Mexican, and the Real del Monte. A Colombian Association

[1] 'I was call'd while at dinner by a note of S.ͬ Martin to go instantly to him. I obeyed the summons and found it was to solicit me to be the bearer of a note of challenge to Rivadavia, whom S.M. thought fit to chastize for his brutal behaviour last night. I thought it was impolite certainly, but everybody expects to receive such conduct from Rivadavia and dissuaded S.M. from so rash a step. Fortunately Garcia soon came in and we succeeded in persuading him to drop this foolish thought altogether.' Journal, 23 March 1825.

[2] J. R. McCulloch, *A Dictionary, Practical, Theoretical, and Historical, of Commerce and Commercial Navigation*, 2 vols. (Philadelphia, 1840), ii. 188.

followed, whose shares, as *The Times* reported, were sought after 'with
avidity';[1] and by December, when an Imperial Brazilian Company,
whose prospectus referred to the lumps of virgin gold to be picked up in
the mountains of Minas Geraes, and a Río de la Plata Mining Association, blessed by Rivadavia, appeared, the boom was in full swing. A
£400 share in Real del Monte, which cost £70 down in October,
fetched £550 in December, and £1,350 in January 1825; and in
January companies were floated in rapid succession—two more
Mexican companies, whose shares sold at a premium of from £200 to
£300 each,[2] two Chilean companies, a Peruvian company, and a
General South American Mining Association. There were a few warning voices, and a Pasco Peruvian Company, in particular, was severely
denounced in the House of Commons.[3] But the effect was only momentary. Still more companies were launched—to operate in Mexico, in
Colombia, in Venezuela, in Haiti, in Central America, in Brazil, in
Chile, in the Río de la Plata. In all, some twenty-six Spanish American
or Brazilian mining companies, with an authorized capital of more than
£24,000,000 (less than a seventh was ever paid up), put shares on the
market in 1824 and 1825[4] before the bubble burst and they were over-
taken, in December 1825, by the panic which followed the boom.

This fascinating scene Paroissien watched with interest. His old
acquaintances, Kinder, Robertson, and the unscrupulous José Antonio
de Irisarri, were all actively engaged in the business of company promotion. Kinder and Robertson, for example, both became directors of
the Famatina Mining Company, which turned out, unfortunately, to
lay claim to the same mines as the Río de la Plata Mining Association.
They were directors also of the Pasco Peruvian Company, which was so
adversely criticized in the House of Commons and in which Paroissien
held shares.[5] Irisarri founded and became president of the Guatemala
Mining Company, in which Paroissien also took shares.[6] And on
4 April 1825, at the very moment when he and García del Río, as the
envoys of Perú, were winding up their accounts, Paroissien 'dined with
Irisarri and had a good deal of conversation about the mines of Potosí

---

[1] *The Times*, 29 Nov. 1824.                    [2] Ibid., 24 Jan. 1825.
[3] *Parliamentary Debates*, n.s., xii. 965, 1048, 9, 22 March 1825.
[4] English, *General Guide*, passim; Rippy, op. cit., p. 128.
[5] Journal, 8 Feb. 1825.                         [6] Ibid., 31 March 1825.

and La Paz'.[1] It was Irisarri who, two days later, concluded a bargain with one of those mining agents who were making hay while the sun shone, for what was later described as 'three-fourth parts of the four celebrated Silver Mines, of the Marquis de Casa Palacio, situate in the Mountain of Potosí, and known as the Mines of Lanacayo', and it was he who, on the 8th April, formed a company to work them (though his name was not mentioned) and took care to reserve a handsome block of shares for himself and for Paroissien and García del Río.[2]

So, on the 27th April, there appeared the Potosí, La Paz and Peruvian Mining Association. Its capital was to be £1,000,000 divided into twenty thousand shares of £50 each, the first instalments of £5 a share to be paid at once and the remainder on call. It proposed to employ this capital 'in working Mines of Gold, Silver, Platina, Quicksilver, Copper, and other Minerals, in the Provinces of Potosí and La Paz, and generally in Upper and Lower Perú'. Its prospectus quoted the opinions of Humboldt and of the less celebrated, but still well-known, Anton Zacharias Helms on the mineral wealth of these regions, stated that, besides the mines of the Marquis de Casa Palacio 'immediately adjoining the city of Potosí', which the Company already owned, it was engaged in negotiating for 'valuable Gold Mines in Tipoani, in the province of La Paz', and alluded to the influence which the late envoys from Perú would be able to exert in acquiring yet further concessions. The board of directors contained six Members of Parliament. Its president was Don Juan García del Río, and its vice-president General James Paroissien, late ministers plenipotentiary from Perú to the Courts of Europe.

In May the Company dispatched an advance agent, one P. A. Garda, to Potosí, with a credit of £5,000, to take possession of the mines.[3] Early in June it invited Paroissien himself to take charge of operations in South America with the rank of chief commissioner. Such an appointment would mean, Paroissien thought, an absence from England for at least two years, and he was engaged to be married. But he was greatly tempted, and, after a hasty visit to Derbyshire, he accepted the offer. 'This was a most important day for me', he wrote in his diary on the 21st June, 'as I agreed today to go to Potosi at a salary

[1] Ibid., 4 April 1825.
[2] Ibid., 6, 8 April 1825; statement by Irisarri, 7 April 1825. P.P.
[3] Journal, 24 May 1825.

of £2,500 per annum';[1] and with that decision the last phase in his varied career opened.

It opened in fevered activity. A secretarial and a technical staff, miners and masons, carpenters and blacksmiths, must all be engaged, and mining equipment, tools, supplies, provisions, ordered. No expense was to be spared, for the Potosí, La Paz and Peruvian Mining Association intended to operate on a grand scale. A chief engineer, J. H. Fryer by name, was secured at a salary of £1,500 a year, and a secretary at Potosí, 'Sir' Edmond Temple—the title had been assumed on the strength of a Spanish decoration gained during the Peninsular wars— at a salary of £500. Accompanied by Fryer, Paroissien hurried up to Cumberland, Northumberland and Durham to recruit miners, order machinery and inspect apparatus. Crossing to the Continent, he visited Humboldt in Paris and left a 'very agreeable impression'. 'Il est spirituel, simple et franc', wrote Humboldt. 'Il conduira tres bien cette grande affaire.'[2] Probably at Humboldt's recommendation, he engaged as chief of the mining department a young mineralogist, Hermann, Baron de Czettritz. Possibly he went on to consult mining experts in Germany; certainly he had intended to do so; and finally he called at Brussels, no doubt to say farewell to San Martín.

Towards the end of September, however, when he addressed a belated memorial to the Government of Perú to reveal the nature of his enterprise, and, as a general officer in the Peruvian army, to ask for two years' leave of absence from his military duties,[3] all was ready, and on the 22nd he left London. He was accompanied by Czettritz, Temple, a young surgeon, John Scrivener, who was to act as an assistant in the mineralogical department and was later to win a certain reputation for his work on yellow fever, and two servants. Miners, carpenters, masons, blacksmiths, clerks, a gardener, a surgeon, and all the equipment and stores of the Company were to follow later with the chief engineer and his family. The party posted down to Falmouth in their own carriage. Then, after two or three days spent in visiting the Cornish copper mines, on the 28th September, Paroissien, in H.M. Packet-Brig *Frolic*, for the second time in his life set sail from England for Buenos Aires.

[1] Journal, 4, 21 June 1825.
[2] Undated, unaddressed letter from Humboldt, c. 28 Aug. 1825. P.P.
[3] Draft, 20 Sept. 1825. P.P.

# CHAPTER X

## CATASTROPHE, 1826-7

GENERAL JAMES PAROISSIEN, late envoy of the state of Perú, and chief commissioner of the Potosí, La Paz and Peruvian Mining Association, landed for the last time on South American soil on 29 November 1825. H.M. Packet-Brig *Frolic* had justified her name. After a long and tedious voyage, for three days she had been driven backwards and forwards by contrary winds in the Río de la Plata till at the last Paroissien put off to shore at the little village of Enseñada, where General Whitelocke and his invading army had disembarked eighteen years earlier, while the rest of his party remained on board to land at Buenos Aires.

Buenos Aires still prospered. 'The benefits of a good Government, which has been at last established', the British consul-general had written eighteen months earlier, 'are now quite sufficiently known and understood to ensure the support of all classes of the people. Every day adds to its moral and physical strength';[1] and time had merely seemed to confirm that judgment. But there were ominous lights upon the horizon. On the opposite shores of the Río de la Plata, where the imperial flag of Brazil still floated, the people of the Banda Oriental of Uruguay had risen in revolt against their alien masters. The insurrection had been encouraged and supported from Buenos Aires, and war between Buenos Aires and Brazil was the inevitable result. It had, indeed, already begun. In the city itself, the Bank of Buenos Aires, founded in 1822 with the strong support of British merchants, was about to fail; and though the union between Buenos Aires and the provinces, shattered in 1820,[2] had been partially restored and a new

---

[1] Humphreys, *British Consular Reports*, p. 25.
[2] Above, pp. 79-80, 105.

Congress of the United Provinces of South America had met, the jealousy and distrust which the provincials felt for the *porteños* had been no whit removed. Nevertheless, the Rivadavian system still held firm. Trade was flourishing and land values were rising, and within a few weeks Rivadavia himself, recently returned from Europe, was to become the first president of the reunited republic.

Paroissien's visit was brief. He was interested in Buenos Aires merely as a financial link between England and the scene of his future mining activities in Potosí. To meet immediate expenses he drew bills on his company in London for £2,000. To finance his future operations in Potosí he drew for another £12,000—a step which was to have momentous results—in favour of a *porteño* merchant, one Félix Castro, who, sent to England as a commissioner to arrange the Buenos Aires loan in London, had agreed to act as the agent of the Potosí, La Paz and Peruvian Mining Association in Buenos Aires. This money he left in Castro's hands, receiving, however, letters of credit on Potosí.[1] Still choosing to regard himself as an Argentine officer, he drafted a long memorial to the Government detailing his services in the cause of South American independence and soliciting formal approval of his journey,[2] and then, on the 28th December, he took the road which he had first travelled fifteen years earlier, the long road which led through Córdoba and Tucumán and Salta to Potosí.

This time he travelled in luxury. His old friend, General Miller, met him four days later, his advent heralded by an immense cloud of dust, riding in a vast four-wheeled coach, known as a *galera*—the elegant travelling carriage brought from England had proved totally unsuitable, as Paroissien might have known, for a journey across the plains—with two baggage carts, a couple of mules, a dozen horses and as many postilions, swelling his train;[3] and his party now consisted not only of Temple, Czettritz, Scrivener and a servant—the second servant had levanted in Buenos Aires—but of two South Americans who had

---

[1] Edmond Temple, *A Brief Account of the Proceedings of the Potosí, La Paz, and Peruvian Mining Association* (London, 1829), pp. 1, 9.

[2] Representation to the Government of Buenos Aires, 24 Dec. 1825. P.P.

[3] Journal, 28 Dec. 1825; *Memoirs of General Miller*, ii. 339; Edmond Temple, *Travels in Various Parts of Peru, including a year's residence in Potosí*, 2 vols. (London, 1830), i. 69–71; L. Tosi de Diéguez, ed., *Memorias del Dr. Juan H. Scrivener* (Buenos Aires, 1937), pp. 22–3. The earlier part of Scrivener's memoirs is unblushingly borrowed from Temple.

entered his employment as well. There was a halt at Córdoba, where Paroissien visited his old *quinta* and bought a mulatto slave—'I mean', he wrote, 'to consider him as an hired servant whose wages I have anticipated'[1]—and a longer pause at Tucumán, a town which had suffered much. 'Discord and Civil War', he noted, 'have indeed made a deplorable difference between the miserable skeleton I now behold, and the industrious, the gay, the hospitable Tucuman I remember.'[2] And at Salta, where it was necessary to dispose of the *galera* and to hire mules for the mountain journey to Potosí, the party was delayed for nearly a month.

For here Paroissien received the welcome news that a ship, itself rechristened the *Potosí*, had been chartered to leave England at once, with the clerks and miners and all the equipment and stores of the company, for the Pacific port of Arica, the nearest and most natural port of entry for goods destined for the great table-land of Upper Perú; and he was at once confronted with the problem of providing transport from the coast to the plateau, acquiring the necessary mule-trains, and arranging for the mules to be taken first to Upper Perú and then to the sea-board.[3] He anticipated, also, a further difficulty. For Upper Perú was no longer a dependency of Perú itself. It had become the independent state of Bolivia. As the political heir of the old Spanish *audiencia* of Charcas, the new state had a coast line—not till the 1880's did Bolivia become a land-locked country—but it had no port of its own, although at the roadless and waterless village of Cobija—a journey of more than five hundred miles from Potosí—the authorities were attempting to form one. Meanwhile, Arica, the port in use, lay within the territory of Perú, and it was only too probable that the cargo of the *Potosí* would be made to pay a double set of customs' duties, first on its entry into Perú and then into Bolivia.[4]

This was a disagreeable prospect, and to lay the matter before the appropriate authorities Paroissien sent Temple forward in advance. The two men heartily disliked each other; Paroissien had resolved to bear with Temple's 'egotism and unpleasant manners' no farther than

[1] Journal, 13 Jan. 1826.
[2] Ibid., 27 Jan. 1826.
[3] Ibid., 3, 18, 23 March 1826.
[4] Ibid., 2, 4 March 1826; Paroissien to Fryer, 14 March 1826. P.P. See also Humphreys, op. cit., pp. 217–18, 144.

Salta if possible; and he was thankful to see him go. 'He is one of those men', he had noted in his journal, 'of whom the public offices in England are full, who only live to take their stipend, and gratify their own individual wants, without caring one penny if the interests of the Govt. or public company they serve, are forwarded or not.'[1] Accordingly, on the 5th March, Temple departed in haste, while Paroissien resumed his journey, more leisurely, ten days later, not by the direct route but, because of rains and floods, by a detour to the west. He finally reached Potosí in mid-April, more than six months after leaving England.[2]

Paroissien had first seen the Imperial City of Potosí in 1810 when as a young and penniless adventurer he had joined the expedition sent from Buenos Aires to liberate the provinces of Upper Perú from Spanish rule. It was in this remote part of what was then the viceroyalty of La Plata that, only a year earlier, the first blood in the revolutions for South American independence had been shed;[3] and it was here, sixteen years later, that the last Spanish soldiers still in the field laid down their arms. Upper Perú, traversed by the great route which led from Lima to Buenos Aires, had been a battle-ground between the patriots and the royalists. Revolt, repression, invasion, counter-invasion, pillage, massacre, it had known them all, not once but many times; and here, in 1825, after the great victory of General Sucre at the battle of Ayacucho, the Spaniards made their final, hopeless stand.

It was soon over. As Sucre advanced from Perú, the country rose to greet him, and its future had now to be determined. In the south there was some sentiment in favour of reunion with the Provinces of the Río de la Plata, though Paroissien himself noted the 'detestation' in which the inhabitants of the United Provinces were generally held by the people of Upper Perú—a hatred, he thought, which 'took its rise in a great measure from the improper conduct' of the officers and men of the liberating army with which he himself had marched in 1810.[4] A few northerners inclined towards incorporation with Perú. But this solution, also, was unacceptable, and the Assembly which Sucre con-

---

[1] Journal, 26 Jan. 1826.

[2] Scrivener's account of this journey in his *Memorias*, pp. 89–95, is sheer invention. It describes a route which was not taken at all.

[3] Above, pp. 41–2, 54–6.                    [4] Journal, 13 April 1826.

vened at the old administrative capital of Chuquisaca boldly pronounced for independence. On the 6th August the new 'República Bolívar' was born—it was christened five days later—and Bolívar, whose name had thus been honoured, was offered the executive power and invited to frame a constitution. Arriving in that same month, he spent several weeks organizing the new state and, on his departure at the end of the year, left Sucre as his deputy. His constitution, a singular document, he presented in the following May. Providing for a life-presidency and a chamber of censors, as well as a bi-cameral legislature, and combining monarchical with republican forms, it embodied, he declared, 'all the guarantees of permanency and liberty, of equality and order', and would, he hoped, prove to be an ark of salvation amid the tide of anarchy which was already threatening to engulf the new Spanish American states.[1] And in May, Sucre, despite his own reluctance, was elected to the presidency.

The territory of the new republic, thus in process of organization when Paroissien arrived at Potosí, stretched from the barren shores of the Pacific to the tropical jungles of the Amazon. But its heart was in the highlands. The bulk of its population of rather more than a million dwelt upon that high plateau where the Andes reach their greatest breadth. Three-fourths were pure-bred Indians. The whites were few, and, like the more numerous body of mestizos, had been demoralized by the experiences which they had endured. La Paz, in its hidden valley, was the chief town, with a population of 40,000, Chuquisaca, a quiet and cloistered oasis, the legal capital, and Cochabamba an important centre of industry and agriculture. But the population of the mining town of Oruro was only a tenth of what it had been a hundred years earlier, and the far-famed silver city of Potosí, with its mint, its unfinished cathedral, and its multitude of churches, was but the ghost of its former greatness.[2] It had once contained a population of 160,000 and now numbered only between eight and nine thousand. Its mines, discovered in 1545, had once produced fabulous wealth. They yielded only $900,000 in 1826. The labour force had once been counted in thousands. But only twelve or fifteen *ingenios*, metallurgical or amalgamation works, were now in operation and they employed fewer than

[1] Lecuna, *Cartas del libertador*, v. 241, 295.
[2] J. B. Pentland, Report on Bolivia, 2 Dec. 1827, F.O. 61/12.

five hundred persons. Out of some five thousand so-called mines tunnelled into the mountain of Potosí, less than a hundred were being worked at all, and of these only ten or twelve were in the principal lodes, while in January 1827 only six could properly be regarded as in a state of activity.[1]

But though the great days of Potosí had long been past, mineral production had risen during the eighteenth century, and the mines were not exhausted. Some had fallen in; others had filled with water; and in late years the *ingenios* had been plundered and destroyed, the labour supply dispersed and capital withdrawn. Technical skill, mining apparatus, quicksilver used in the process of separating silver from the ore, all were lacking. Nevertheless, once the revolutionary disturbances were over, the coinage at the mint of Potosí again began to increase, and so did the city's population.[2] The mines of Bolivia as a whole produced in 1826 $2,619,918 in silver and $800,000 in gold. Though there were great and obvious difficulties in the way of the introduction of modern machinery, whether for drainage or for the extraction of ore, while in some mines it could not be used at all, no country, in the opinion of a competent British investigator who had been sent to report on the state of Bolivia, afforded better prospects for the foreign miner;[3] and the British consul-general in Perú, no lenient critic of the extravagance and ill-judgment of the newly formed mining companies, reached the conclusion that with prudence and care British capital, skill and industry could not fail to restore the mines both of Bolivia and of Perú to active operation.[4]

The mineral wealth of the great altiplano of Bolivia was not merely a figment of the overheated imagination of the British public. And in 1826 the opportunities afforded for its exploitation to the foreign entrepreneur seemed favourable enough. It was true that the country was poverty-stricken, and that its social and political foundations were precarious, but Sucre's government promised well. Under his guiding hand the administrative and fiscal systems were reformed, schools and

---

[1] J. B. Pentland, Report on Bolivia, 2 Dec. 1827, F.O. 61/12; H. Czettritz, 'Descripción del Cerro de Potosí'. P.P.; Temple, *Travels*, i. 308–10; *Memoirs of General Miller*, ii. 238 ff.

[2] *Memoirs of General Miller*, ii. 248.

[3] J. B. Pentland, Report on Bolivia, 2 Dec. 1827, F.O. 61/12.

[4] C. M. Ricketts to Canning, 16 Sept. 1826, F.O. 61/8.

colleges opened, peace and order secured. For the moment a 'bright dawn of prosperity' shed its lustre over Bolivia,[1] and so flattering were the prospects that the British consul-general in Perú could even contemplate the recognition of Bolivia by England and the negotiation of a commercial treaty between the two countries.[2]

The dawn was false. Within two years, when Sucre retired, repudiated, its illusory gleams had vanished, while Sucre himself was soon to die, at the early age of thirty-five, by the hand of an assassin. But at the time when Paroissien reached Potosí the outlook both for Bolivia and for the Potosí, La Paz and Peruvian Mining Association was still unclouded. The attitude of the Government to foreign enterprise—and the population of Potosí had been swollen by mining agents and their staffs—was liberal and welcoming. From Chuquisaca Sucre himself wrote to congratulate Paroissien upon the arrival of one who had not only 'so distinguished himself in the cause of American independence' but who held also a commission 'so likely to benefit' Bolivia.[3] A petition which Paroissien presented asking for governmental protection and support of his enterprise was at once granted,[4] and as for the cargo of the *Potosí*, the Government was quite prepared to admit the whole either at its new port of Cobija, or at any other point, duty-free.[5]

Paroissien had, also, other grounds for satisfaction, for the agent sent out from England to take possession of the Company's mines, P. A. Garda, had displayed considerable energy. The Association now owned not four mines in the Cerro de Potosí but nine, of which two were already producing a rather low-grade ore, and the *ingenio*, which had also been acquired, was being repaired.[6] It was true that when the mines came to be surveyed, the mining expert, Czettritz, arrived at the conclusion that both their economic exploitation and the gratification of the high expectations which the Company's directors entertained in London depended on the acquisition and joint working of other properties.[7] But this was Paroissien's intention. He was, for example,

[1] Ricketts to Dudley, 15 Dec. 1827, F.O. 61/12.
[2] Ibid.; Humphreys, op. cit., pp. 221–5.
[3] Sucre to Paroissien, 24 April 1826. P.P.
[4] Decree of 8 May 1826. P.P.; Temple, *Brief Account*, pp. 10–11.
[5] Decrees of 25 March and 12 May 1826. P.P.
[6] Czettritz, 'Descripción del Cerro de Potosí'. P.P.; Temple, *Brief Account*, pp. 4–8, 22, 84.                      [7] Czettritz, loc. cit.

greatly interested in the mines of Puno in the neighbourhood of Lake
Titicaca, which had formerly yielded great wealth,[1] and these, though
more than four hundred miles away, Czettritz was sent to inspect in
May. Equally distant, and still more inaccessible, were the gold-mines,
or, more properly, gold washings of Tipuani, which, before the outbreak of the revolutionary movements in South America, had produced
some $1,000,000 a year,[2] and tentative negotiations for the acquisition
of these had been begun in London. There were, also, other properties
to which Paroissien's attention was drawn and which he hoped to purchase. He proposed to work on a grand scale, 'and even whole districts',
and his specific for the Potosí, La Paz and Peruvian Mining Association
was, indeed, not intensive but extensive exploitation, even, apparently,
if it should mean operating in areas so far apart as Potosí and Puno, or
so difficult of access as Tipuani.[3]

But the time was now approaching when the *Potosí* might be
expected to arrive from England, though her sailing had, in fact, been
greatly delayed, first by the procrastination of her owner, a Captain
Henry Templer—'without exception', wrote the chief engineer of the
Company to Paroissien, 'the most unprincipled scoundrel I ever met
with'[4]—and then by accident. She had at last left London early in
January for Falmouth, where she was to pick up some Cornish miners,
but, blown by a violent tempest from outside Falmouth harbour to the
Scilly Islands, she was forced to put back to Plymouth, where her crew
deserted.[5] She finally sailed on March 10th. She carried, besides the
chief engineer, J. H. Fryer, and his family, a surgeon, a book-keeper,
clerks, a blacksmith, a surveyor, a gardener, mechanics, carpenters,
miners from the north of England and from Cornwall, in all some forty-
five passengers. And her cargo, valued at £20,000, included not only
gunpowder and quicksilver, machinery and mining instruments, iron
and bricks, but glassware and hardware, mahogany desks for the
counting house, plants and trees, beers and wines, a piano for Mrs.
Fryer, and a carriage for Paroissien.

[1] Ricketts to Canning, 14 May 1827, enclosure, F.O. 16/11.
[2] Pentland, Report on Bolivia, 2 Dec. 1827, F.O. 61/12.
[3] Temple, *Brief Account*, p. 7; Paroissien to Channon, 20 Oct. 1826.
English Letter Books. P.P.
[4] Fryer to Paroissien, 21 Dec. 1825. P.P.
[5] J. Crosland to Paroissien, 1 March 1826. P P.

Leaving Temple to hire the largest house in Potosí for the reception of this company, Paroissien, early in May, visited Sucre at Chuquisaca and then turned his steps to the coast. After an adventurous journey, during which his mulatto slave absconded with two of his best mules and a part of his wardrobe, he arrived at the little town of Tacna, only forty miles from Arica, but a more salubrious site, on the 11th June.

Here, and at the more northerly city of Arequipa, where a British vice-consul was in residence, the British merchants in Lima, Paroissien's old friend, John Begg, among them, had hastened to establish agencies to tap the trade of southern Perú and Bolivia.[1] And here Paroissien's representative, Garda, had been anxiously waiting since April for news of the *Potosí*. He had attempted, also, to secure from the Peruvian authorities in the district of Arequipa permission for the ship's cargo, when it should arrive, to be landed free of duty, or at least on payment of no more than transit charges. The local officials, however, dared not commit themselves. They were prepared to give provisional approval, but the matter, they declared, was of such importance that it must be referred to Lima.[2]

According to the new commercial code of Perú, machinery and mining equipment could be imported free, but charges, possibly of thirty per cent and upwards, on the value of the rest of the cargo of the *Potosí*, might amount, Paroissien thought, to more than $45,000,[3] and if these dues were to be avoided, there was nothing for it but to go to Lima. There was still no news of the ship itself, and he decided to undertake the journey. His mule-trains were already coming down from the mountains to the coast; to change the destination of the *Potosí* from Arica to the new Bolivian port of Cobija, where there would be no difficulty in landing the cargo but much in transporting it to the highlands, was in fact impracticable; and, besides, he had private accounts to settle with the Peruvian Government. When he and García del Río, as the envoys of Perú in Europe, had wound up their affairs, they had claimed from that Government the sum of £28,000, and of this not one penny had been admitted, let alone paid. Moreover, in

---

[1] Humphreys, op. cit., pp. 173–4.

[2] Garda to Paroissien, 16 May 1826. P.P.

[3] Paroissien to Company Directors, 23, 26 June 1826. English Letter Books. P.P. For the tariff see Humphreys, op. cit., pp. 198 ff.

1821, before they had left for Europe, they had been presented, as a reward for their services, with shares in an estate—the Caucato estate —valued at $25,000 each. Rumours had reached them that, because of the bankruptcy of this estate, other of the shareholders had been given a monetary compensation, but nothing had been given to them; and the agent whom they had recently authorized to look after their interests had advised Paroissien that it might be advantageous if he came to Lima himself.[1]

This was unsound advice, and John Begg, in Lima, knew better. 'I am sorry to see', he had written to Paroissien in May, 'a strong prejudice against you in the Government.' Nothing, he had added, could be expected of the Caucato estate.[2] The ex-envoys were held to have been 'very extravagant' in their conduct, if not worse.[3] All the troubles of the Peruvian loan were laid at their door. Bolívar was still at the head of affairs in Perú, and Bolívar, Paroissien reported to García del Río, was 'endemonado contra nosotros'.[4] Yet Paroissien decided to go. He reached Lima on the 5th July, to be kept waiting in impatient suspense while his petition for the remission of the duties on the cargo of the *Potosí* was considered. He was able to forward neither his own nor his Company's interests. All he gained was formal permission to absent himself from the military service of Perú—for he still held the rank of a brigadier-general—for two years![5] The Peruvian treasury was empty. There was not a penny to spare, and certainly not for the late envoys of Perú in Europe. 'We are considered enemies of the country', he wrote to García del Río.[6] As for the question of the customs' dues, he could obtain no favourable ruling.[7] After a fruitless stay of more than six weeks, he boarded a Colombian vessel, suffered a frightful voyage of twenty-seven days, instead of the normal three or four, to Pisco and was nearly shipwrecked, was forced to complete his journey by land, and arrived at Tacna in the second week of October to find that the

[1] F. López Aldana to Paroissien, 8 March 1826. P.P.
[2] Begg to Paroissien, 17 May 1826. P.P.
[3] Paroissien to García del Río, 10 June 1826. P.P.
[4] Paroissien to García del Río, 27 April 1826. P.P.
[5] Representation to the Government of Perú, approved 22 July 1826. P.P.
[6] Paroissien to García del Río, 16 Aug. 1826. P.P.
[7] Petitions endorsed 21, 31 July 1826. P.P.; Paroissien to Channon, 13 Sept. 1826. English Letter Books. P.P.; Temple, *Travels*, ii. 191.

Potosí, La Paz and Peruvian Mining Association had been overwhelmed with disaster.

For, just as when Paroissien had represented a South American state in England, so now, when he represented an English company in South America, time and distance were his enemies. Already when he had left England in September 1825, there had been signs of uneasiness in the money market and the rage for joint-stock enterprises was declining, and at the moment of his arrival in Buenos Aires in December the crash came. The speculative bubble burst; a financial panic swept the country; and while the Bank of England was drained of gold and the country banks closed their doors, merchant houses were ruined and the Spanish American loan market and the Spanish American mining companies alike collapsed. By March 1826, the shares even of such companies as the Real del Monte, the United Mexican and the Anglo-Mexican had become positively unsaleable. 'The general pecuniary and commercial concerns of this country', wrote the solicitor for the Potosí, La Paz and Peruvian Mining Association to Paroissien, 'are at an ebb of misery and distress, of which you can form no conception. . . . You must at present refrain from drawing upon the Company. . . . Drafts . . . coming . . . by surprize until the present overwhelming difficulties of the country are removed may produce irreparable evils.'[1]

The position of the Potosí, La Paz and Peruvian Mining Association was, indeed, highly vulnerable. The Company had issued 20,000 shares. All of these had been appropriated, but on barely more than half had the first deposit of £5 a share been paid. In March 1826, two of the directors, Paroissien and García del Río themselves, together with the original promoter of the Company, Antonio José de Irisarri, were credited with 3,599 shares between them, though Paroissien seems to have been strangely ignorant of his own holdings. A third director, who had been closely associated with Irisarri in promoting the Company, held no fewer than 2,628 shares. And on not one of these 6,227 reserved shares had a penny been paid.[2] The Company might have been supposed to have had an initial capital of £100,000. In fact its

[1] J. Crosland to Paroissien, 1 March 1826. P.P.

[2] Directors to Paroissien, 28 March 1826. P.P.; Temple, *Brief Account*, p. 23; Paroissien to Directors, 19 Oct. 1826; Paroissien to Channon, 20 Oct. 1826. English Letter Books. P.P.

paid-up capital at the end of 1825 was certainly not more than £54,000.

Yet the Company had begun its operations on a prodigal scale. Its staff was large, expensive, and lavishly equipped. The cargo of the *Potosí* was valued at £20,000, and cost more. Incidental expenses seem to have been heavy. And by the end of March 1826, when the Association had met Paroissien's first drafts from Buenos Aires to the extent of £2,000, its resources were already almost exhausted. It was quite unable to make a call upon the shareholders, for if it were to do so, wrote the directors, the shareholders would probably themselves meet 'and break up the Association rather than pay it'. There was no alternative, therefore, but to practise rigid economy, until conditions should improve. The establishment at Potosí, Paroissien was instructed, must be cut down; no new contracts must be made; no bills must be drawn; and one bill, already drawn, the directors declined to honour.[1]

This was the bill for £12,000 which Paroissien, before his departure from Buenos Aires, had drawn in favour of Félix Castro, the Company's agent there. Its arrival, before Paroissien himself announced it, had caused a 'great sensation'. The directors were dumbfounded. They had already received bills from Buenos Aires for £2,000. Paroissien, they argued, would have in his possession not only this sum but also the balance of the £5,000 earlier given to the Association's advance agent, Garda, and he would soon have available the cargo of the *Potosí*, some of which could, if necessary, be sold. They could not believe that he needed yet more money, and they concluded that no damage would be done by protesting a bill which in fact they could not pay.[2]

This was a doubly optimistic view. By the time that the directors' exhortations and reproof reached Potosí, the Association's expenses and obligations in South America already exceeded the funds in Paroissien's hands. As for the bill for £12,000, it was true that Paroissien had intended to leave this money on deposit at Buenos Aires, where it would earn a high rate of interest and could be drawn on in the future. It was true also that on his arrival at Potosí he decided, because of the difficulties of the exchange between Buenos Aires and Potosí, not to

---

[1] Directors to Paroissien, 28 March 1826. P.P.
[2] Directors to Paroissien, 28 March, 18 April 1826; Channon to Paroissien, 29 March 1826. P.P.

draw on Castro's letter of credit but to use instead the house of his old friend, John Begg, in Perú.[1] But bills on Castro to the extent of $17,000 had already been presented and honoured—the mules which Paroissien had bought at Salta on his way to Potosí were, for example, paid for in this way—and other bills were outstanding. These bills, of course, Castro now in turn protested. He calculated, moreover, that what was due to him on account of interest charges on his money and the expenses in which he was involved more than doubled the sums paid on behalf of the Association. He embargoed such moneys as had been left at interest in Buenos Aires, either belonging to Paroissien or to the Association, and he began to take other steps for the recovery of his debts.[2]

The news of the directors' action reached Temple at Potosí on the 5th July, the very day on which Paroissien arrived at Lima. Temple was horror-struck. This 'act of suicide', he wrote, must 'terminate fatally all the golden prospects of one of the first and best, if not the very best, of all the speculations of the year 1825'.[3] Already, he reported a few days later, 'bills, protested by Don Felix Castro, have been returned, and are returning upon us from all parts'.[4] 'For God's sake', he wrote to Paroissien, 'send me some money.'[5]

But though the shock to the credit of the Company was severe, the damage was not irretrievable, for within three weeks the *Potosí* arrived at Arica. Her cargo was valuable. By selling some of it the Company could meet its obligations and still continue its operations, though on a reduced scale. Confidence was partially restored, and, recovering from his despair, Temple hastened to Chuquisaca to implore the protection of Sucre lest Castro should attempt to seize the Association's property at Potosí. '*Los señores Ingleses*', Sucre dryly observed— if Temple is to be believed—'must have been reading the history of El Dorado with a little more credulity than it deserves, if they imagined that the precious metals were to be obtained without labour and expense; for, although it is true that they abound in this country, they cannot be had for *nothing*, any more than the materials of which we

[1] Paroissien to Begg, 28 April 1826. P.P.
[2] Castro to Paroissien, 3 June 1826. P.P.
[3] Temple to Directors, 5 July 1826. P.P.; Temple, *Travels*, i. 365–6.
[4] Temple, *Brief Account*, p. 22; *Travels*, i. 370–1.
[5] Temple to Paroissien, 5 July 1826. P.P.

build our houses.' Nevertheless, he promised to afford the Company all the protection he could.[1]

The *Potosí*, having reached Arica on the 21st July, was now unloading. In accordance with the instructions which Paroissien had left behind him when he went to Lima,[2] her cargo was placed in the customs house and her passengers were accommodated at Tacna. This took time, but by the 22nd August the cargo had been discharged and Paroissien's return was impatiently expected. Money was scarce, tempers were short, the clerks and miners discontented. And on the 14th September, the day after Paroissien's storm-tossed vessel had at last landed him at Pisco on his journey back to Tacna, the blow fell which was to prove fatal to his enterprise. William Templer, who was the brother of the owner of the *Potosí* and who had sailed with her, attached the whole of her cargo for the payment of freight.[3]

The explanation of this proceeding lay in London, and whatever faults of carelessness or improvidence might be attributed to Paroissien in his conduct of the Association's affairs in South America, the folly of the board of directors in England was still more glaring. In November 1825, three of the directors had chartered the *Potosí* in their own names. Legally, therefore, they alone were responsible to the owner for the freight or hire of the ship, though the charges would in fact be met by the Company. Payments were to be made every two months until the final discharge of the cargo. But, partly through the owner's personal responsibility, the sailing of the ship was intolerably delayed. She did not finally sail till early in March, and the Company then disputed the owner's right to claim the whole of the freight during the period of delay. The three directors who had chartered the vessel demanded, for their part, that the Company should indemnify them against the consequences of their liability to the owner. To this the other directors were prepared to agree, but on one condition only, namely that the three charterers should obey a call to pay up the deposits on their reserved shares. The charterers refused, and thereupon joined with the owner of the *Potosí*, with whom they seem to have been on remarkably good terms, in an agreement that the freight should be paid, not in

[1] Temple, *Travels*, i. 401–2; Temple to Paroissien, 11 Aug. 1826. P.P.
[2] Paroissien to Fryer, 26 June 1826. P.P.
[3] Templer to Fryer, 14 Sept. 1826. P.P.

England, according to the terms of the original charterparty, but in South America on the discharge of the ship. They sent out to Templer a power of attorney to act on their behalf,[1] and Templer, attaching the cargo, claimed upwards of £4,000 for freight due before the voyage began and another £5,000 for freight earned by the time it was completed.[2]

The Association was now doomed, though the directors in London were slow to grasp that fact. 'In an agony of mind little short of madness', Paroissien, when at long last he arrived at Arica, sat down to give a picture of the ruin wrought: the cargo of the *Potosí*, much of which turned out to be 'rubbish', embargoed in the customs house; the mules, brought down from the mountains to convey the cargo to Bolivia, embargoed by the Company's book-keeper on account of his wages; 'our people starving and very clamorous'; and he himself 'without a dollar to purchase even bread for them' and assailed by creditors 'from every quarter'.[3] And in a letter to his fiancée in Derbyshire he added: 'I am the victim of a set of scoundrels who have sent these unfortunate people to this barren coast to starve, without absolutely affording the means to get into the Interior or anywhere else. My blood boils with indignation to think I have been such a dupe, for the Speculation in itself was good, was excellent.'[4]

The catastrophe was, indeed, complete. A small portion of the cargo of the *Potosí* had been sold, in order to meet immediate expenses, before the embargo was laid, but the funds thus realized were soon exhausted. 'We are now living on the bounty of the British merchants here', wrote the chief engineer in November.[5] 'So rigorous has Mr. Templer been in enforcing the embargo', Paroissien informed the directors, 'that I have not been able to obtain even my own private baggage . . . even the very chair I sit upon is embargoed.'[6] And, while an ugly spirit soon showed itself among some of the men brought out in the

---

[1] Charterparty, 4 Nov. 1825; Counsel's opinion, 15 May 1826; Directors to Paroissien, 18 May 1826; Power of Attorney to Templer, 23 May 1826. P.P.

[2] Templer to Fryer, 19 Sept. 1826. P.P.; Temple, *Brief Account*, p. 42.

[3] Paroissien to Directors, 19 Oct. 1826. English Letter Books. P.P.

[4] Paroissien to Isabel Wilson, 23 Oct. 1826. Copying Book No. 1. P.P.

[5] Fryer to Directors, 13 Nov. 1826. English Letter Books. P.P.; Temple, *Brief Account*, p. 47.

[6] Paroissien to Directors, 3 Nov. 1826. English Letter Books. P.P.

*Potosí*, and the muleteers, whom Paroissien had hired to carry her cargo to the mountains, clamoured for the fulfilment of their contracts or for compensation, an attorney, representing Félix Castro at Buenos Aires, appeared with a claim for payment on the unlucky bill protested in London as well as for enormous damages. To crown all, Paroissien himself was stricken with a severe fever, from which he never fully recovered.[1]

But he struggled on. Temple was instructed to dismiss all the Association's employees at Potosí, except Czettritz and Scrivener, and in January 1827, notice was given of the termination of their contracts also. A few of the newly arrived miners were induced to return to England through the good offices of the merchant house in which John Begg was a partner, though others of the late passengers of the *Potosí* to whom notice of dismissal was given preferred to remain, in order, wrote Fryer, to try 'to enforce the payment of their salaries, and an allowance for their passage home'.[2] As for Templer, Paroissien was resolved to fight him. An appeal was lodged with the local *intendente*, who appointed a judge, in the person of the curate of Tacna, and in December Paroissien won his case. Templer's action was condemned, the embargo removed, and the cargo of the *Potosí* handed back to its consignees.[3] But though this victory was won, its fruits were at once snatched away, for Castro's attorney now solicited a re-embargo in the interests of his client. With him Paroissien went to arbitration, agreeing to pay $40,000; and when the cargo of the *Potosí* was sold—as it now had to be—slowly and at ruinous losses, and the duties on it had been paid, it seems to have been Castro who got most of the proceeds.[4]

Gradually, however, the affairs of the Association were liquidated, in so far as they could be liquidated. At Potosí the Company's establishment was closed and its effects sold. Temple, who seems to have made himself thoroughly disliked by all his colleagues, left for Buenos Aires

---

[1] Paroissien to Directors, 3, 24 Nov. 1826; Fryer to Directors, 13 Nov. 1826. Ibid.

[2] Paroissien to Temple, 20 Oct. 1826; Fryer to Directors, 13 Nov. 1826. Ibid.

[3] Paroissien to Directors, 23 Dec. 1826. Ibid.; Temple, *Brief Account*, p. 58, *Travels*, ii. 199.

[4] Paroissien to Channon, 8 Dec. 1826. Copying Book No. 2; Paroissien to Directors, 23 Dec. 1826, 14 March 1827. English Letter Books. P.P.

and England in April 1827; Scrivener retired to Salta, where he settled down to practise as a physician; and Garda alone remained, to keep legal possession of the mines. He remained, indeed, till 1829, for it was not till that year that the directors of the Potosí, La Paz and Peruvian Mining Association, who had continued to nourish ridiculous illusions, finally recalled him and closed their doors.

As for Paroissien, he was impatient to leave the 'most miserable of all possible places upon earth', to return to England, and there to 'bring an action against Templer and his associates in iniquity'.[1] But until the cargo of the *Potosí* had all been sold it was impossible for him to go, and he then still waited in the vain hope that a promised consignment of quicksilver would arrive which would enable him to relieve his necessities. His private resources—such moneys as he had had in the hands of John Begg at Lima—were exhausted. 'We must all perish', he wrote despairingly in April, or 'return to England as distressed British subjects.'[2] His health grew worse and he was confined to his bed three days a week. Confirmed dropsy set in. He was advised that his life was in danger. But it was not till the end of August, when letters arrived recalling both him and Fryer, that he felt equal to beginning his journey, and, with the strong premonition that he would never again see England,[3] he set sail from Arica in the ship *Olive Branch*, bound for Valparaíso, on the 4th September. He died at sea on the 23rd September.[4]

Paroissien was only forty-three. His life had ended in failure and he died a ruined man. And as the waters closed over him they seemed about to close over Spanish America also. The mining companies were collapsing and the colonization schemes failing. Governments began to default on their loans and merchant houses to go bankrupt; and nowhere in South America, except, perhaps, in the empire of Brazil, was there apparent any promise of free and stable institutions, of peaceful and orderly growth. Of the great figures whom Paroissien had

[1] Paroissien to Haigh, 6 Nov. 1826; Paroissien to Udney Passmore, 9 Feb. 1827. Copying Books Nos. 1 and 3. P.P.

[2] Paroissien to Directors, 1 April 1827. English Letter Books. P.P.

[3] Paroissien to Directors, 31 Aug. 1827; Paroissien to Channon, 31 Aug. 1827. P.P.

[4] Edward Widder to Stephen Beuzeville, J. C. Myles and García del Río, 9 Oct. 1827. P.P.

M

known, San Martín and O'Higgins had already trod the path of exile, the one to survive till 1850, the other till 1842, and amidst the disorders of the countries which they had helped to found no one could yet foresee the sure and rapid rise of Chile, few could be blind to the difficulties which must beset Perú. Sucre was soon to leave Bolivia. Yet Sucre was Bolivia's brightest hope; and for him an assassin lurked on a lonely road. In the United Provinces Rivadavia had already fallen, his hopes undone, his policies rejected. Buenos Aires was still at war with Brazil, and as that struggle ended, with the establishment at long last of a buffer state between the rival powers, the independent state of Uruguay, the clouds of civil strife were gathering once more over the lands of the River Plate, and there anarchy was to father despotism. As for Bolívar and his favourite child, Colombia, 'I believe all lost for ever and the country and my friends submerged in a tempest of calamities',[1] was the Liberator's despairing cry; and when, in 1830, Bolívar died, waiting to leave Colombian shores, the splendid fabric of his vision had already faded, and barely a wrack remained.

It was, indeed, no encouraging picture that Spanish America presented in the late 1820's to the would-be immigrant, to the foreign investor, to the statesmen of Europe and the United States, or to the Spanish Americans themselves. But Bolívar and his embittered contemporaries were wrong. All was not lost. El Dorado had vanished, though some day the myth would be revived. False hopes, glittering illusions, had been swept away. But the map of the New World had been transformed. A continent had been born anew. The twenty years that had seen the fall of the empires of Spain and Portugal and the opening of Latin America to the trade of the world were of immense significance in modern history, and between America and Europe new links had been forged, new interests created. Trader, doctor, soldier, diplomat, company promoter and mining entrepreneur, Paroissien, in the course of his varied career, had illustrated them all.

[1] Lecuna, *Cartas del libertador*, ix. 326.

# APPENDICES

## I. *Note on the Territorial Organization of the Spanish Empire in South America*

AT the end of the eighteenth century there were three viceroyalties in Spanish South America, those of Perú, New Granada and La Plata, with their capitals at Lima, Santa Fé de Bogotá and Buenos Aires respectively, and two independent captaincies-general, that of Chile, created in 1778, and that of Caracas, or Venezuela, established in 1777. In South America the distinction between a viceroyalty and a captaincy-general had become merely one of name, except that a viceroy continued to enjoy a greater dignity and a larger salary than did a captain-general.

The capital of each of these five dominions was the seat of a royal *audiencia*, or high court of justice, which exercised quasi-legislative and administrative as well as judicial powers and acted also as an advisory council to the viceroy or captain-general. The three viceroyalties, however, each possessed a second *audiencia*. That of Cuzco, within the viceroyalty of Perú, was a late creation and was merely a judicial tribunal. The *audiencia* of Charcas, within the viceroyalty of La Plata, and the *audiencia* of Quito, within the viceroyalty of New Granada, were more important. They were far older than the viceroyalties to which they belonged. Their presidents, though politically subject to viceregal authority, exercised wide powers within the area under the *audiencia*'s jurisdiction, and the regions which they in effect governed were known as presidencies. The modern state of Bolivia is the political heir of the *audiencia*, or presidency, of Charcas, that of Ecuador of the *audiencia*, or presidency, of Quito. The jurisdictional boundaries of the colonial *audiencias* were often exceedingly vaguely defined. But they

were in general to form the basis of the territorial claims of the new Spanish American states.

Viceroyalties and captaincies-general were, of course, divided and subdivided into smaller territorial districts. Provincial administration, however, was greatly changed by the introduction in the late eighteenth century of the system of intendancies, administrative areas which superseded the old provincial jurisdictions and were presided over by governors *intendentes*. In the viceroyalty of La Plata Paraguay was one such *intendencia*, Córdoba another.

## II. *Glossary*

*alcalde*: municipal magistrate. Small towns had one *alcalde*, larger towns two *alcaldes*. They acted as judges of first instance and were elected annually by the *regidores* or town councillors.

*audiencia*: high court of justice and its territorial jurisdiction. See Appendix I.

*cabildo*: town council.

*cabildo abierto*: a meeting of the town council at which the principal citizens were invited to be present.

*captain-general*: a royal governor independent of a viceroy and directly responsible to the Crown in Spain. See Appendix I. But the title is also used in a purely military sense.

*caudillo*: chieftain, 'boss', or leader.

*consulado*: a merchant guild, established by royal charter, which combined the functions of a chamber of commerce with certain administrative and judicial duties. The *consulados* safeguarded the privileges of the merchant importers.

*cortes*: parliament.

*creole*: properly 'criollo'. One born of European parents in Spanish America.

*estanciero*: owner of an estate, farm, or ranch.

*gaucho*: originally a smuggler of the countryside dealing in cattle hides. The name was later applied to the herdsman of the plains, and indeed to all inhabitants of the pampas, and became at last the popular term for the Argentine cow-boy.

*hacendado*: landowner or rancher.

*hacienda*: country estate.

*inquilino*: a tenant. The name given to the labourer on a Chilean estate.

*intendente*: governor of an administrative area known as an *intendencia*. See Appendix I.

*junta*: council, committee, or board.

*mestizo*: half-breed, part Spanish, part Indian.

*montoneras*: bands of gaucho cavalry, individually known as *montoneros*.

*orientales*: the name applied to the inhabitants of the Banda Oriental of Uruguay.

*peninsulares*: Spaniards.

*porteños*: port-dwellers. The name specifically applied to the people of Buenos Aires.

*presidency*: see Appendix I.

*sierra*: ridge of mountains.

*travesía*: passage, crossing, stretch. In Argentina the word is used to denote a large desert region.

*yerba maté*: the herb known as Paraguayan tea.

## III. *Note on Sources*

THE chief manuscript sources on which I have drawn in writing this book are the Foreign Office, War Office, Admiralty, and Customs Records in the Public Record Office, London, and the Paroissien Papers in the possession of Messrs. Cunnington Son and Orfeur of Braintree, Essex. These last were collected together by Paroissien's relatives after his death. They consist of considerable fragments of the rough and ready journal which Paroissien seems to have kept for most of his life, a number of letter and account books, a voluminous correspondence both in English and Spanish, legal and official documents relating to various episodes in Paroissien's career, and family archives. I have also cited, from time to time, a number of other manuscript collections, but to these the references are few and the collections themselves call for no especial comment.

The newspapers which I have used are the London *Times* and the *Morning Chronicle*, together with the *Gaceta de Buenos Aires*, the *Argos de Buenos Aires*, the *Southern Star*, or *Estrella del Sur*, of Montevideo, and the *Gaceta*

*del Gobierno* of Lima. The *Gaceta de Buenos Aires* has been reproduced in facsimile by the Junta de Historia y Numismática Americana (6 vols., Buenos Aires, 1910–15), the *Argos de Buenos Aires* by the Academia Nacional de la Historia of Argentina (5 vols., Buenos Aires, 1931–42), the *Southern Star* by the Instituto Histórico y Geográfico del Uruguay (Montevideo, 1942), and the *Gaceta del Gobierno* of Lima (vols. 1–3) by the Universidad Nacional de La Plata (La Plata, 1950).

# INDEX OF AUTHORS AND SHORT TITLES

The names of the authors and editors of works cited, together with the short titles used in referring to certain books, pamphlets, and printed collections of documents, are indexed below. The numbers after each entry refer to the page where, in a footnote, a first citation is made and full bibliographical details will be found.

Amunátegui Solar, D. — 76
*Archivo de Belgrano* — 11
*Archivo de O'Higgins* — 121
*Archivo de San Martín* — 71
Archivo [general] de la nación argentina — 63
Arguedas, Alcides — 42

Barros Arana, Diego — 71
Beverina, Juan — 3
Bischoff, E. U. — 57
Blanco Acevedo, Pablo — 34
Búlnes, Gonzalo — 75
Burgin, Miron — 49

Carranza, A. P. — 55
Castlereagh, *Memoirs* — 12
Centner, C. W. — 76
Chaves, J. C. — 26
Constable, T. — 135
Cruz, Ernesto de la — 67, 114

Davila, Vicente — 26
*Documentos referentes a la guerra de la independencia* . . . — 63
Donoso, Ricardo — 121
Dundonald, Thomas Cochrane, Earl of — 84

Encina, F. A. — 65
English, Henry — 139 (bis)

*Exposición de la conducta del teniente general Brayer* — 71

'First Report . . . on Joint Stock Companies' — 140

García Reyes, A. — 75
Goebel, D. B. — 5
Graham, Maria — 77
Gray, W. H. — 112

Haigh, Samuel — 72
Hall, Basil — 59
Head, Sir Francis B. — 140
Heaton, Herbert — 17
Helms, A. Z. — 50
*Historia de la nación argentina* — 78
Holland, Henry Richard [Vassall Fox], Lord — 5
Humphreys, R. A. — 5, 83

Jeaffreson, J. C. — 139
*Justificación de la conducta pública seguida por . . . García del Río i . . . Paroissien* — 102

Keen, Benjamin — 40
Kirkpatrick, F. A. — 58

Lecuna, Vicente — 64, 114
Levene, Ricardo — 20, 78, 114

Lohmann Villena, G. 84
Loza, Emilio 63

Mabragaña, H. 108
McBride, G. M. 65
McCulloch, J. R. 141
Manchester, A. K. 17
Manifiesto de las acusaciones . . .
   contra . . . Lord Cochrane 104
Manifiesto de las sesiones tenidas
   en . . . Miraflores 87
Manning, W. R. 49
Martius, C. F. P. von 16
Masur, G. 114
Matienzo, J. N. 35
Mawe, John 11
Memorias de los virreyes del Río
   de la Plata 37
Miller, John 46
Mitre, Bartolomé 13, 58
Molinari, D. L. 24, 39
Museo Histórico Nacional 84
Museo Mitre 11, 71

Neumann, W. H. 75
Notes on the Viceroyalty of La
   Plata 11

O'Leary, D. F. 112
Otero, J. P. 59

Parliamentary Debates 4
Paz Soldán, F. M. 100, 103
Pereira Salas, Eugenio 75, 76
Peruvian Pamphlet 121
Pezuela, Joaquín de la 84 (bis)
Presas, José 29
Proceedings of a General Court
   Martial . . . for the Trial of
   . . . Whitelocke 10

Proctor, Robert 77
Puente Candamo, J. A. de la 94
Pueyrredón, Carlos A. 31

René-Moreno, Gabriel 41
Report of the Trial of Kinder
   versus Everett 101
Rippy, J. F. 139
Roberts, Carlos 3
Robertson, J. P. 4, 60
Robertson, W. P. 4, 60
Robertson, W. S. 12
Robinson, William 6
Rodríguez Casado, V. 84
Rojas, Ricardo 114
Rosenblat, Ángel 49
Rubio, J. M. 23
Ruiz-Guiñazú, Enrique 22

San Martín. Su correspondencia 84
Sarmiento, D. F. 106
Schmidtmeyer, Peter 80
Scrivener, J. H. 146
Spix, J. B. von 16
Stapleton, A. G. 137
Stevenson, W. B. 85

Temperley, H. W. V. 137
Temple, Edmond 146 (bis)
Tosi de Diéguez, L. 146

Vane, Charles William, third
   Marquis of Londonderry 12
Vicuña Mackenna, B. 75, 101

Webster, Sir Charles K. 87, 119
Whitaker, A. P. 120
Williams, J. B. 5

Yrarrázaval Larraín, J. M. 98

# GENERAL INDEX

Abascal y Souza, José Fernando de, 85
Abreu, Manuel, 94
Aconcagua, 68
Aconcagua, river, 69
Addington, Henry, Viscount Sidmouth, 8
*Admiral Berkeley*, the, 32
*Águila*, the, 74
Alvarez, Ildefonso Antonio, 57 n.
Alvarez de Condarco, José Antonio, 57 n.,
70, 74, 75, 76
Álzaga, Martín de, 10, 11, 27, 28, 36–7,
40, 42
Amazon, river, 2, 25
American Revolution, war of the, 2–3
Ancón, 89, 97, 104
Andalucía, French occupation of (1810),
45
Andes, Army of, 59, 62, 63, 64, 68, 69,
78, 80
Anglo-Mexican Mining Company, 141,
155
Anglo-Portuguese Commercial Treaty
(1810), 17–18
Araucania, 65
*Araucano*, the, 75
Arenales, Juan Antonio Alvarez de, 82,
88, 90, 91, 93, 96
Arequipa, 91, 153
Argentina, 2, 52. *See also* Buenos Aires;
La Plata, viceroyalty of; and United
Provinces of the Río de la Plata
*Argos de Buenos Aires*, 108
Arica, 93, 147, 153, 158, 161
Artigas, José Gervasio, 52, 61–2, 78, 79
Asturias, Junta of, 20
Asunción, 24, 50, 52, 53
Auchmuty, Sir Samuel, 5, 7, 9, 11
Austerlitz, battle of, 1
Ayacucho, battle of (1824), 138, 148

Bahia, 15, 16
Baird, Sir David, 2
Balcarce, Antonio González, 54, 55, 80
Banda Oriental, Portuguese designs on,
23–5; repudiates authority of Buenos
Aires, 52–3; 60–2; effects of revolu-
tion in, 60; annexation by Brazil (1816),
53, 79; insurrection of 1825, 145; in-
dependence of, 162. *See also* Monte-
video; Uruguay
Bank of Buenos Aires, 145
Baring Brothers and Company, 139.
Barking, Essex, 6
Barnard, J. J., 80, 91–2
Bayonne, scandal of, 20
Begg, John, 80, 91–2, 97, 100, 112,
114–15, 128, 153, 154, 157, 160, 161
Belgrano, Manuel, political and economic
ideas of, 25, 36, 38, 40, 43, 62, 87; part
in emancipation of Buenos Aires, 45–6,
47, 56, 62; expedition to Paraguay, 53
Bentham, Jeremy, 106
Beresford, William Carr, 2, 3, 4, 5, 7–8,
22
Beuzeville, Stephen, 21
Bío-Bío, river, 65, 73, 77
Bolívar, Simón, character, 113, and
political ideas, 111–14, 149; liberates
Venezuela and New Granada, 64, 86;
enters Quito and Guayaquil, 113;
interview with San Martín, 111–14;
liberation of Perú, 129, 133, 138, 154;
organization of Bolivia, 149; despair
and death, 162
Bolivia, 2, 41, 163; creation of, 147–51;
mining in, 149–51; ports of entry to,
147, 151, 153; prospects of, 151, 162.
*See also* Upper Perú
Bonaparte, Joseph, 20

Bonaparte, Napoleon, 1, 4, 6, 16, 20, 24; and Spanish America, 21, 33, 34, 36

Brayer, Michel, 71

Brazil, arrival of Portuguese Court in (1808), 16; independence of, 109–10; empire of, 110, 161.

Opening of ports, 16; British trade, 11, 16–18; London loan, 139; British mining companies, 142

Designs on Banda Oriental and proposed invasion of viceroyalty of La Plata, 23–4; intrigues of Carlota Joaquina, 24–32; annexation of Banda Oriental (1816), 53, 79; recognizes independence of United Provinces, 118; war with Buenos Aires, 145, 162

British and Foreign Bible Society, 102

Brougham, Henry Peter, Baron Brougham and Vaux, 118, 121, 131

Buenos Aires, population and growth, 1–2, 60, 106–7; trade with interior provinces, 2, 50–2; with Rio de Janeiro, 19; with Britain (1806–10), 4–5, 7–8, 11–13, 20–1, 38–40, (after 1810 Revolution), 48–9, 60, 129, 137, 145; London loan, 139

British invasions of, 1–5, 7–10, 12–14, 22; British recognition of independence, 136–7

Preliminaries of revolution in, 13–14, 22–32, 33–40, 42–4; Revolution of 1810, 44–9; Junta of 1810, 47–9, 52, 60–1; Triumvirates, 61, 105; Assembly of 1813, 61–2, and Congress of Tucumán, 62; Administration of Rodríguez, 105–7, 145

Relations with interior provinces, 49, 52, 53–4, 60–2, 78–9, 80, 105–7, 145–6, 162; with Montevideo and Banda Oriental, 13–14, 31, 33–4, 49, 52–3, 58, 60, 61–2, 79, 145, 162; with Upper Perú, 52, 54–8, 59, 60, 62, 102, 107; with Paraguay, 52, 53, 62; with Chile, 59–60, 64–6, 68, 70–1, 73; with Perú, 77–9, 102, 105, 107–8; with Brazil, 23–32, 118, 145, 162

See also United Provinces of Río de la Plata; La Plata, viceroyalty of

Burke, James, 27

Cádiz, 4, 34, 78, 85; Consulado of, 38, 39; mutiny at, 86

Calcutta, 77

Caledonia, the, 91 n.

Callao, 76, 84, 89, 129; blockade of, 90–2; surrender of (1821), 95–7; mutiny at, 133; final surrender (1826), 138

Cancha Rayada, battle of (1818), 72

Canning, George, policy and opinions (1806–8), 4, 15, 21, 25, 26; (1822), 118–21; (1823), 127, 131; (1824–5), 136–8

Canterac, José, 95–6, 97

Caracas, 113, 139, 163

Carlota Joaquina, Princess, arrival in Brazil, 16; intrigues in viceroyalty of La Plata, 21–32, 34–6, 41, 43–5; return to Portugal, 109

Carnfield Hall, Derbyshire, 134

Carrera, José Miguel, 67–8, 71, 74

Carta Régia, the, of 1808, opens Brazilian ports, 16

Castelli, Juan José, and monarchical plot of 1808, 25, 27; his defence of Paroissien, 36, 43–5; and Revolution of 1810, 45–7; expedition to Upper Perú, 54–8

Castlereagh, Robert Stewart, Viscount, 9, 20–1, 27, 117–19

Castro, Félix, 146, 156, 157, 160

Catamarca, 57

Caucato, 100, 154

Cauquenes, 79

Chacabuco, battle of (1817), 70, 71, 72

Chacabuco, the, 75

Chamberlain, Henry, 108

Charcas, audiencia of, 163; and see Upper Perú

Charles IV, of Spain, 16, 20, 36

Chile, captaincy-general of, 163; projected British conquest of, 5, 6, 8, 9; trade links with viceroyalty of La Plata, 51, 52; extent, population and social structure, 65–6

Chile, Republic of, establishment and destruction of 'first Republic', 66–8; liberating expedition of 1817, 68–70, and military operations, 71–3; proclamation of independence, 72; creation of navy, 74–6; Directorate of O'Higgins, 70, 74, 102–3, 104, 137–8, 162

Relations with United Provinces, 59–60, 64, 66, 68, 70–1, 73, 77; liberating expedition to Perú, 77, 79, 80–4, 86–98, and relations with Peruvian Government, 102–4

Relations with Great Britain: opening of ports, and British trade, 66–7, 76–7; London loan, 122; British recognition of independence, 137, 138; British mining companies, 142
  Relations with U.S.A., 70, 71, 74–5, 76, 118
Chiloé, Island of, 76, 103
Chuquisaca, 41, 42, 55, 149, 153, 157
Chuquisaca, University of, 22, 25, 39, 41
Cisneros, Baltasar Hidalgo de, 37–8, 40, 42, 45–8
Cobija, 147, 151, 153
Cochabamba, 55, 149
Cochrane, Thomas, Earl of Dundonald, enters service of Chile, 75–6; and liberating expedition to Perú, 82–4, 86, 88–93; his quarrel with San Martín, 84, 92–3, 97–8, 102–4
Cock, Simon, 121
Colombia, creation of, 86, 89; negotiations with Perú, 110–11; Guayaquil annexed to, 112–13; London loan, 121, 123, 124, 125; recognition of independence by U.S.A., 118, and by Great Britain, 136, 137; fall of Bolívar, 162
Colombian Mining Association, 141–2
Concepción (Chile), 65, 66, 68, 71–2
Copiapó, 65
Coquimbo, 83
Córdoba, 50, 51, 59, 147, 164; and Revolution of 1810, 52, 53–4; gunpowder factory at, 57, 63
Córdoba, University of, 22, 25, 50
Correo de Comercio, 40
Corrientes, city, 50, 51
Corrientes, Province, 24, 62
Courcy, Admiral de, 31
Craufurd, Robert, Brigadier-General, 5, 6, 8, 9
Creoles, 164; in Buenos Aires, 13, 22, 25, 33–4, 36–40, 42–9, 52; in Chile, 66–8, 70; in Paraguay, 53; in Perú, 85, 89, 90; in Upper Perú, 41–2
Creutzer, Pedro, 102, 132
Cumberland, the, 75
Cuyo, Province, 51, 59, 82
Cuzco, 91
Cuzco, audiencia of, 163
Czettritz, Hermann, Baron de, 144, 146, 151–2, 160

Delano, Paul, 82
Desaguadero, river, 55

Ecuador, 112, 163
Edinburgh Review, the, 116
Egaña, Mariano, 140
Elío, Francisco Javier, appointed Governor of Montevideo, 13; and Carlota Joaquina, 31, 32, 34–5; repudiates authority of Buenos Aires, 33, 34, 36, 37; Viceroy of La Plata, 52
Elizabeth, the, 7
Encalada, Manuel Blanco, 74, 75
Enseñada, 10, 145
Entre Ríos, Province, 50, 62
Esmeralda, the, 89
Essex, the, 76
Everett, Walker, Maltby and Ellis, 123, 124, 125–6, 130, 131

Falmouth, 110, 144, 152
Famatina Mining Company, 142
Ferdinand VII, of Spain, renounces throne of Spain (1808), 20; loyalty to in Spanish America, 34, 36, 41, 43, 44; attitude of Junta of Buenos Aires towards, 47–8; his restoration and despotism, 62, 86, 116
Fox, Charles James, 1
France, and war of American Independence, 2–3; Napoleonic wars, 1, 4, 6, 17, 20, 45; invasion of Spain in 1823, 135; and Spanish America, 20–1, 24, 33, 34, 36, 135–6; and Portugal, 16–17
Francia, José Gaspar Rodríguez de, 22, 53
Frolic, H.M. Packet-Brig, 144–5
Fryer, J. H., 144, 152, 159, 160, 161
Frys and Chapman, 139

Gaceta de Buenos Aires, 48, 54
Gallant Schemer, the, 5, 6
Galup, Bernardo, 108 n.
Galvarino, the, 75
García, José Manuel, 106–7
García del Río, Juan, participation in liberating expedition to Perú, 82–3, and in armistice negotiations at Miraflores, 86–7; appointed Foreign Minister of Perú, 95; missions as Peruvian Envoy, with Paroissien, in Chile, the United Provinces, and

England, 98–9, 101–8, 110–11, 114–16, 119–37; association with the Potosí, La Paz and Peruvian Mining Company, 143, 154, 155

Garda, P. A., 143, 151, 153, 156, 161

Gardner, Daniel, 6, 9, 11, 15, 18, 21

Gardner, John, 21

General South American Mining Association, 142

George IV, 119, 137

Gil de Castro, José, 80

Goldschmidt, B. A., and Company, 139

Goyeneche, José Manuel, 41, 42, 54, 55

Great Britain, and Spanish colonies: (1776–1806), interest in and designs on, 2–3, 4, 5; (1806–7), invasions of Río de la Plata, 1–14, 22; (1807–8), liberation proposals, 12, 20; (1808–10), under Anglo-Spanish Alliance, 20–1, 27

and South American emancipation: attitude towards and interest in, 116; neutrality and trade policy, 117–18; *de facto* recognition of new states, 118–119; diplomatic recognition and commercial treaties, 131, 136–8

and South American trade: (1806–7), 3, 5, 9, 12, 13, 15; (1808), 17–18, 20; (post-1810), 116–19; (1822), 122–4; speculative and mining boom (1824–5), 135–7, 138–44, 155, 161. Trade with Bolivia, 151–3; with Brazil, 11, 16–18, with Buenos Aires, 4–5, 7–8, 11–13, 20, 21, 38–40, 48–9, 60, 129, 137, 145; with Chile, 76–7; with Montevideo, 9, 11, 32; with Perú, 91–2, 96–7, 124–5, 128, 129, 153

and South American loans, 135, 138–140, 155, 161; to Brazil, 139; to Buenos Aires, 139; to Chile, 122; to Colombia, 121, 123, 124, 125, 139; to Guatemala, 139; to Mexico, 139; to Perú, 101, 111, 121–32, 133, 134–5, 138, 139

Colonization schemes, 161; in Chile and Colombia, 140; in Río de la Plata, 132, 140, 141

Relations with France: war of American Revolution, 2–3; Napoleonic wars, 1, 4, 6, 17, 20; Polignac memorandum (1823), 136. With Portugal, 16, 20, 17–18, 24–5. With Spain: wars, 1, 3, 20; alliance, 20–1, 31, 117; offers of mediation to, 117–19; recognition of independence of Spanish

American colonies, 136–8; seizure of British ships in Spanish American waters, 121. With U.S.A.: Non-importation Act and Embargo, 4, 17; war of 1812, 76; commercial rivalry in South America, 118, 137; Monroe doctrine, 136

Grenville, William Wyndham, Baron, 4

Grey, Charles, Viscount Howick, 4

Guadalajara, State, 139

Guatemala, 139

Guatemala Mining Company, 142

Guayaquil, 76, 92, 111; revolution in, 89; annexation to Colombia, 112–13; San Martín's meeting with Bolívar in, 112–14

Guido, Tomás, 82, 83, 86–7

Hackney, Borough of, 6

Haigh, Samuel, 80

Hall, Basil, 90, 95, 96, 135

Hardy, Sir Thomas, 99, 108

Helms, Anton Zacharias, 143

Herring, Graham and Powles, 121–2

Huacho, 89, 90

Huaquí, battle of (1811), 55

Huaura, 89, 91, 93

Hullett Brothers, 122

Humahuaca, 56

Humboldt, Alexander von, 141, 143, 144

Hurtado, Manuel, 133, 134

Ica, 88, 91

Imperial Brazilian Company, 142

*Independencia*, the, 75

Indians, in Bolivia, 149; in Chile, 65; in Perú, 85, 88; in Río de la Plata, 49, 64

Inquisition, the, 61

*Intrépido*, the, 75

Irisarri, Antonio José de, 122, 131, 140, 142–3, 155

Jauja Valley, 88

Jena, battle of, 1

João, Dom, Prince Regent of Portugal, 16, 18–19, 23–4, 25, 109, 118

Jones, Jenkin, 126

Jujuy, 51, 54, 57

Junín, battle of (1824), 138

Kinder, Thomas, 122–4, 125, 131, 134, 139, 142

La Guaira, proposed railway to Caracas, 139

Lancastrian Schools, 102, 107

La Paz, city, 41, 42, 55, 149

La Paz, Junta of, 42

La Plata, viceroyalty of, area, population and administration, 1–2, 49–52, 163–4; British invasions of (1806–7), 1–15; economic problems and trade (1808–1810), 11, 18, 20, 38–40; and Court of Rio de Janeiro, 23–32, 34–6, 41

Internal dissensions: in Montevideo, 33–5, 37; in Buenos Aires, 33–4, 36–40; in Upper Perú, 40–2. Eventual dismemberment: Buenos Aires and the 1810 Revolution, 42–9; Montevideo, 52–3, 61–2; the interior provinces, 52, 53–4; Paraguay, 53; Upper Perú, 52, 54–8, 60, 62, 102, 107, 147–8

La Rioja, 57, 69

La Serena, 65

La Serna, José de, 90, 94–5

Las Heras, Juan Gregorio de, 69, 71, 82, 98

Lautaro, the, 75

Letters on Paraguay, 132

Letters on South America, 132

Lima, as capital of viceroyalty of Perú, 2, 13, 22, 51; population, 85; liberating expedition to, 70, 73–4, 83–4, 86, 88, 89, 90, 91; San Martín's occupation of, 95–6, 98, and departure from, 114; gift to Paroissien from municipality of, 100, 153–4; and London loan, 123–5, 128–9; military and political crisis of 1823–4, 129, 133, 138; Paroissien's visit to in 1826, 153–4

Liniers, Santiago, in defence and reconquest of Buenos Aires (1806–7), 3, 10, 36; attitude towards British merchants and trade, 11, 20, 38; appointed Viceroy of La Plata, 13; rivalry with Elío, 13, 33–4, 35; and Carlota Joaquina, 28, 30, 32, 34; and creoles, 34, 36–7, 39; superseded as Viceroy, 35; his execution, 52, 53–4

Lisbon, 4, 17

Liverpool, 92, 119

Logia Lautaro, the, 79

Los Patos pass, 69

Lucca, Duke of, 87, 101

Luccock, John, 17

Luján, 3

Luptons and Co., 17

Luzuriaga, Toribio de, 82

Madrid, 20

Magé, 18

Maipú, battle of (1818), 72–3

Maldonado, 7

Maria I, of Portugal, 16

María Isabel, the, 75

Martínez de Rozas, Juan, 66, 67

Mary, the, 21, 28, 32

Mawe, John, 11, 15, 17, 18, 19

Medusa, frigate, 7

Melville, Henry Dundas, Viscount, 8

Mendoza, 51, 66, 105; San Martín's base for expedition to Chile, 59, 62, 63, 64, 68, 69, 72, 78, 79; Paroissien's landed estate in, 73, 100; execution of Carrera brothers in, 74

Mexico, proposed British expeditions to, 12, 20; monarchy in, 111; independence recognized by U.S.A., 118, and by Great Britain, 136, 137; London loans, 139; British mining companies, 141–2, 155

Middleton, Ralph Dodsworth, 21

Miguel, Julián de, 28, 32

Miller, William, 80, 93, 110, 137–8, 146

Minas Geraes, 142

Ministry of All-the-Talents, 4

Miraflores, Armistice of, 86–8, 94

Miranda, Francisco de, 3, 8–9, 26, 67

Misiones, District, 24

Monroe Doctrine, 136

Monteagudo, Bernardo, 82–3, 95, 98, 103, 107, 110–12, 125

Montevideo, population, 2; British occupation of (1807), 3, 5, 7, 9–15, 22; proposed Portuguese invasion, 23–4; Paroissien's arrest and imprisonment in (1808), 32, 33, 34–5

Rivalry with Buenos Aires, 13–14, 31, 33, 34, 37; repudiates Junta of Buenos Aires (1810), 49, 52; sieges of, 52–3, 61; conquest by Brazil, 53

Montezuma, the, 75

Moreno, Agustín Gutíerrez de, 104 n.

Moreno, Mariano, 38–9, 43, 47, 48, 54, 55–6, 60

Morning Chronicle, the, 116, 120

Mosquera, Joaquín, 110

Murillo, Pedro Domingo, 42

Myles, Charles John, 120

Negroes, 59, 61, 83–4, 85, 98
New Granada, viceroyalty of, 86, 90, 112, 163; *and see* Colombia
Nieto, Vicente, 42, 54, 55
*Notes on the Viceroyalty of La Plata*, 13
*Numancia* battalion, 90

O'Higgins, Bernardo, early career, 67–8; crossing of Andes and election as Supreme Director of Chile, 68–70; campaigns in southern and central Chile, 71–3; political difficulties, 74, and creation of navy, 74–5; and liberating expedition to Perú, 74, 77, 79; rejects monarchist proposals, 102–104; resignation and exile, 137–8, 162
*O'Higgins*, the, 75, 83
*Olive Branch*, the, 161
Orleans, Duke of, 87
Oruro, 55, 149
Osorio, Mariano, 72
Osorno, 65

Panamá, isthmus of, 51, 111
Paraguay, population, trade routes, administration, etc., under viceroyalty of La Plata, 2, 4, 49, 50, 52, 164; repudiates authority of Junta of Buenos Aires (1810–11), 52, 53; under dictatorship of Francia, 22, 53, 60, 62
Paroissien, Anna Maria, 21 n.
Paroissien, George, 6
Paroissien, James, early life, 5–6, and voyage to Montevideo, 7–9; joins militia, 10; is refused permission to settle in Buenos Aires, 11; leaves Montevideo for Santa Catarina, 15, and Rio de Janeiro, 16; his activities and impressions in Brazil, 17–19; plans return to Buenos Aires and acts as secret political agent on behalf of Carlota Joaquina, 21–31; arrest and imprisonment in Montevideo and Buenos Aires, 32, 34–6, 43; his defence by Castelli, 43–5, and release, 47
    Serves in liberating expedition to Upper Perú, 54–7; granted letters of naturalization, 56, 63; appointed director of gunpowder factory in Córdoba, 57, 63; meets San Martín, 59; serves in liberating expeditions to Chile, 63–4, 69–73, 79–80, and Perú, 81 ff.

Appointed envoy to Europe of Peruvian Government, 98–9; his private financial affairs, 100–1; his instructions as envoy, 101–2, 110–11; mission in Chile, 102–4, and in United Provinces, 102, 105, 107–8; impressions of Rio de Janeiro, 108–10; his secret instructions revoked, 114–15, 127
    Arrival in England, 115–16, 119, and reception by Canning, 119–20; diplomatic and propagandist activities, 120–1, and negotiation of Peruvian loan, 121–32; superseded as commercial agent, 128, 131–2; continues to regard himself as envoy, 133, 136, 137; concerts with San Martín abortive plans for aid to Perú, 133–4; presents accounts to, and claims on, Peruvian Government, 134–5
    Interest in South American speculations, 140, 142–3; appointed Vice-president and Chief Commissioner of Potosí, La Paz and Peruvian Mining Company, prepares for expedition to Potosí and leaves England, 143–4; arrival and financial transactions in Buenos Aires, 145–6; journey to Potosí, 146–8; favourable prospects in Bolivia and Perú, 151–2; visit to Lima, 153–4; financial embarrassments of the Company in London, 155–6; and in South America, 156–60; its liquidation, and Paroissien's illness and death, 160–2
Paroissien, Jesse, 5
Paroissien, Louis, 6
Paroissien, Mary, 6 n.
Pasco, battle of (1820), 90
Pasco Peruvian Mining Company, 142
Paso de la Cumbre, 68
Patagonia, 2, 37
Paula, Francisco de, 87
Pedro I, of Brazil, 19, 109–10*
Pernambuco, 15
Perú, Republic of, declaration of independence (1821), 95; San Martín's government, 95, 98, 110, and monarchist projects, 87, 94–5, 98–9, 100–4, 111, 114–15, 120, 126; fall of Monteagudo, 111–12; San Martín's retirement and the Constituent Congress and Junta, 114–15; Presidency of Riva-Agüero and crisis of 1823, 128–30; Bolívar's dictatorship, 138

Opening of ports, 96; commercial code, 147, 153, 154

Relations with Chile, 102–4; with Colombia, 110–11, 112–14; with Spain, 120–1; with United Provinces, 102, 106–7; with Upper Perú, 102, 107, 148; with U.S.A., 102, 118

Relations with Great Britain: Peruvian mission to London, 98–9, 101, 111, 114–15, 119–21, 128–9, 131–3; British recognition of independence, 136, 137, 138; London loan, 101, 111, 121–32, 134–5, 138, 139, 154; British trade, 91–2, 96–7, 153; British mining companies, 142–4, 150, 151–2

*Peruvian Pamphlet*, 120–1

Perú, viceroyalty of, 2, 13, 41, 55, 163; population and social structure, 85–6; and Upper Perú, 41, 42, 52, 85; and Chile, 67–73; San Martín and liberation of, 58–9, 62, 68, 70, 73–99, 110; Bolívar and liberation of, 114, 128, 129–30, 133, 138

Pezuela, Joaquín de la, 86–7, 90, 93, 95

Pichincha, battle of (1822), 113

Pisco, 83–4, 86, 90, 91, 93, 100, 110, 154, 158

Pitt, William, 1, 4, 8, 9

Polignac, Prince Jules de, 133, 136

Popham, Sir Home Riggs, 2, 3, 4, 5, 7, 8, 12

Portugal, emigration of royal family to Brazil, 16; relations with England, 16, 20, and Anglo-Portuguese Commercial Treaty of 1810, 17–18; colonial policies, 16, 23–4, 53, 79, 109–10; return of the Court, 109

Potosí, 37, 50, 54–5, 56, 58, 148, 157, 160; silver mines of, 41, 149–52

*Potosí*, the, 147, 152, 153, 154, 156, 157, 158, 159, 160, 161

Potosí, La Paz and Peruvian Mining Association, 142–4, 146–8, 151–61

Poyais, Kingdom of, 122

Presas, José, 28–9

Proctor, Robert, 123–4, 125, 127–8, 129, 130, 131

Pueyrredón, Juan Martín de, 3, 56, 62, 64, 70, 79, 87

*Pueyrredón*, the, 74

Punchauca, Armistice of, 94

Puno, 152

Punta del Este, 7

Putaendo, river, 69

Quito, city, 113

Quito, presidency of, 112, 163

Rancagua, 79, 80

Rancagua, battle of (1814), 68

Reach, Captain, 5

Real del Monte Mining Company, 141, 142, 155

*Representación de los Hacendados*, 39–40

Riachuelo, river, 10

Rio de Janeiro, population and growth under Prince Regent, 16; British trade with, 16–18; trade with Buenos Aires, 20; Paroissien's impressions of, in 1808, 18–19, and in 1822, 109–10

Río de la Plata Mining Association, 142

Riva-Agüero, José de la, 128–9

Rivadavia, Bernardino, 105–8, 140–1, 142, 146, 162

Robertson, John Parish, 4, 11, 106–7, 128–9, 131–2, 134, 139, 141–2

Robertson, William Parish, 129, 132

Robinson, Jeremy, 102

Rodríguez, Martín, 46, 105, 107

Rodríguez Peña, Nicolás, 25, 27, 28, 34, 45, 47, 54

Rodríguez Peña, Saturnino, 22, 23, 25–32, 34, 43–5, 87

Rousseau, Jean-Jacques, 48

Royal Philippine Company, 4

Rush, Richard, 120, 136, 138, 140

Russia, 101

Saavedra, Cornelio, 37, 45, 47

*Salisbury Packet*, the, 110

Salta, 50–1, 54, 56, 58, 147, 157, 161

San Juan, 51, 69

San Luis, 51, 68, 83

San Marcos, University of (Lima), 22

San Martín, José de, early career, 58–9; character, 59; his great 'strategic design', 58, 68, 70, 73; as Governor of Cuyo, 59, 62–4; crossing of Andes, 68–70; Chilean campaigns, 72–3; preparations for invasion of Perú and relations with Governments of Buenos Aires and Chile, 73–81; liberating expedition to Perú, 81–96; assumption of Protectorate of Perú, 95; quarrel with Cochrane, 84, 92–3, 97–8, 102–4; monarchical designs, 87–8, 94–5, 98–9, 101–2,

111; work in Perú, 98; meeting with Bolívar, 111–14; resignation, 112, 114; comments on events in Perú, 129; visit to London in 1824, 133–4; settles in Brussels, 134; quarrel with Rivadavia, 107, 140–1; death, 162
*San Martín*, the, 75, 83, 89
Santa Catarina, Island of, 15, 18, 19
Santa Cruz (Brazil), 18, 19
Santa Fe, city, 50, 51, 78
Santa Fe, province, 62, 78
Santa Fé de Bogotá, 163
Santa Rosa de los Andes, 70
Santiago de Chile, 65, 66, 69–70, 71, 72, 73, 77, 80, 102
Santiago del Estero, 50, 57
Saxe-Coburg, Prince Leopold of, 101, 120
Scrivener, John, 144, 146, 160, 161
Seville, 45; Junta Central at, 37, 40, 44, 45, 46; Junta of, 20, 41, 44
Slavery, emancipation from, in the United Provinces, 61; in Perú, 98
Smith, Charles, 30
Smith, Sir Sidney, 19, 22–32, 35, 44
Sobremonte, Rafaél, 3, 10, 28
Soler, Miguel Estanislao de, 69, 70
*Southern Star*, the, 9, 11
Souza e Coutinho, Rodrigo de, 18, 23
Spain, wars with England, 1, 2–3, 20; French invasions, rising of 1808, and reversal of alliances, 20–1, 31, 37, 44–5; Regency of 1810, 45; restoration of Ferdinand VII (1814), 62; mutiny at Cádiz (1820) and Constitution of 1812, 86; French invasion of 1823, 135
  Colonial policy of: imperial administration, 2, 163–4; commercial monopoly, 3–4, 20, 21, 38–40, 48, 116–117; Junta of Seville and, 37, 41; proposed expedition to Río de la Plata (1819), 78, 86; pacificatory proposals (1820), 86; seizure of British ships, 121; British offers of mediation rejected, 117–18
Staples, Robert Ponsonby, 123–4
Stephenson, Robert, 139
Stevenson, W. B., 90 n.
Strangford, Percy Clinton Sydney Smythe, Viscount, 23–6, 29, 31, 35, 56
Sucre, Antonio José de, 113, 129, 148–9, 150–1, 153, 157, 162
Suipacha, battle of (1810), 54

Sussex, Augustus Frederick, Duke of, 101, 120

Tacna, 153, 154, 158, 160
Talcahuano, 71, 72
Temple, Edmond, 144, 146, 147–8, 153, 157, 160–1
Templer, Henry, 152
Templer, William, 158–9, 160, 161
*Thais*, the, 91 n.
Thomson, James, 102
*Times, The*, 1, 4, 8, 12, 116, 139, 142
Tipuani, 143, 152
Titicaca, Lake, 2, 55, 152
Toro, Domingo Santiago, 104 n.
Trafalgar, battle of, 1, 37
Trujillo, 90, 129
Tucumán, 50, 51, 57, 58, 147
Tucumán, Congress of, 62, 78–9
Tupungato, 68

Ulm, battle of, 1
Unánue, Hipólito, 95, 98
United Mexican Mining Company, 141, 155
United Provinces of South America, *see* United Provinces of the Río de la Plata
United Provinces of the Río de la Plata, Constituent Assembly of 1813, 61; monarchical ideas in, 62, 87, 106; Declaration of Independence of (1816), 62; anarchy of 1820, 78–80, 105; recognition by Brazil and U.S.A., 118, and by Great Britain, 136–7; Presidency of Rivadavia, 146, 162
  Colonization schemes in, 132, 140, 141
  *See also* Buenos Aires
United States of America, Non-importation Act and Embargo, 4, 17; war of 1812, 76; and liberation of Chile, 70, 71, 74–5; naval commanders in Pacific, 76, 102; recognition of Spanish American independence, 118; Monroe Doctrine, 136
Upper Perú, population, 41, 149; trade routes, 50–1; and mining industry, 2, 41, 149–50
  Transfer from viceroyalty of Perú to that of La Plata in 1776, 41; Carlota Joaquina's offer of protection in 1808, 41; premature revolution of 1809, 41–2; reattachment to viceroyalty of Perú,

52, 85; liberating expeditions from Buenos Aires in 1810–12, 54–8, and in 1813 and 1815, 58, 60; representatives-in-exile at Congress of Tucumán in 1816, 62; royalist opposition, 102, 107, ended in 1825 by Sucre's advance, 148; creation of independent State of Bolivia, 147, 148–9
*See also* Bolivia

Uruguay, 2, 14, 23, 145, 162; *and see also* Banda Oriental; Montevideo

Uspallata, 68, 69, 105

Valdivia, 65, 76, 103
Valparaíso, 65–6, 71, 74, 75, 77, 82, 92, 102, 161

*Vencedor*, the, 15
Venezuela, captaincy-general of, 163; expedition of Miranda to, 8; liberation of, 64, 85, 113; La Guaira-Caracas railway project, 139

Waine, Captain, 7
Walton, William, 120–1
Wellesley, Arthur, Duke of Wellington, 20
Wellesley, Richard Colley, Marquis, 117
Whitelocke, John, 9, 10, 11, 12, 22, 145
Wilson, Isabel, 159
Windham, William, 4, 5, 8, 9
*Windham*, the, 74

Zea, Francisco, 121, 124

N

Map 1: The Spanish and Portuguese Empires in South America in 1808

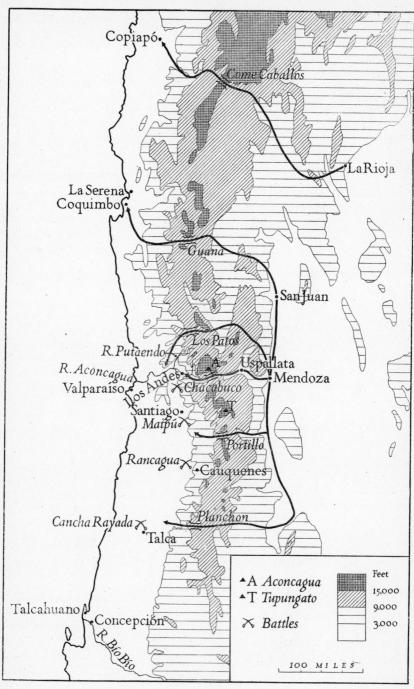

Copiapó

Cerro Caballos

La Rioja

La Serena
Coquimbo

Guana

San Juan

R. Putaendo
Los Patos

R. Aconcagua
▲A
Uspallata
Valparaíso
Los Andes
Mendoza
Chacabuco
Santiago
▲T
Maipú

Portillo

Rancagua
Cauquenes

Cancha Rayada
Planchon

Talca

Talcahuano
Concepción

R. Bío Bío

▲A Aconcagua
▲T Tupungato
✕ Battles

Feet
15,000
9,000
3,000

100 MILES

Map 2: The Invasion of Chile

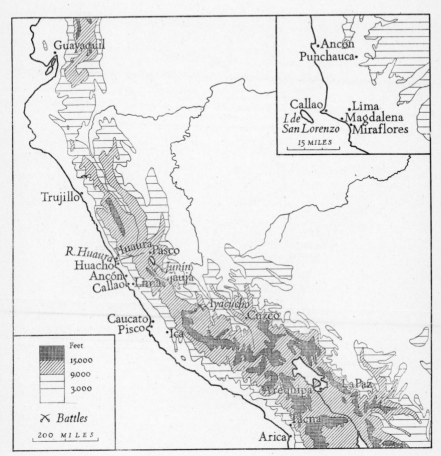

Map 3: The Invasion of Perú

Map 4: South America in 1826